Saint Peter's University Library
Withdrawn

Best Loved Poems of
the American West

Best Loved Poems of the American West

Selected by John J. and
Barbara T. Gregg

DOUBLEDAY & COMPANY, INC.
GARDEN CITY, NEW YORK
1980

Copyright © 1980 by Doubleday & Company, Inc.
ISBN: 0-385-13309-X
Library of Congress Catalog Card Number 78-1241
All Rights Reserved
Printed in the United States of America

Library of Congress Cataloging in Publication Data
Main entry under title:

Best loved poems of the American West.

Includes indexes.
1. American poetry. 2. The West—Poetry.
I. Gregg, John J. II. Gregg, Barbara T.
PS595.W39B4   811′.008′03278

ACKNOWLEDGMENTS

For arrangements made with various authors, estates, and publishing houses where copyrighted material was permitted to be reprinted, and for the courtesy extended by them, the following acknowledgments are gratefully made. All possible care has been taken to trace the ownership of every selection included and to make full acknowledgment for its use. If any errors or omissions have accidentally occurred, they will be corrected in subsequent editions, provided notification is sent to the publisher.

"At Cheyenne" by Eugene Fields from *Poems Of Eugene Fields* and "Desert Song" by John Galsworthy from *Caravan* (copyright 1925 Charles Scribner's Sons) are reprinted with the permission of Charles Scribner's Sons.

"Idaho" by Frank French from *Songs of the American West,* edited by Richard E. Lingenfelter and Richard A. Dwyer. Copyright 1968 by The Regents of The University of California; reprinted by permission of The University of California Press.

"Land's End" and "The Last Trail" by Stanton A. Coblentz from *Redwood Poems* are reprinted with the permission of Naturegraph Publishers, Inc.

"Shasta," "A Dance For Rain," "Vinegaroon," "New Mexican Desert," and "An Adobe House" by Witter Bynner are reprinted with the permission of the Witter Bynner Foundation for Poetry, Inc.

"The Water-Hole" and "Sagebrush" by Charles Erskin Scott Wood are reprinted with the permission of The Vanguard Press.

"Early Moon," from *Cornhuskers* by Carl Sandburg, copyright 1918 by Holt, Rinehart, and Winston, Inc.; copyright 1946 by Carl Sandburg. Reprinted by permission of Harcourt Brace Jovanovich, Inc. "Buffalo Dusk," from *Smoke and Steel* by Carl Sandburg, copyright 1920 by Harcourt Brace Jovanovich, Inc.; copyright 1948 by Carl Sandburg. Reprinted by permission of the publishers.

"Quivira" by Arthur Guiterman from *A Ballad Maker's Pack,* copyright 1921; "The Oregon Trail" by Arthur Guiterman from *I Sing the Pioneers,*

PS
595
W39
B4

copyright 1926; "Coyote and the Star," "Ephraim and the Grizzly," "The Dance of the Gray Raccoon," and "The Prairie Dog," from *Wildwood Fables,* copyright 1927. All of the above are reprinted by permission of Louise H. Sclove.

"Tall Men Riding," "Fine!," "The Law West of the Pecos," "The Sheep Beezness," "When Billy the Kid Rides Again," "Jackrabbits," and "To a Jackrabbit," copyright S. Omar Barker. Reprinted by permission of the author.

"Indian Song" by Willard Johnson from *Southwest Review,* Vol. X, No. 2 (January 1925). Reprinted by permission of the publisher.

"Indian Death" by Alice Corbin and "Sheep Country" by Margaret Pond from *Folk-Say IV: This Land is Ours,* edited by B. A. Botkin. Copyright 1932, 1960 by B. A. Botkin. Printed by The University of Oklahoma Press. Reprinted 1970 by Johnson Reprint in one volume with *Folk-Say, A Regional Miscellany, 1931.* Edited by B. A. Botkin. Copyright 1931, 1959 by B. A. Botkin. Printed by The University of Oklahoma Press. "The Golden Stallion" by Paul Thompson from *Folk-Say, A Regional Miscellany: 1929.* Edited by B. A. Botkin. Copyright 1929, 1957 by B. A. Botkin. Norman: The Oklahoma Folklore Society, printed by The University of Oklahoma Press. Reprinted 1970 by Johnson Reprint in one volume with *Folk-Say, A Regional Miscellany: 1930.* Edited by B. A. Botkin. Copyright 1930, 1958 by B. A. Botkin. The University of Oklahoma Press. The above reprinted with the permission of Gertrude Botkin.

"An Indian Summer Day on the Prairie" by Vachel Lindsay. Reprinted with the permission of Macmillan Publishing Co., Inc., from *Collected Poems* by Vachel Lindsay. Copyright 1914 by Macmillan Publishing Co., Inc., renewed 1942 by Elizabeth C. Lindsay. "The Broncho That Would Not Be Broken" and "The Ghost of the Buffaloes" by Vachel Lindsay. Reprinted with permission of Macmillan Publishing Co., Inc., from *Collected Poems* by Vachel Lindsay. Copyright 1917 by Macmillan Publishing Co., Inc., renewed 1945 by Elizabeth C. Lindsay.

"The Death of Crazy Horse" and "Red Cloud" by John G. Neihardt from *The Song of the Indian Wars,* currently published in *The Twilight of the Sioux.* Copyright 1925, 1935, 1949 by Macmillan Publishing Company; copyright 1943, 1946, 1953 by John G. Neihardt. Reprinted with the permission of the John G. Neihardt Trust.

"The Shallows of the Ford," "Riders of the Stars," and "The Desert" by Henry Herbert Knibbs from *Riders of the Stars* by Henry Herbert Knibbs. Copyright 1916 by Henry H. Knibbs and renewed 1944 by Ida Julia Knibbs. Reprinted by permission of the publisher, Houghton Mifflin Company.

"The Bosky Steer," "The Ballad of Billy the Kid," and "Boomer Jackson" by Henry Herbert Knibbs from *Songs of the Lost Frontier* by Henry Herbert Knibbs. Copyright 1930 by Henry Herbert Knibbs and renewed 1958 by Ida Julia Knibbs. Reprinted by permission of the publisher, Houghton Mifflin Company.

"The Long Road West," "The Oro Stage," and "Waring of Sonora-town" by Henry Herbert Knibbs from *Songs of the Trail* by Henry Herbert Knibbs.

Copyright 1920 by Henry H. Knibbs and renewed 1948 by Ida Julia Knibbs. Reprinted by permission of the publisher, Houghton Mifflin Company.

"Little Papoose," "Blanket Injun," "The Sheep-Herder's Lament," and "The Sheriff's Report" by Arthur Chapman from *Out Where the West Begins* by Arthur Chapman. Copyright 1916 by Arthur Chapman and renewed 1944 by Kathleen Chapman. Reprinted by permission of Houghton Mifflin Company.

"The Santa Fe Trail" by Arthur Chapman from *The Cactus Center* by Arthur Chapman. Reprinted by permission of Houghton Mifflin Company.

"Ode to the Norther" by William Lawrence Chittenden from *Ranch Verses* by William Lawrence Chittenden.

"The Flower-Fed Buffaloes" by Vachel Lindsay, reprinted by permission of Nicholas C. Lindsay on behalf of the estate of Vachel Lindsay.

"Spanish Johnny" from *April Twilights and Other Poems,* by Willa Cather. Copyright 1923 by Willa Cather and renewed 1951 by the Executors of the Estate of Willa Cather. Reprinted by permission of Alfred A. Knopf, Inc.

"The City by the Sea," "The Cool, Grey City of Love," "The Abalone Song," "Pumas," "Father Coyote," and "The Black Vulture" by George Sterling are reprinted with the permission of The Bancroft Library at the University of California, Berkeley, owner of the literary property rights of the Estate of George Sterling.

"A Peck of Gold" and "Once by the Pacific" from *The Poetry of Robert Frost,* edited by Edward Connery Latham. Copyright 1928, © 1969 by Holt, Rinehart and Winston. Copyright © 1956 by Robert Frost. Reprinted by permission of Holt, Rinehart and Winston, Publishers.

"Lewis and Clark," "Western Wagons," and "Jesse James," from *A Book of Americans* by Rosemary and Stephen Vincent Benét. Copyright 1933 by Rosemary and Stephen Vincent Benét. Copyright renewed © 1961 by Rosemary Carr Benét. Reprinted by permission of Brandt & Brandt Literary Agents, Inc.

Contents

Introduction

Our purpose in assembling this collection has been to offer in one volume an extensive and varied sampling of all kinds of poetry, culled from many sources, written about life in the Old West.

We wanted it to contain as many as possible of the well-known poems of the cowboys, the prairies, the mountain country, and the gold country of the Far West, so that a reader seeking an old favorite could find it; but we also wished to offer a more varied spread not easily come by elsewhere.

The book, however, is not intended to be encyclopedic or all-inclusive. Railroad, Hobo, Mississippi riverboat and Black poetry are very special and mostly southern, and are available in fine collections devoted to them alone.

Indian poetry, also a very special thing, is represented only by selected examples of "interpretations" by poets capable of expressing in English the thought and spirit of the Indian originals—feelings both of pathos and humor. The Indians certainly were premier poets of the West. The poems included *about* Indians are just a few we especially liked.

So what should be included in a collection of this kind? Where does the West begin? How far north or south does it extend? The boundaries have been more clearly set since Arthur Chapman wrote his poem in reply to the question, and Horace Greeley pronounced his well-known admonition—he meant upstate New York. The West is now undoubtedly the Far West beyond the Rockies. But that would exclude some good poetry of the prairies that we like very much, so we will start west of the broad Missouri.

We hope you like our choices.

. —JOHN J. AND BARBARA T. GREGG

Out Where the West Begins

Out where the hand-clasp's a little stronger,
Out where the smile dwells a little longer,
   That's where the West begins;
Out where the sun is a little brighter,
Where the snows that fall are a trifle whiter,
Where the bonds of home are a wee bit tighter,
   That's where the West begins.

Out where the skies are a little bluer,
Out where friendship's a little truer,
   That's where the West begins;
Out where a fresher breeze is blowing,
Where there's laughter in every streamlet flowing,
Where there's more of reaping and less of sowing,
   That's where the West begins.

Out where the world is in the making,
Where fewer hearts in despair are aching,
   That's where the West begins;
Where there's more of singing and less of sighing,
Where there's more of giving and less of buying,
And a man makes friends without half trying
   That's where the West begins.

ARTHUR CHAPMAN

I

Wagons West!

Lewis and Clark

Lewis and Clark
Said, "Come on, let's embark
For a boating trip up the Missouri!
It's the President's wish
And we might catch some fish,
Though the river is muddy as fury."

So they started away
On a breezy May day,
Full of courage and lore scientific,
And, before they came back,
They had blazed out a track
From St. Louis straight to the Pacific.

Now, if *you* want to go
From St. Louis (in Mo.)
To Portland (the Ore. not the Me. one),
You can fly there in planes
Or board limited trains
Or the family car, if there be one.

It may take you two weeks,
If your car's full of squeaks
And you stop for the sights and the strangers,
But it took them (don't laugh!)
Just one year and a half,
Full of buffalo, Indians and dangers.

They ate prairie-dog soup
When they suffered from croup,
For the weather was often quite drizzly.
They learned "How do you do?"
In Shoshone and Sioux,
And how to be chased by a grizzly.

They crossed mountain and river
With never a quiver,
And the Rockies themselves weren't too big for them,

For they scrambled across
With their teeth full of moss,
But their fiddler still playing a jig for them.

Missouri's Great Falls,
And the Yellowstone's walls
And the mighty Columbia's billows,
They viewed or traversed,
Of all white men the first
To make the whole Northwest their pillows.

And, when they returned,
It was glory well-earned
That they gave to the national chorus.
They were ragged and lean
But they'd seen what they'd seen,
And it spread out an Empire before us.

ROSEMARY AND STEPHEN BENÉT

Western Wagons

They went with axe and rifle, when the trail was still to blaze
They went with wife and children, in the prairie-schooner days
With banjo and with frying pan—Susanna, don't you cry!
For I'm off to California to get rich out there or die!

We've broken land and cleared it, but we're tired of where we
    are.
They say that wild Nebraska is a better place by far.
There's gold in far Wyoming, there's black earth in Ioway,
So pack up the kids and blankets, for we're moving out today.

The cowards never started and the weak died on the road,
And all across the continent the endless campfires glowed
We'd taken land and settled—but a traveler passed by—
And we're going West tomorrow—Lordy, never ask us why!

We're going West tomorrow, where the promises can't fail.
O'er the hills in legions, boys, and crowd the dusty trail!
We shall starve and freeze and suffer. We shall die, and tame
    the lands.
But we're going West tomorrow, with our fortune in our hands.

                  ROSEMARY AND STEPHEN BENÉT

The Covered Wagon

Through a mist of tears I watch the years
Of my youth go by again—
The golden years when the pioneers
First peopled an unknown plain.

By our camp fire's gleam on a far off stream,
Like a light in a drifting haze,
I journey back by the old dim track
That leads to the vanished days:

As the phantom trains of the wind-swept plains
In shadowy outline pass,
The cottonwood trees stir with the breeze
That ripples the prairie grass.

The prairies swoon in the radiant noon,
And I catch the lost perfume
Of the cactus blent with the faint sweet scent
Of the yucca's waxen bloom.

The cattle drink at the river's brink
At the close of the peaceful day—
They are dim-seen ghosts of the trampling hosts
That, far-flung, once held sway.

I hear the beat of a horse's feet
And a note from a night-bird's throat,—

The deadly purr of a rattler's whir,
And the bark of a lone coyote:

And the muffled thrum of the Indian drum
As it beats a weird tattoo
For the wild war dance—the old romance
Still stirs me through and through!

The trail grows dim . . . Ah, now the rim
Of the sunset sky bends low,
And the gray-green sedge at the prairie's edge
Is bathed in a blood-red glow!

The measured breath of my mustang's feet
Still lures me down the years—
And I want to ride back by the strong man's track
That I see tonight through tears.

LENA WHITTAKER BLAKENEY

The Mule-skinners

In readin' the story of early days, it's a cause of
    much personal pain
At the way the author-men leave out us in charge
    of the wagon train;
Granted the rest of 'em worked and fit in the best
    way that they could do—
If it wasn't for us that skinned the mules, how
    would the bunch have come through?

We have frosted ourselves on the prairie sweeps
    a-bringin' the Sioux to book,
And the sojer men never had no kick that the front
    rank had been forsook;

They cussed warm holes in the blizzard's teeth
    when waitin' fer grub and tents,
But the comforts of home we allus brung though
    at times at our expense.

We have sweated and swore in the desert land
    where the white sand glares like snow,
A-rompin' around forty rods from hell playin' tag
    with Geronimo;
We larruped the jacks when the bullets flew and
    then when 'twas gettin' too hot,
We used for our breastworks mules, dead mules,
    and we give 'em back shot for shot.

We never was rigged up purty, of course, and we
    didn't talk too perlite,
But we brung up the joltin' wagon train to the trail
    end of every fight;
We made a trail through the hostile lands and our
    whip was the victory's key,
So why in the name of all that's fair can't we figger
    in history?

          ATTRIBUTED TO JOHN CALDWELL

The Last Trail

I.

Across the bison-dotted plain
    Where plodding thousands pressed,
He wandered with a wagon train
    To seek the fabled West.

Not twenty yet!—but lithe and stout
    As a gale-resisting pine,

He had heard the golden bugles shout
  In the airs of 'Forty Nine;

And forth from his green Virginia home,
  He had burst like a colt set free,
Called by the wind and sky to roam,
  And beckoned by peak and tree.

But as he lumbered along the trail
  Over the rutted grass,
His goal seemed less than a dreamer's tale
  Beside one twinkling lass,—

Ellen, the daughter of their guide,
  A maiden rosy-fair;
Supple of limb, and amber-eyed,
  And dowered with auburn hair,
Whose gaze had a flash of stinging pride
  That was the lad's despair!

Long in his memory, like a scourge,
  He heard her scorn recur,
When, faltering-tongued, he tried to urge
  A rendezvous with her.

"O Danny Long!" her laughter trilled,
  But shook him like a blast.
"Your wish perhaps shall be fulfilled
  When you're a man at last!"

And, laughing still, she tripped away;
  But ever he bore the scar.
And ever vowing, "I'll have my day!"
  He worshipped from afar.

II

Among the weedy flats they rolled,
  And toiled up long inclines
Where mountains loomed remote and cold,
  Like white, Titanic shrines.

And over the winding timber land,
   Peopled by wolf and bear . . .
Till they saw the salt plateaux expand
   With a far, eye-wounding glare.

Then on, across a starving vast
   Where the thirsty oxen fell,
And the mountains, strewn with sagebrush, cast
   A spirit-clouding spell.

Even their leader's granite brow
   Was furrowed with grim alarm:
"Make haste! We're late already now!"
   He shouted, with upraised arm.

"Make haste! The winter comes! It comes,
   And frosty mounds pile high!
Hear how the winds, like threatening drums,
   Roar from the chilling sky!"

But slower and slower lagged the horde,
   And the weak began to quail.
And half a score could trudge no more
   Along the weary trail.

And half a score in silence lay,
   With crosses to mark their rest,
Far on the huge and lonely gray
   Of the desert's broken breast.

III

Scarce forty rovers, tattered and torn
   And gaunt with the rationed fare,
Arrived, when autumn was newly born,
   Where the carved Sierras stare,—

The bleak Sierras, snowy-browed
   And ragged with fir and pine,
Beyond whose spires, the guide avowed,

Were valleys free of snow or cloud
  And flowing in milk and wine!

But oh, the miles and miles between!—
  The twisted hundred miles
Along the rim of the gnarled ravine
  And the shadowy forest aisles!

Had but the mountains raised a rod
  And bidden the wind to rest,
The tired wanderers would have trod
  The warm and honeyed West;

But surely some maniac hand controlled
  The leashes of the gale.
Too early came the winter cold,
  And whitened the pilgrim trail.

Too early came the winter cold,
  With snow-drifts shoulder-tall,
And solid ranks of icy banks,
  Like some beleaguering wall! . . .

How wracked the faces Danny Long
  Viewed in the shivering camp,—
Trail-hardened men, once iron-strong,
  Now with a skeleton stamp!—

And whimpering women, thin and white
  As ghosts that came and passed,
Where the blazing logs threw back the night
  But not the chattering blast.

"If only the storm will end, will end,
  We'll push to the sunlit vale!"
But the sleet continued to descend,
  Lashed by a scourging gale.

And the sleet continued to descend,
  And famine was prowling nigh.

And the lean, sick oxen had to lend
   The only food supply.

"When these are gone? When these are gone?"
   The feverish plaint arose.
But the men, their brooding eyes withdrawn,
   Stared at the gathering snows.

"Rations for barely three weeks more!
   Three hungry weeks!" they said.
And the wind let out a screech and a roar
   Like mockery of their dread.

"There is one hope!" the whispered word
   Went flashing round the camp.
And the forlorn, desperate scheme they heard
   Burned like a smoldering lamp.

"Should any man, as a last resort,
   Plunge to the plain below,
He'll find a place—called Sutter's Fort—
   Whence help for all may flow!"

Now on the men a silence fell,
   And they nodded with mirthless smiles.
Who would set out on that frozen route
   For a hundred trackless miles?

Better to die where warm lights glow,
   With their women and their kin,
Than to fall alone in the night and snow
   Where engulfing blizzards spin!

IV

As Danny Long, with sunken eyes,
   Gazed on the blue-lipped crowd,
A startled hope began to rise
   From his spirit's wrack and cloud.

Beside an icy-hooded van
  He peered at the wasted face
Of her who, when their course began,
  Had laughed with a lily grace.

And a message in her desolate glance,
  Her ghostly-fragile cheeks,
Lashed out, and smote him like a lance:
  "We die, and no man speaks!"

"Hear me! I speak!" cried Danny Long.
  "I go! I take the trail!"
And the weary eyes of the wondering throng
  Answered, "To what avail?"

But careless of all his comrades said,
  He hastened the reckless flight.
For in the eyes of a maid he read
  A sudden grateful light.

V

The clearing sky was palely blue
  And the hooting wind had died,
When Danny waved a brisk adieu
  And mounted a white divide;
While three companions—a haggard crew—
  Stalked grayly at his side.

Over a bouldery ridge, and down
  An iced precipitous aisle,
And through ravines with a piny crown,
  They wandered in single file.

For hours, amid the mounded snow
  That piled about their knees,
Their weakening footsteps pressed below
  Through winding leagues of trees.

For hours they followed a river track,
    And recognized the way
By tatters of clothes, and heaps of black
    Where abandoned wagons lay.

And horns of cattle lined their path;
    And sleek wolves nosed in sight.
And here and there, with grisly glare,
    A skull of glittering white.

By evening the chargers of the gale
    Tore through a shrieking land.
And the damp-log fires, smoky and pale,
    Blinked on a cowering band;

While in the morning's pelted gloom
    They crept to the trail again
Like shadows stealing from a tomb,—
    Shadows that once were men.

Like shadows stealing from a tomb
    After some ghoulish rite,
Mutely they dared the tempest-doom
    And the billowing sweeps of white.

But long before that howling day
    Had snorted to a close,
One of the starved adventurers lay
    Silent amid the snows.

Shallow the grave they dug for him
    There in the screeching cold.
But the living three heard distantly
    Their own bleak dirges tolled.

Then forth once more into the blast
    Where the creaking pine-trees strained . . .
Till, when another dawn was past,
    But two of the men remained.

Now Danny, as he dragged his way
  Across the sneering wild
Beheld his sole companion sway
  And whimper like a child . . .

Then fall to earth . . . and the rainy sky
  Sobbed like a lost soul's moan.
And the youth knelt down; and, with a sigh,
  Followed the trail alone.

VI

Far through the canyon's dim descent
  He made his faltering way,
To slopes where dwarfish oaks were bent
  Under a roof of gray.

And down and down, unceasingly,
  Gnawing at roots for food,
Where, through wide hill-lands, he could see
  No end to the solitude.

Only the thought of an ice-bound camp
  In a spectral, bluish waste,
Upheld his steps on the tortured tramp
  And murmured and cried, "Make haste!"

Only the memory of a maid
  Pleading with ravaged eyes,
Stabbed at his heart as he knelt, and prayed
  To the showery, heedless skies.

"O Danny Long!" her laughter trilled
  Out of the mocking past.
"Your wish for me shall be fulfilled
  When you're a man at last!"

"Oh, may my wish be soon fulfilled!"
  He muttered, half aloud.

But "Never!" the jeering north wind shrilled
   From her rags of scudding cloud.

Now, with delirium in his brain
   And a trembling in his limbs,
He sees the stretch of the great brown plain,
   A plain that whirls and swims . . .

And he droops and sinks, to rise once more
   And stumble along the trail,
Devoured by fires that shrivel and roar,
   And demons that howl, "You fail!"
But he staggers still by pond and hill,
   Moaning, "I must prevail!"

VII

Sprawled in the mire beneath an oak
   In the mirthful valley sun,
Two Indians saw the mud-stained cloak
   Of him who was spent and done.

And they carefully gathered up the lad,
   Hoping he yet might live,
But saw that he gasped for speech, and had
   A message of blood to give.

"High up the trail—they waste away—
   Help them—the time is short!"
Such was the prayer they heard him pray
   When hastened to Sutter's Fort.

But as he tossed on a new-made bed,
   Huddled in warm, dry clothes,
He knew that a rescuing party sped
   Over the hills and snows;

And again he saw a maiden's face
   And the sparkling glance she cast;

And she smiled with the olden, rose-hued grace:
"O Danny Long, you've won the race
  And earned your wish at last!"

And the weary lids drew closed once more,
  And quiet slumber came;
And the final word his faint lips bore
  Was the echo of her name.

The final word his faint lips bore
  Was, "Tell her I shall wait
Where never numbing snow can pour
  Nor storm-gale scream its hate."

Then, with that smile of bright content
  Known to the blessèd few,
He slipped away like one who went
  To a lovers' rendezvous.

STANTON A. COBLENTZ

Pioneer Woman

Beneath these alien stars
  In darkness I have stood alone,
Barriers more than mountains
  Between me and my home.

And I have seen the shadows fall
  Grim patterned on the floor,
As onward passed the faces
  Beyond the cabin door.

The desert wind has waved my hair;
  Desert sands have etched my face,

And the courage of the mountains
Has bound me to this place.

And something of its peace I've won,
Triumphant now my day is done.
Oh, I have stood with only God
Between me and the sun.

VESTA PIERCE CRAWFORD

The Prairie Schooner

When I see a prairie schooner
With the tongue a-pointing west,
What a mighty nameless longing
Always swells and fills my breast;
For it's headed toward a country
I shall always love the best,
Toward a land of stars and sunshine,
Toward the prairies of the West.

It's a wide and wondrous region;
Naught its virgin beauty mars
Where the plains are strewn with blossoms
As the sky is strewn with stars,
Where the air so keen and bracing
Gives to life a joy and zest,
Makes the pulses leap and tingle;
In the blood there runs the West.

And I know within the schooner
'Neath its cover worn and brown,
There are hearts with hope a-tingle,
There is faith that will not down.
Though a man may meet misfortune,

Failure never is confessed
When he mounts a prairie schooner
With the tongue a-pointing west.

So when from the ties that bind me
I at last shall break away,
Leave each sordid task behind me,
As I surely shall some day,
When I choose a craft for cruising,
Love or Fortune as my quest,
It will be a prairie schooner
With the tongue a-pointing west.

EDWARD EVERETT DALE

The Pioneer

Fill up your glass, O comrade true,
   With sparkling wine that cheers,
And let us drink a bumper to
   The sturdy pioneers:
The honest men, the women fair,
   Who, years and years ago,
Had steady hearts and heads to dare
   Deeds we may never know,
   Nor page in history show.

They had their uses then, and now
   They have their uses too,
For oh! they live to tell us how,
   In eighteen sixty-two
The summer was the hottest time
   That ever scorched our State,
And then, with earnestness sublime,
   They hasten to relate
   Tales vast to contemplate,

And speak of bitter wintry woe.
　Why, mercy sakes alive!
There fell a fifteen foot of snow
　In eighteen sixty-five!
Three foot of water in the Platte
　Was frozen ten foot thick,
And, seeming not content with that,
　Each man and wife and chick
　With rheumatiz took sick.

And should we smile? The years gone by
　With martyr lives are strewn;
We're gaily treading, you and I,
　The path which they have hewn,
Hewn from the desert and the mine,
　Posterity to cheer.
Let's toast them in the sparkling wine,
　Drink to the mem'ries dear!
　Drink to the pioneer!

EUGENE FIELD

Idaho

1

They say there is a land,
　Where crystal waters flow,
O'er beds of quartz and purest gold,
　Way out in Idaho.

CHORUS:
O! wait, Idaho!
　We're coming, Idaho;
Our four "hoss" team
　Will soon be seen
Way out in Idaho.

2

We're bound to cross the plains
  And up the mountains go;
We're bound to seek our fortunes there,
  Way out in Idaho.
CHORUS

3

We'll need no pick or spade,
  No shovel, pan, or hoe;
The largest chunks are 'top of ground,
  Way out in Idaho.
CHORUS

4

We'll see hard times no more,
  And want we'll never know,
When once we've filled our sacks with *gold,*
  Way out in Idaho.
CHORUS

FRANK FRENCH

The Gift of Water

"Is water nigh?"
  The plainsmen cry,
As they meet and pass in the desert grass.
  With finger tip
  Across the lip
I ask the sombre Navajo.
The brown man smiles and answers "Sho!"
With fingers high, he signs the miles
  To the desert spring,
And so we pass in the dry dead grass,
  Brothers in bond of the water's ring.

HAMLIN GARLAND

Lost in a Norther

There are voices of pain
In the autumn rain.
There are pipings drear in the grassy waste,
There are lonely swells whose summits rise
Till they touch and blend with the sombre skies,
Where massed clouds wildly haste.

I sit on my horse in boot and spur
As the night falls drear
On the lonely plain. Afar I hear
The honk of goose and swift wing's whir
Through the graying deeps of the upper air—
Like weary great birds the clouds sail low—
The winds now wail like women in woe,
Now mutter and growl like lions in lair.

Lost on the prairie! All day alone
With my faithful horse, my swift Ladrone.
And the shapes on the shadow my scared soul cast.
Which way is north? Which way is west?
I ask Ladrone, for he knows best,
And he turns his head to the blast.
He whinnies and turns at my voice's sound,
And then impatiently paws the ground.

The night's gray turns to a starless black,
And the drifting drizzle and flying wrack
Have melted away into rayless night.
The wind like an actor, childish with age,
Plays all his characters—now sobs with rage,
Now flees like a girl in fright.

I turn from the wind, a treacherous guide,
And touch my knee to the glossy side
Of my ready horse, and the prairie wide
Slips by like a sea under bounding keel:
As I pat his neck and feel the swell

SAINT PETER'S COLLEGE LIBRARY
JERSEY CITY, NEW JERSEY 07306

Of his mighty chest and swift limbs' play,
The sorrowful wind-voice dies away.

The coyote starts from a shivering sleep
On the grassy edge of a gully's steep,
And silently slips through wind-blown weeds.
The prairie hen from before my feet
Springs up in haste with swift wings' beat,
And into the dark like a bullet speeds.

Which way is east? Which way is south?
Is not to be answered when dark as the mouth
Of a red-lipped wolf the night shuts down.
I look in vain for a star or light;
Ladrone speeds on in steady flight,
His ears laid back in an anxious frown.

The long grass breaks on his steaming breast
As foam is dashed from the billow's crest
By a keen-prowed ship.
I see it not, but I hear it whip
On my stirrup-shield, and feel the rush
And spiteful lash of the hazel brush.

The night grows colder—the wind again—
Ah! What is that? I pull at the rein
And turn my face to the blast.
It was sleet on my cheek. Ay—thick and fast
The startled snow through the darkness leaps,
As massed in the mighty north wind's wing
Like an air-borne army's rushing swing,
The dreaded norther upon me sweeps.

I bowed my head till the streaming mane
Of my panting horse warmed cheek again
And plunged straight into the night amain.

Day came and found me slowly riding on
With senses bound as in a chain.
Through drifting deeps of snow, Ladrone

Dumbly, faithful plodded on, the rein
Flung low upon his weary neck.
I long had ceased to fear or reck
Of death by cold or wolf or snow,
Bent grimly on my saddle-bow.

My limbs were numb; I seemed to ride
Upon some viewless, rushing tide—
My hands hung helpless at my side.
The multitudinous, trampling snows,
With solemn, ceaseless, rushing din,
Swept round and over me: far and wide
A *roaring silence* shut the senses in.
Above me through the hurtling shrouds
The far sky, red with morning glows,
Looked down at times
And then was lost in clouds.

But were my tongue with poet's spell
Aflame, I could not tell
The tale of biting hunger—cold—the hell
Of fear that age-long night!
How life seemed only in my brain; the wind,
The foam-white breeze of wintry seas
That roared in wrath from left to right,
Striking the helpless deaf and blind

The third morn broke upon my sight,
Streamed through the window of the room
In which I woke, I know not how—
Broke radiant in a golden bloom
As though God smiled away the night.
Like an eternal, changeless sea
Of marble lay the plain
In dazzling, moveless, soundless waste,
Horizon-girt, without a stain.

The air was still; no breath or sound
Came from the white expanse—
The whole earth seemed to wait in trance,

In hushed expectant silence bound.
And oh the beauty of the eastern sky,
Where glowed the herald banners of the King—
And as I looked with famished eye,
Lo, day came on me with a spring!

Along the iridescent billows of the snow
The sun-god shot his golden beams,
Like flaming arrows from the bow.
He broke on every crest, and gleams
    Of radiant fire
    Alit on every spire,
Along the great sun's pathway as he came,
And cloudless, soft, serene as May,
Opened the jocund day.

HAMLIN GARLAND

The Oregon Trail

Two hundred wagons, rolling out
    to Oregon
  Breaking through the gopher holes,
    lurching wide and free,
Crawling up the mountain pass, jolting,
    grumbling, rumbling on,
  Two hundred wagons, rolling to the sea.

From East and South and North they
    flock, to muster, row on row,
A fleet of ten-score prairie ships beside
    Missouri's flow.
The bullwhips crack, the oxen strain, the
    canvas-hooded files
Are off upon the long, long trail of sixteen
    hundred miles.

The women hold the guiding-lines; beside
    the rocking steers
With goad and ready rifle walk the bearded
    pioneers
Through clouds of dust beneath the sun,
    through floods of sweeping rain
Across the Kansas prairie land, across
    Nebraska's plain.

Two hundred wagons, rolling out to Oregon
    Curved around the campfire flame at halt
    when day is done,
Rest awhile beneath the stars, yoke again
    and lumber on,
    Two hundred wagons, rolling with the
    sun.

Among the barren buttes they wind beneath
    the jealous view
Of Blackfoot, Pawnee, Omaha, Arapahoe
    and Sioux.
No savage threat may check their course,
    no river deep and wide;
They swim the Platte, they ford the Snake,
    they cross the Great Divide.
They march as once from India's vales
    through Asia's mountain door
With shield and spear on Europe's plain
    their fathers marched before.
They march where leap the antelope and
    storm the buffalo
Still Westward as their fathers marched ten
    thousand years ago.

Two hundred wagons, rolling out to Oregon
    Creeping down the dark defile below the
    mountain crest,
Surging through the brawling stream, lunging,
    plunging, forging on,

Two hundred wagons, rolling toward the
    West.

Now toils the dusty caravan with swinging
      wagon-poles
Where Walla Walla pours along, where
      broad Columbia rolls.
The long-haired trapper's face grows dark
      and scowls the painted brave;
Where now the beaver builds his dam the
      wheat and rye shall wave.
The British trader shakes his head and
      weighs his nation's loss,
For where those hardy settlers come the
      Stars and Stripes will toss.
Then block the wheels, unyoke the steers;
      the prize is his who dares;
The cabins rise, the fields are sown, and
      Oregon is theirs!

    They will take, they will hold,
    By the spade in the mold,
    By the seed in the soil,
    By the sweat and the toil,
    By the plow in the loam,
    By the School and the Home!

Two hundred wagons, rolling out to Oregon,
    Two hundred wagons, ranging free and
      far,
Two hundred wagons, rumbling, grumbling,
      rolling on,
    Two hundred wagons, following a Star!

ARTHUR GUITERMAN

Away Out West

Away, away from city and street;
Away from the tread of thronging feet
That hurry and crowd, but never know
The trails where man may joy to go.
Away where the pines are green and tall,
And skies are blue, and high hills call.
Away from the things that cry and clamor,
And beat on the heart like an iron hammer—
The needless needs that chain the soul
In a ceaseless round to a useless goal.
Away where the stars are big and bright
As lamps of God in the desert night;
When silence lies like a waveless sea
That reaches from now to eternity—
Till dawn comes up on the peaks above
Like the light of joy in the eyes you love.
Away where the earth is strong and free,

With room for the men who are yet to be;
Where hope is truest and life is best—
    Away out West.

Out from the things that cramp and hold,
And shape man's life in an iron mold.
Out from walls on every side;
Out to the spaces clean and wide;
Sky for roof and the earth for floors;
Home as big as all outdoors;
Wind in the pines for a singing harp,
Camp-fire high on a granite scarp;
Rustlings soft in the leaves and grass,
Shy and quick where the wild things pass;
Life of the wilderness, better to meet
Than the things of night on a city street.
Out where we turn from yesterday
And wash our hearts in the clean today.
Out where a man is free to make
New roads of life for new hope's sake—
Free to dream of the greater man
He meant to be when life began;
Where the soul has room for its highest quest
        Away out West.

West of the lands where life is old,
Choked by the past till its blood is cold;
Dumb and dull with toil and fret;
Numb with the pain of old regret;
Dead men's hopes and memories
That whisper and call in every breeze;
Dead men's work and dead men's bones
That clog the earth and crowd the stones;
Till the heart is hushed and the pulse goes still
Lest it wake the dead and cross their will.
West, O West, where the sun each day
Bids the feet to be up and away;
Where new trails run and new lands wait,
And a man and God are his only fate.

Where the far blue peaks and the valleys wide
Cleanse the heart of its hasty pride,
And the open sky and boundless space
Carve something great on the poorest face;
Where a man's on honor to be his best—
   Away out West.

                    SHARLOT M. HALL

Laramie Trail

Across the crests of the naked hills,
   Smooth-swept by the winds of God.
It cleaves its way like a shaft of gray,
   Close-bound by the prairie sod.
It stretches flat from the sluggish Platte
   To the lands of forest shade;
The clean trail, the lean trail,
   The trail the troopers made.

It draws aside with a wary curve
   From the lurking, dark ravine.
It launches fair as a lance in air
   O'er the raw-ribbed ridge between;
With never a wait it plunges straight
   Through river or reed-grown brook;
The deep trail, the long trail,
   The trail of force and fear.

For the stirring note of the bugle's throat
   Ye may hark to-day in vain,
For the track is scarred by the gang-plow's shard
   And gulfed in the growing grain.
But wait to-night for the moonrise white;

Perchance ye may see them tread
The lost trail, the ghost trail,
   The trail of the gallant dead.

Twixt cloud and cloud o'er the pallid moon
   From the nether dark they glide
And the grasses sigh as they rustle by
   Their phantom steeds astride.
By four and four as they rode of yore
   And well they know the way:
The dim trail, the grim trail.
   The trail of toil and fray.

With tattered guidons spectral then
   Above their swaying ranks.
With carbines swung and sabres slung
   And the gray dust on their flanks.
They march again as they marched it then
   When the red men dogged their track.
The gloom trail, the doom trail.
   The trail they came not back.

They pass, like a flutter of drifting fog.
   As the hostile tribes have passed.
As the wild-wing'd birds and the bison herds
   And the unfenced prairies vast.
And those who gain by their strife and pain
   Forget, in the land they won.
The red trail, the dead trail.
   The trail of duty done.

But to him who loves heroic deeds
   The far-flung path still bides.
The bullet sings and the war-whoop rings
   And the stalwart trooper rides.
For they were the sort from Snelling Fort
   Who traveled fearlessly
The bold trail, the old trail.
   The trail to Laramie.

          JOSEPH MILLS HANSON

The Long Road West

Once I heard a hobo, singing by the tie-trail,
   Squatting by the red rail rusty with the dew:
Singing of the firelight, singing of the high-trail,
   Singing to the morning as the dawn broke through:

"Saddle, rail, or packsack—any way you take it:
   Choose a pal and try him, but on your own is best.
Sand, clay, or cinders—any way to make it,
   Looking for tomorrow down the long road west."

Far across the ranges, over where the sea swings,
   Battering the raw ledge, booming up the sand:
There I heard a sailor telling what the sea sings,
   Sings to every sailor when he longs for land:

"When you've saved your cash and when you've done
     your hitch, sir;
   Holystone and hardtack, buckle to the test—
When you're back in port and your feet begin to itch, sir,
   Think about tomorrow, and the long road west."

Slowly came a cowboy riding round the night herd;
   Silver was the starlight, slender was the moon:
Then I heard him singing, lonely as a night bird,
   Pony's head a-nodding to the queer old tune:

"Wind, rain, and sunshine—every kind of weather:
   Sweating on the mesa, freezing on the crest:
Me and just my shadow, jogging on together,
   Jogging on together down the long road west."

Lazy was the cool stream slipping through the far light
   Shadowing the buckthorn high along the hill,
When I heard a bird sing softly in the starlight,
   Singing in the evening when the trees were still:

"Valley, range, and high trail, mesa, butte, and river:
Sun across the lowlands, rolling down to rest:
There'll always be the skyline, running on forever,
Running on forever, down the long road west."

HENRY HERBERT KNIBBS

Babies of the Pioneers

Tired cattle stumbled on the dusty trail,
Men's hearts grew faint and women's cheeks turned pale.
But some there were who knew no cares nor fears—
The laughing babies of the pioneers.

EUNICE W. LUCKEY

Oregon Trail: 1851

Out they came from Liberty, out across the plains,
Two-stepping, single-footing, hard-boiled and easy-shooting
Whips cracking: oaths snapping . . .
                              Hear those banjos wail—
Emigratin' westward on the Oregon Trail.

Fight through the heathens, Rickarees and Sioux,
Aim across the wagon-wheel and drill the varmints through.
Line 'em up, line 'em out, pray the tugs'll hold,
Wheels a-screeching glory through the sunset's gold;
Keep y'r musket handy, trigger on the cock,
Peel y'r eyes, kid, if you'd see old Independence Rock!
Took our luck right in our hands; can't afford to fail—
Hittin f'r the westward on the bone-strewn trail.

Milt's woman had a kid. Nary doctor nigh,
Milt thought he'd lose 'em; figured that they'd die;
God's mercy pulled 'em through; Hallelujah, sing!
Put y'r faith in God, friends, and conquer everything!
Line them millin' leaders out; get the bulls a-goin'—
Got to get to Oregon!

   West winds blowing
Bitter from the Stonies, looming blue ahead,
Wagons bogged in prairie mud, teams stuck fast,
Heave the tumbled baggage off, clean the wagon bed,
Sweat and curse and on again, freed at last,
On again and buck the rain, buck the wind and hail—
Emigration westward on the Oregon Trail.

Onward through the mountains, lifting to the blue,
Up and through the rock cuts, weaving to the pass;
Old Ezra stopped here, where his spirit flew,
Left his little gran'child, such a pretty lass;
Ben's a-goin' to take her; that'll make him eight—
God sure'll bless him for his kindly thought.
Hitch up and roll again. Hit's getting late
And this old defile ain't no place to be caught;
No time for sorrowing, tear-eyed and pale—
Got to keep a-movin' on the Oregon Trail.

Can't see the wagon-tracks; trail's pinched out;
Nothing but the snow peaks and shale-rock slopes,
Outspan the bull-teams; we'll heave them wagons
Upside and over with the rawhide ropes—
Let's buck the mountains! Let's whip the snow crusts!
Pounding through the chill wind, shirts sweat-black . . .
Gee! But I wish I was back in Liberty!
Pull, there, you quitter! for y'u can't turn back—
Top of the mountains now, keen in the starlight,
Sunup's a-comin' in the western sea,
Yellow beams of glory-glow, floodin' the snow peaks—
There lies Oregon! Glory to Thee!

Punch up the bull teams, tune up the banjo,
Hallelujah! Praise God, kneeling in the snow,
Land of the dripping fir, land of the homestead,
Oregon! Oregon! Beckoning below—
All out for Liberty, out across the ranges,
Two-stepping, single-footing, hard-boiled and glory-singing,
Whips cracking, oaths snapping, bull teams charging on,
Babes a-borning, me a-dying, trail shouts ringing—
Here come the conquerors (and there lie the frail)
Roaring to the sunset on the Oregon Trail!

JAMES MARSHALL

Crossing the Plains

What great yoked brutes with briskets low,
With wrinkled necks like buffalo,
With round, brown, liquid, pleading eyes,
That turned so slow and sad to you,
That shone like love's eyes soft with tears,
That seemed to plead and make replies,
The while they bowed their necks and drew
The creaking load; and looked at you.
Their sable briskets swept the ground,
Their cloven feet kept solemn sound.

Two sullen bullocks led the line,
Their great eyes shining bright like wine;
Two sullen captive kings were they,
That had in time held herds at bay,
And even now they crushed the sod
With stolid sense of majesty,
And stately stepped and stately trod,
As if't were something still to be
Kings even in captivity.

JOAQUIN MILLER

Exodus for Oregon

A tale half told and hardly understood;
The talk of bearded men that chanced to meet,
That lean'd on long quaint rifles in the wood,
That look'd in fellow faces, spoke discreet
And low, as half in doubt and in defeat
Of hope; a tale it was of lands of gold
That lay below the sun. Wild-wing'd and fleet
It spread among the swift Missouri's bold
Unbridled men, and reach'd to where Ohio
  roll'd.

Then long chain'd lines of yoked and patient
  steers;
Then long white trains that pointed to the west,
Beyond the savage west; the hopes and fears
Of blunt, untutor'd men, who hardly guess'd
Their course; the brave and silent women, dress'd
In homely spun attire, the boys in bands,
The cheery babes that laugh'd at all, and bless'd
The doubting hearts, with laughing lifted
  hands! . . .
What exodus for far untraversed lands!

The Plains! The shouting drivers at the
  wheel;
The crash of leather whips; the crush and roll
Of wheels; the groan of yokes and grinding steel
And iron chain, and lo! at last the whole
Vast line, that reach'd as if to touch the goal,
Began to stretch and stream away and wind
Toward the west, as if with one control;
Then hope loom'd fair, and home lay far behind;
Before, the boundless plain, and fiercest of their
  kind.

At first the way lay green and fresh as seas,
And far away as any reach of wave;

The sunny streams went by in belt of trees;
And here and there the tassell'd tawny brave
Swept by on horse, look'd back, stretch'd forth
     and gave
A yell of warn, and then did wheel and rein
Awhile, and point away, dark-brow'd and grave,
Into the far and dim and distant plain
With signs and prophecies, and then plunged on
     again.

Some hills at last began to lift and break;
Some streams began to fail of wood and tide,
The somber plain began betime to take
A hue of weary brown, and wild and wide
It stretch'd its naked breast on every side.
A babe was heard at last to cry for bread
Amid the deserts; cattle low'd and died,
And dying men went by with broken tread,
And left a long black serpent line of wreck and
     dead.

Strange hunger'd birds, black-wing'd and still
     as death,
And crown'd of red with hooked beaks, blew
     low
And close about, till we could touch their
     breath—
Strange unnamed birds, that seem'd to come
     and go
In circles now, and now direct and slow,
Continual, yet never touch the earth;
Slim foxes slid and shuttled to and fro
At times across the dusty weary dearth
Of life, look'd back, then sank like crickets in a
     hearth.

Then dust arose, a long dim line like smoke
From out of riven earth. The wheels went
     groaning by,
Ten thousand feet in harness and in yoke,

They tore the ways of ashen alkali,
And desert winds blew sudden, swift and dry.
The dust! it sat upon and fill'd the train!
It seem'd to fret and fill the very sky.
Lo! dust upon the beasts, the tent, the plain,
And dust, alas! on breasts that rose not up again.

   They sat in desolation and in dust
By dried-up desert streams; the mother's hands
Hid all her bended face; the cattle thrust
Their tongues and faintly call'd across the lands.
The babes, that knew not what this way through
      sands
Could mean, did ask if it would end today . . .
The panting wolves slid by, red-eyed, in bands
To pools beyond. The men look'd far away,
And, silent, saw that all a boundless desert lay.

   They rose by night; they struggled on and on
As thin and still as ghosts; then here and there
Beside the dusty way before the dawn,
Men silent laid them down in their despair,
And died. But woman! Woman, frail as fair!
May man have strength to give to you your due;
You falter'd not, nor murmur'd anywhere,
You held your babes, held to your course, and
      you
Bore on through burning hell your double burdens
      through.

   Men stood at last, the decimated few,
Above a land of running streams, and they?
They push'd aside the boughs, and peering
      through
Beheld afar the cool, refreshing bay;
Then some did curse, and some bend hands to
      pray;
But some look'd back upon the desert, wide
And desolate with death, then all the day

They mourned. But one, with nothing left
    beside
His dog to love, crept down among the ferns and
    died.

JOAQUIN MILLER

William Brown

Poor William did what could be done;
  He swung a pistol on each hip,
  He gathered up a great ox-whip
And drove right for the setting sun.

He crossed the big backbone of earth,
  He saw the snowy mountains rolled
  Like mighty billows; saw the gold
Of great big sunsets; felt the birth

Of sudden dawn upon the plain;
  And every night did William Brown
  Eat pork and beans and then lie down
And dream sweet dreams of Mary Jane . . .

JOAQUIN MILLER

The Wanderer's Grave

Away from friends, away from home
  And all the heart holds dear,
A weary wand'rer laid him down,—
  Nor kindly aid was near.

And sickness prey'd upon his frame
    And told its tale of woe,
While sorrow mark'd his pallid cheeks
    And sank his spirit low.

Nor waiting friends stood round his couch
    A healing to impart,—
Nor human voice spoke sympathy,
    To sooth his aching heart.

The stars of night his watchers were,—
    His fan the rude winds breath,
And while they sigh'd their hollow moans,
    He closed his eyes in death.

Upon the prairie's vast expanse
    This weary wand'rer lay;
And far from friends, and far from home,
    He breath'd his life away!

A lovely valley marks the spot
    That claims his lowly bed;
But o'er the wand'rer's hapless fate
    No friendly tear was shed.

No willing grave received the corpse
    Of this poor lonely one;—
His bones, alas, were left to bleach
    And moulder 'neath the sun!

The night-wolf howl'd his requiem,—
    The rude winds danced his dirge;
And e'er anon, in mournful chime,
    Sigh'd forth the mellow surge!

The Spring shall teach the rising grass
    To twine for him a tomb;
And, o'er the spot where he doth lie,
    Shall bid the wild flowers bloom.

But, far from friends, and far from home
   Ah, dismal thought, to die!
Oh, let me 'mid my friends expire,
   And with my fathers lie.

                RUFUS B. SAGE

The Wagon Train

Forward! The crackling lashes send
   A thrill of action down the train,
Their brawny necks the oxen bend
   With creaking yoke and clanking chain;
The horsemen gallop down the line,
And swerve around the lowing kine
   That straggle loosely on the plain . . .

And now the sun is dropping down,
The light and shadows, red and brown,
   Are weaving sunset's purple spell:
The teams are freed, the fires are made,
Like scarlet night-flow'rs in the shade,
And pleasant groups before, between,
Are thronging in the fitful sheen—
   The day is done and all is well . . .

A hundred nights, a hundred days;
Nor folded cloud nor silken haze
Mellow the sun's midsummer blaze.
   Along the brown and barren plain
   In silence drags the wasted train;

The dust starts up beneath your tread,
Like angry ashes of the dead,
   To blind you with a choking cloud

And wrap you in a yellow shroud . . .
Alas, it is a lonesome land
Of bitter sage and barren sand,
    Under a bitter, barren sky
That never heard the robin sing,
Nor kissed the lark's exultant wing,
    Nor breathed the rose's fragrant sigh!

A weary land—alas! alas!
The shadows of the vultures pass—
    A spectral sign across your path;
The gaunt, gray wolf, with head askance,
Throws back at you a scowling glance
    Of cringing hate and coward wrath,
And like a wraith accursed and banned
Fades out before your lifted hand.

A dim, sad land, forgot, forsworn,
By all bright life that may not mourn,
    And crazed with glistening ghost of seas . . .
Only to taunt the thirst and fly
From withered lip and lurid eye . . .

The sun is weary overhead,
And pallid deserts round you spread
    A sorrowful eternity . . .
And so the dust and grit and stain
Of travel wears into the grain,
    And so the hearts and souls of men
    Were darkly tried and tested then,
So that in happy after years,
When rainbows gild remembered tears,
    Should any friend enquire of you
    If such or such an one you knew—
I hear the answer, terse and grim,
"Ah, yes, I crossed the plains with him!"

SAM L. SIMPSON

Western Lines

The Missourian crosses the plains, toting his wares and his cattle.

*   *   *

Oxen that rattle the yoke and chain, or halt in the leafy shade!
what is that you express in your eyes?
It seems to me more than all the print I have read in my life.

*   *   *

I see the vast deserts of Western America.

*   *   *

The prairie grass dividing—its special odor breathing . . .

*   *   *

Where sun-down shadows lengthen over the limitless and
lonesome prairie;
Where the herds of buffalo make a crawling spread of the square
miles far and near.

* * *

See, beyond the Kansas, countless herds of buffalo, feeding
on short, curly grass.

* * *

Aware of the buffalo herds, grazing the plains—the hirsute and
strong-breasted bull.

* * *

Night on the prairies;
The supper is over—the fire on the ground burns low;
The wearied emigrants sleep, wrapt in their blankets:
I walk by myself—I stand and look at the stars, which I think
now I never realized before.

WALT WHITMAN

The Oregon Trail

Away down yonder in the Wahee Mountains,
Where folks don't know about books nor
    countin's,
There lived a Zeke, an old galoot,
And all he knew was how to shoot.
He had a girl and he would always tell 'er
Not to monkey with a city feller;
The city feller came without fail
And old Zeke shot him on the Oregon Trail.

On the Oregon Trail, that's where he shot 'im;
On the Oregon Trail, they came down and got
    'im.
The city feller came without fail
And old Zeke shot 'im on the Oregon Trail.

Hezekiah had a lovely daughter,
Never did a thing she hadn't oughter,

She married Zeke and they went alone
Up in the mountains and built a home.
It wasn't long until the stork came flying,
Brought a kid that was always crying.
The poor stork died he grew so frail—
Couldn't stand it on the Oregon Trail.

On the Oregon Trail, that's where they killed
    'im.
On the Oregon Trail a tomb they built 'im.
They dug his grave and on it wrote:
"This poor bird was the family goat."
He carried kids until his back was broke on the
    Oregon Trail.

UNKNOWN

Star of the Western Skies

Lonely caravan a-rollin' through the night.
    Lonely caravan, you know the trail is right,
For a guiding star shines from afar,
    Leads the wagon train along.

Stars of the western skies, keep guiding me
    Over hill and dale and winding trail and over the great divide.
Land of the western skies, abide in me,
    For on the darkest night your light shall be my guide.

Wheels a grinding as we're winding on and on
    Through the night and through the coming dawn.
Stars of the western skies, keep on guiding me
    Till my restless heart is satisfied.

UNKNOWN

Sweet Betsy from Pike

Oh do you remember sweet Betsy from Pike,
Who crossed the wide prairies with her lover Ike?
With two yoke of oxen, a big yeller dog,
A tall Shanghai rooster, and one spotted hog.

    CHORUS:
Sing-a oralei, oralei, oralei aye,
Sing-a oralei, oralei, oralei aye.

Out on the prairie one bright starry night,
They broke out the whisky and Betsy got tight;
She sang and she shouted and danced o'er the plain,
And made a great show for the whole wagon train.
    CHORUS

The Injuns came down in a wild yelling horde,
And Betsy was skeered they would scalp her adored;
Behind the front wagon wheel Betsy did crawl,
And fought off the Injuns with musket and ball.
    CHORUS

They soon reached the desert, where Betsy gave out,
And down in the sand she lay rolling about;
While Ike in great terror looked on in surprise,
Saying, "Get up now, Betsy, you'll get sand in your eyes."
    CHORUS

The wagon tipped over with a terrible crash,
And out on the prairie rolled all sorts of trash;
A few little baby clothes done up with care,
Looked rather suspicious—though 'twas all on the square.
    CHORUS

The Shanghai ran off and the cattle all died,
The last piece of bacon that morning was fried;
Poor Ike got discouraged, and Betsy got mad,
The dog wagged his tail and looked wonderfully sad.
    CHORUS

They swam the wide rivers and crossed the tall peaks,
And camped on the prairie for weeks upon weeks.
Starvation and cholera and hard work and slaughter,
They reached California spite of hell and high water.
    CHORUS

Long Ike and sweet Betsy attended a dance,
Where Ike wore a pair of his Pike County pants;
Sweet Betsy was covered with ribbons and rings,
Said Ike, "You're an angel, but where are your wings?"
    CHORUS

A miner said, "Betsy, will you dance with me?"
"I will that, old hoss, if you don't make too free;
But don't dance me hard. Do you want to know why?
Doggone you, I'm chock-full of strong alkali."
    CHORUS

Long Ike and sweet Betsy got married of course
But Ike, getting jealous, obtained a divorce;
And Betsy, well satisfied, said with a shout,
"Good-by, you big lummux, I'm glad you backed out."
    CHORUS

                                                  UNKNOWN

II

Rhymes of the Gold Country

The Dead Prospector

The hills shall miss him—while the pines,
    Through which he wandered o'er the slopes,
Shall ask the nodding columbines
    Of him—the Man of Living Hopes.

He loved the mountains—when came Spring
    He turned unto the greening way,
And, as one hoards a priceless thing,
    He counted grudgingly each day.

The heights were his—let those who would
    Seek ease in vales stretched far beneath;
Where gleams yon gaunt peak's snowy hood
    His camp-fire smoke curled like a wreath.

His quest was vain—and yet who knows
    How little meant the gold he sought;
Enough for him Fall's golden glows,
    And colors in the sunset wrought.

ARTHUR CHAPMAN

The Miner's Progress

A Pilgrim from the Eastern shore
    Stood on Nevada's strand:
A tear was in his hither eye,
    A pickaxe in his hand.
A tear was in his hither eye—
    And in his left, to match,
There would have been another tear,
    But for a healing patch.

And other patches, too, he wore,
   Which on his garments hung,
And two were on that ill-starred spot
   Where mothers smite their young.
His hat, a shining "Costar" once,
   Was broken now, and dim,
And wild his bearded features gleamed,
   Beneath the tattered rim.

The Pilgrim stood: and, looking down,
   As one who is in doubt,
He sighed to see how fast *that* pair
   Of boots was wearing out.
And while he filled an ancient pipe,
   His wretchedness to cheer,
He stopped, with hurried hand, to pick
   A flea from out his ear.

Then spake this Pilgrim from the East,
   "I am a wretched man,
For lust of gold hath lured me to
   The shovel and the pan.
I saw, in dreams, a pile of gold
   Its dazzling radiance pour;
No more my visions are of gold,
   Alas! my hopes are *ore*."

"Thrice have I left this cursed spot,
   But mine it was to learn
The fatal truth, that 'dust we are,
   To dust we shall *return*.'
So, here condemned, by Fates unkind,
   I rock illusive sand,
And dream of wailing babes at home,
   Unrocked, an orphan band."

The Pilgrim paused, for now he heard
   His distant comrades' shout,
He drew a last whiff from his pipe,
   Then knocked the ashes out.

And, stooping, as he gathered up
   His shovel and his pan,
The breeze his latest accents bore,
   "I am a wretched man!"

Once more returned, at close of day,
   To a cheerless, dismal home,
He vows, if he was back in Maine,
   He never more would roam.
Now hunger makes "his bowels yearn,"
   For "yams" or "Irish roots,"
But these he looks in vain to find—
   Then tries to fry his boots.

The night is passed in happy dreams
   Of youth and childhood's joys:
Of times when he got flogged at school
   For pinching smaller boys.
His wife, whose smile hath cheered him oft,
   And rendered light his care,
He sees, in far New England's clime,
   Enjoying better fare.

But morn dispels these fairy scenes,
   And *want* arouses pluck;
He shoulders pick and pan once more,
   Again to try his luck.
He digs in dark, secluded depths,
   The spots where *slugs* abound,
And oh! what raptures fill his breast—
   His "pile" at last is found.

He drops his pick, his pan is left,
   He e'en neglects his pipe,
He leaves the diggings far behind,
   His purse he holds with iron gripe.
Resolved to dig and toil no more,
   Nor more in dreams to trust,
His well filled bag upon his back,
   Of pure and shining dust.

His wardrobe changed, behold him now,
   In affluence and pride,
Surrounded by the forms he loves,
   With joy on every side!
Pressed closely to his heart he holds
   His wife and children dear,
The latter shouting madly, while
   The former drops a tear.

ATTRIBUTED TO ALANZO DELANO

The Song of the Flume

Awake, awake! for my track is red,
  With the glow of the coming day;
And with tinkling tread, from my dusty bed,
    I haste o'er the hills away,
Up from the valley, up from the plain,
    Up from the river's side;
For I come with a gush, and a torrent's rush,
    And there's wealth in my swelling tide.

I am fed by the melting rills that start
    Where the sparkling snow-peaks gleam,
My voice is free, and with fiercest glee
    I leap in the sun's broad beam;
Tho' torn from the channels deep and old,
    I have worn through the craggy hill,
Yet I flow in pride, as my waters glide,
    And there's mirth in my music still.

I sought the shore of the sounding sea,
    From the far Sierra's hight,
With a starry breast, and a snow-capped crest
    I foamed in a path of light;
But they bore me thence in a winding way,
    The've fettered me like a slave,
And as scarfs of old were exchanged for gold,
    So they barter my soil-stained wave.

Thro' the deep tunnel, down the dark shaft,
    I search for the shining ore;
Hoist it away to the light of day,
    Which it never has seen before.
Spade and shovel, mattock and pick,
    Ply them with eager haste;
For my golden shower is sold by the hour,
    And the drops are too dear to waste.

Lift me aloft to the mountain's brow,
    Fathom the deep "blue vein,"
And I'll sift the soil for the shining spoil,
    As I sink to the valley again.
The swell of my swarthy breast shall bear
    Pebble and rock away,
Though they brave my strength, they shall yield at
       length,
    But the glittering gold shall stay.

Mine is no stern and warrior march,
    No stormy trump and drum;
No banners gleam in my darkened stream,
    As with conquering step I come;
But I touch the tributary earth
    Till it owns a monarch's sway,
And with eager hand, from a conquered land,
    I bear its wealth away.

Awake, awake! there are living hearts
    In the lands you've left afar;
There are tearful eyes in the homes you prize
    As they gaze on the western star;
Then up from the valley, up from the hill,
    Up from the river's side;
For I come with a gush, and a torrent's rush,
    And there's wrath in my swelling tide.

                      ANNA M. FITCH

Sutter's Fort, Sacramento

I stood by the old fort's crumbling wall,
    On the eastern edge of the town:
The sun through clefts in the ruined hall,
    Flecked with its light the rafters brown.

Charmed by the magic spell of the place,
  The present vanished, the past returned;
While rampart and fortress filled the space,
  And yonder the Indian camp-fires burned.

Around me were waifs from every clime,
  Blown by the fickle winds of chance—
Knight errants, ready at any time,
  For any cause, to couch a lance.

The staunch old Captain with courtly grace,
  Owner of countless leagues of land,
Benignly governed the motley race,
  Dispensing favors with open hand. . . .

Only a moment the vision came;
  Where tower and rampart stood before
Where flushed the night with the camp's red flame—
  Dust and ashes and nothing more!

                              LUCIUS HARWOOD FOOTE

Miners

ALONE IN A STOPE

It's worse than death, that hush
And the black beyond my lamplight,
I can hear the hanging pushing—
Forcing at the mine props—
Even that is silent—sure
As ever-ready death. And when I work
There is no echo of my shovel's scrape—
Nothing but the dry-boned sound
Of ghastly grey-green ore
Rattling in the shute.

GHOSTS

Hear them knocking—listen—there!
Ghosts of miners—fighting for air.
Faint—far away—down the stope—
Picking the cave in—and no hope.
You hear them knocking in the Elm Orlu,
In Leadville mines, and at Granite, too—
In the Cœur d'Alenes, and the Comstock lodes,
And in soft coal mines, where gas explodes—
Hear them! Listen—quiet—there!
Ghosts of miners—wanting air.

JOHN C. FROHLICHER

Dickens in Camp

Above the pines the moon was slowly drifting,
    The river sang below;
The dim Sierras, far beyond, uplifting
    Their minarets of snow.

The roaring camp-fire, with rude humor, painted
    The ruddy tints of health
On haggard face and form that drooped and fainted
    In the fierce race for wealth;

Till one arose, and from his pack's scant treasure
    A hoarded volume drew,
And cards were dropped from hands of listless leisure
    To hear the tale anew.

And then, while round them shadows gathered faster,
    And as the firelight fell,
He read aloud the book wherein the Master
    Had writ of "Little Nell."

Perhaps 't was boyish fancy,—for the reader
    Was youngest of them all,—
But, as he read, from clustering pine and cedar
    A silence seemed to fall;

The fir-trees, gathering closer in the shadows,
    Listened in every spray,
While the whole camp with "Nell" on English meadows
    Wandered and lost their way.

And so in mountain solitudes—o'ertaken
    As by some spell divine—
Their cares dropped from them like the needles shaken
    From out the gusty pine.

Lost is that camp and wasted all its fire;
    And he who wrought that spell?
Ah! towering pine and stately Kentish spire,
    Ye have one tale to tell!

Lost is that camp, but let its fragrant story
　　　Blend with the breath that thrills
With hop-vine's incense all the pensive glory
　　　That fills the Kentish hills.

And on that grave where English oak and holly
　　　And laurel wreaths entwine,
Deem it not all a too presumptuous folly,
　　　This spray of Western pine!

BRET HARTE

The Society Upon the Stanislaus

I reside at Table Mountain, and my name is Truthful James;
I am not up to small deceit, or any sinful games;
And I'll tell in simple language what I know about the row
That broke up our Society upon the Stanislow.

But first I would remark, that it is not a proper plan
For any scientific gent to whale his fellow-man,
And, if a member don't agree with his peculiar whim,
To lay for that same member for to "put a head" on him.

Now nothing could be finer or more beautiful to see
Than the first six months' proceedings of that same Society,
Till Brown of Calaveras brought a lot of fossil bones
That he found within a tunnel near the tenement of Jones.

Then Brown he read a paper, and he reconstructed there,
From those same bones, an animal that was extremely rare;
And Jones then asked the Chair for a suspension of the rules,
Till he could prove that those same bones was one of his lost mules.

Then Brown he smiled a bitter smile, and said he was at fault—
It seemed he had been trespassing on Jones' family vault.
He was a most sarcastic man, this quiet Mr. Brown,
And on several occasions he had cleaned out the town.

Now I hold it is not decent for a scientific gent
To say another is an ass—at least, to all intent;
Nor should the individual who happens to be meant
Reply by heaving rocks at him, to any great extent.

Then Abner Dean of Angel's raised a point of order—when
A chunk of old red sandstone took him in the abdomen,
And he smiled a kind of sickly smile, and curled up on the floor,
And the subsequent proceedings interested him no more.

For, in less time than I write it, every member did engage
In a warfare with the remnants of a palæozoic age;
And the way they heaved those fossils in their anger was a sin,
Till the skull of an old mammoth caved the head of Thompson in.

And this is all I have to say of these improper games,
For I live at Table Mountain, and my name is Truthful James;
And I've told in simple language what I know about the row
That broke up our Society upon the Stanislow.

BRET HARTE

The Emigrant's Dying Child

Father! I'm hungered! give me bread;
   Wrap close my shivering form!
Cold blows the wind around my head,
   And wildly beats the storm.
Protect me from the angry sky;
   I shrink beneath its wrath,
And dread this torrent sweeping by,
   Which intercepts our path.
Father! These California skies,
   You said, were bright and bland—
But where, tonight, my pillow lies,—
   Is this the golden land?

'Tis well my little sister sleeps,
   Or else she too would grieve;
But only see how still she keeps—
   She has not stirred since eve.
I'll kiss her, and perhaps she'll speak;
   She'll kiss me back I know;
Oh! father, only touch her cheek,
   'Tis cold as very snow.
Father! You do not shed a tear
   Yet little Jane has died:—
Oh! promise, when you leave me here,
   To lay me by her side.
And when you pass this torrent cold,
   We've come so far to see,
And you go on beyond, for gold,
   O think of Jane and me.

G. W. PATTON

In the Mines

Leave the sluice and "tom" untended,
   Shadows darken on the river;
In the canon day is ended,
   Far above the red rays quiver;
Lay aside the bar and spade,
   Let the pick-axe cease from "drifting,"
See how much the claim has paid
   Where the gold dust has been sifting.

Tell no tales of wizard charm,
   In the myths of ages olden,
When the sorcerer's potent arm
   Turned all earthly things to golden;—
Pick and spade are magic rods
   In the brawny hands of miners;

Mightier than the ancient gods,
   Laboring men are true diviners.

Gather round the blazing fire
   In the deepening darkness gleaming,
While the red tongues leaping higher
   Seem like banners upward streaming;
Stretched around the fiery coals,
   Lulled into luxurious dreaming,
Half-a-dozen hungry souls
   Watch the iron kettle steaming.

Break the bread with ready hand,
   Labor crowns it with a blessing,—
Now the hungry crowd looks bland,
   Each a smoking piece possessing;
Pass the ham along this way,
   Quick! before the whole is taken;
Hang philosophy, we say,
   If we only save our bacon!

Spread the blankets on the ground,
   We must toil again to-morrow;
Labor brings us slumber sound
   No luxurious couch can borrow;
Watch the stars drift up the sky,
   Bending softly down above us,
Till in dreams our spirits fly
   Homeward to the friends who love us.

As the needle, frail and shivering,
   On the ocean wastes afar,
Veering, changing, trembling, quivering,
   Settles on the polar star;
So in souls of those who roam,
   Love's magnetic fires are burning,
To the loved ones left at home
   Throbbing hearts are ever turning.

JOHN SWETT

He Done His Level Best

Was he a mining on the flat—
    He done it with a zest;
Was he a leading of the choir—
    He done his level best.

If he'd a reg'lar task to do,
    He never took no rest;
Or if 'twas off-and-on—the same—
    He done his level best.

If he was preachin' on his beat,
    He'd tramp from east to west,
And north to south—in cold and heat
    He done his level best.

He'd yank a sinner outen (Hades),*
    And land him with the blest;
Then snatch a prayer 'n waltz in again,
    And do his level best.

He'd cuss and sing and howl and pray,
    And dance and drink and jest,
And lie and steal—all one to him—
    He done his level best.

Whate'er this man was sot to do,
    He done it with a zest;
No matter *what* his contract was,
    HE'D DO HIS LEVEL BEST.

MARK TWAIN

* Here I have taken a slight liberty with the original MS. "Hades" does not make such good metre as the other word of one syllable, but it sounds better. [Mark Twain's note. Supposedly the verse was written by Simon Wheeler, narrator of the Jumping Frog tale.]

The Miner's Lament

High on a rough and dismal crag,
  Where Kean might spout, "Ay, there's the rub,"
Where oft, no doubt, some midnight hag
  Had danced a jig with Beelzebub,
There stood beneath the pale moonlight
  A miner grim with visage long,
Who vexed the drowsy ear of night
  With dreadful rhyme and dismal song.

He sang: "I have no harp or lute
  To sound the stern decrees of fate;
I once possessed a two-holed flute,
  But that I sold to raise a stake.
Then wake thy strains, my wild tin-pan,
  Affright the crickets from their lairs,
Make wood and mountain ring again,
  And terrify the grizzly bears.

"My heart is on a distant shore,
  My gentle love is far away,
She dreams not that my clothes are tore!
  And all besmeared with dirty clay;
She little knows how much of late,
  Amid these dark and dismal scenes,
I've struggled with an adverse fate,
  And lived, ah me! on pork and beans.

"Oh! that a bean would never grow,
  To fling its shadow o'er my heart;
My tears of grief are hard to flow,
  But food like this must make them start,
The good old times have passed away,
  And all things now are strange and new;
All save my shirts and trousers gray,
  Three stockings and one cowhide shoe!

"Oh, give me back the days of yore,
    And all those bright though fading scenes
Connected with that happy shore
    Where turkeys grew, and clams and greens—
Those days that sank long weeks ago
    Deep in the solemn grave of time,
And left no trace that man may know
    Save trousers all patched up behind!
And boots all worn, and shoes all torn,
    Or botched with most outrageous stitches.
Oh, give me back those days of yore,
    And take these weather beaten breeches!"

ATTRIBUTED TO MARK TWAIN

The Ballad of Tonopah Bill

Tonopah Bill was a desert rat who had traveled the gold
    camps through;
He was first to hear of the latest strike wherever the rumors flew.
In the frozen north or the Rio Grande he had looked for
    elusive pay,
And the tales of his wonderful luck would spread in a most
    remarkable way.

He talked in an optimistic vein, as fitted the mining game,
And he carried his art to the Other Side when he staked his
    final claim,
For he started forth in the Milky Way and he rapped on the
    pearly gates,
And when St. Peter confronted him he asked for permanent rates.

But the good Saint shook his head and said, "No place in here
    for you!
We want no more within our door of the lawless mining crew.

They are blasting the golden streets at night to search for the
    hidden vein,
With hammer and drill and a double shift they prospect a
    copper stain.

"They have pitched their tents and staked their claims as far as
    the eye can see,
For they cannot forget the lure of the gold in all eternity."
Now Tonopah Bill grinned a knowing grin and spoke in a
    forceful way,
"Good Saint," quoth he, "there's a trick or two on that gang
    I would like to play.

"With a word or two I will send them hence and peace once
    more will reign.
They will pass at night through the pearly gates and never
    return again."
It sounded remarkably like a bluff but the need of the Saint
    was sore,
And Bill had a confident way with him, as I have remarked before.

So the gates flew wide and he entered in, and straight to the
    camp he drew,
Where he told a marvelous tale to that restless mining crew.
No thought they gave that the tale was wild, no time did they
    take to prove,
But straight as the news was flashed around the camp was
    on the move.

St. Peter looked in a vast amaze and, "Tell me," he began,
"What means you used to start so quick this mining caravan."
"I told them news of a strike," said Bill, "that just was
    made Below.
A million dollars it ran to the ton, and plenty there to show.

"Free milling rock in a fissure vein, well worth a heavy bet,
And I said if they hurried up a bit some ground was open yet."
The good Saint looked aghast and said, "This story is absurd."
"Perhaps," said Bill with a cheerful grin. " 'Tis a rumor that
    I heard."

It was not long ere the watchful Saint saw Bill approach again,
His mining tools were on his back and argument was in vain.
"I am mighty sorry to go," said he, "and to say good bye to you,
But I'm off to join the others, for the rumor might be true."

UNKNOWN

Californy Stage

Thar's no respect fer youth er age
   A-board the Californy Stage:
Yu pull an' haul an' push an' yank
   Ontill ye're ga'nted lean an' lank.
They crowd you in with Chinese men,
   Like fat hawgs packed into a pen;
They're bound your stomick to provoke
   With musty plug-terbacker smoke.

Oh, they started this dam thievin' line
   Back in th' days o' Forty-Nine:
All peace an' comfort they defy;
   You pay, then ride "Root hawg er die!"

The ladies is compelled to sit
   With dresses in terbacker spit.
The gold-crazed men don't seem to care;
   Just talk an' lie, an' sing an' swear.
The dust lays deep in summertime,
   The mountains steep an' hard to climb;
The drivers yell, "Whoa, Moll! Whoa, Bill!
   Climb out, all hands, an' push up hill!"

When them dam drivers feel inclined
   They make you walk along behind,
An' on your shoulders lug a pole
   To help 'em through some big mud-hole.

They smile an' promise, when you pay,
  "You'll have to walk 'bout half the way!"
Them lying skunks kin dam well laugh . . .
  You have to push the other half!

Thar's no respect fer youth er age
  A-board the Californy Stage!
You pull an' haul, an' cuss the day
  You left a good home fur away:
An' when at last, all pale an' sore,
  You reach the Sacremento's shore,
You're too dam heartsick fer to scold,
  And too dam weak to pick up gold!

                    UNKNOWN

"The Days of 'Forty-Nine"

You are looking now on old Tom Moore,
  A relic of bygone days;
Bummer, too, they call me now,
  But what care I for praise?
For my heart is filled with the days of yore,
  And oft I do repine
For the Days of Old, and the Days of Gold,
  And the days of 'Forty-Nine.

  REFRAIN:
Oh, my heart is filled with the Days of Yore,
  And oft I do repine
For the Days of Old, and the Days of Gold,
  And the Days of 'Forty-Nine.

I had comrades then who loved me well,
  A jovial, saucy crew:
There were some hard cases, I must confess,
  But they were all brave and true;
Who would never flinch, whate'er the pinch,
  Who never would fret nor whine,
But like good old Bricks they stood the
    kicks
  In the Days of 'Forty-Nine.
  REFRAIN

There was Monte Pete—I'll ne'er forget
  The luck he always had.
He would deal for you both day and night,
  So long as you had a scad.
He would play you Draw, he would Ante
    sling,
  He would go you a hatfull Bline—
But in a game with Death Pete lost his breath
  In the Days of 'Forty-Nine.
  REFRAIN

There was New York Jake, a butcher boy,
   That was always a-getting tight;
Whenever Jake got on a spree,
   He was spoiling for a fight.
One day he ran against a knife
   In the hands of old Bob Cline—
So over Jake we held a wake,
   In the Days of 'Forty-Nine.
      REFRAIN

There was Hackensack Jim, who could out-roar
   A Buffalo Bull, you bet!
He would roar all night, he would roar all day,
   And I b'lieve he's a-roaring yet!
One night he fell in a prospect-hole—
   'T was a roaring bad design—
For in that hole he roared out his soul
   In the Days of 'Forty-Nine.
      REFRAIN

There was Poor Lame Ches, a hard old case
   Who never did repent.
Ches never missed a single meal,
   Nor he never paid a cent.
But Poor Lame Ches, like all the rest,
   Did to death at last resign,
For all in his bloom he went up the Flume
   In the Days of 'Forty-Nine.
      REFRAIN

And now my comrades all are gone,
   Not one remains to toast;
They have left me here in my misery,
   Like some poor wandering ghost.
And as I go from place to place,
   Folks call me a "Travelling Sign,"
Saying "There goes Tom Moore, a Bummer, sure
   From the Days of 'Forty-Nine."
      REFRAIN

UNKNOWN

The Dying Californian

Lay up nearer, brother, nearer
  For my limbs are growing cold,
And thy presence seemeth dearer
  When thine arms around me fold.
I am dying, brother, dying,
  Soon you'll miss me in your berth,
And my form will soon be lying
  'Neath the ocean's briny surf.

Harken, brother, closely harken.
  I have something I would say,
Ere the vale my visions darken
  And I go from hence away.
I am going, surely going,
  For my hope in God is strong,
I am willing, brother, knowing
  That he doeth nothing wrong.

Tell my father when you greet him
  That in death I prayed for him,
Prayed that I might one day meet him
  In a world that is free from sin.
Tell my mother God assist her
  Now that she is growing old,
Tell her child would glad have kissed her
  When his lips grew pale and cold.

O my children, heaven bless them,
  They were all my life to me,
Would I could once more caress them
  Ere I sink beneath the sea.
Listen, brother, catch each whisper,
  'Tis my wife I speak of now,
Tell, O tell her how I missed her
  When the fever burned my brow.

Tell her she must kiss my children
Like the kiss I last impressed.
Hold them as when last I held them
Folded closely to my breast.
Give them early to their maker,
Putting all their trust in God,
And he never will forsake them
For he said so in his word.

Tell my sister I remember
Every kindly parting word,
And my heart has been kept tender
With the thought this memory stirred.
'Twas for them I crossed the ocean—
What my hopes were I'll not tell;
And I've gained an orphan's portion,
Yet he doeth all things well.

Tell them I never reached that haven
Where I sought the "precious dust,"
But I've gained a port called Heaven
Where the gold will never rust.
Hark, I hear my Saviour speaking,
'Tis his voice I know so well.
When I am gone, O don't be weeping.
Brother, here is my last farewell.

UNKNOWN

Humbug Steamship Companies

A Forty-niner Song

When you start for San Francisco,
They treat you like a dog,

The victuals you're compelled to eat
   Ain't fit to feed a hog.
And a drunken mate a-cursing
   And a-ord'ring you around,
And wishing that the boat would sink
   And everyone be drowned.

   CHORUS:
Then come along, come along,
   You that want to go;
"The best accommodations,"
   And "the passage very low."
Our boats they "are large enough,"
   Don't be afraid,
The *Golden Gate* is going down
   To beat the *Yankee Blade*.

The captain goes to dinner
   And begins to curse the waiter;
Knocks him out of hearing
   With a thundering big potater.
The cabin maid, half crazy, breaks
   The meat dish all to smash,
And the steward comes a-running
   With a plate of moldy hash.
   CHORUS

You are driven 'round the steerage
   Like a drove of hungry swine,
And kicked ashore at Panama
   By the Independent Line;
Your baggage it is thrown overboard,
   The like you never saw.
A trip or two will sicken you
   Of going by Panama.
   CHORUS

UNKNOWN

My Sweetie's a Mule in the Mine

My sweetie's a mule in the mine,
I drive her without any lines,
On the rumble I sit,
Tobacco I spit
All over my sweetie's behind.

UNKNOWN

III

Texas: The Lone Star State

Tall Men Riding

This is the song that the night birds sing
   As the phantom herds trail by,
Horn by horn where the long plains fling
   Flat miles to the Texas sky:

Oh, the high hawk knows where the rabbit goes,
   And the buzzard marks the kill,
But few there be with eyes to see
   The Tall Men riding still.
They hark in vain on the speeding train
   For an echo of hoofbeat thunder,
And the yellow wheat is a winding sheet
   For cattle trails plowed under.

Hoofdust flies at the low moon's rise,
   And the bullbat's lonesome whir
Is an echoed note from a longhorn throat
   Of a steer, in the days that were.
Inch by inch time draws the cinch,
   Till the saddle will creak no more,
And they who were lords of the cattle hordes
   Have tallied their final score.

This is the song that the night birds wail,
   Where the Texas plains lie wide,
Watching the dust of a ghostly trail,
   Where the phantom Tall Men ride!

                 S. OMAR BARKER

The Texas Ranger

In the old, old days when the West was young,
The Ranger rode the trail.
The thunder of hoof-beats was his song,
And the Right his Holy Grail.

He was tall and straight as Indian corn;
Weathered and brown as a berry.
His draw was as quick as the redstart's flight;
He was Law on the Texas prairie.

The sky was his roof; the earth his bed;
His saddle a ready pillow.
His friends were the quail, the wild curlew
And the shade of the button willow.

You say the Ranger rides no more?
Listen, some night, if you will
When the wind is soft as a bluebird's call,
And the prairies are dark and still,

And you may hear the pound of hoofs,
You may catch the fleeting shadow
Of a horse and rider charging across
The grassy moonlit meadow.

Through windy darkness and brittle dawn,
He follows his mighty quest,
For the trail he cut so long ago
Runs straight through the heart of the West.

MARGIE B. BOSWELL

The Cowboys' Christmas Ball

To the Ranchmen of Texas

'Way out in Western Texas, where the Clear Fork's
    waters flow,
Where the cattle are "a-browzin'," an' the Spanish ponies
    grow;
Where the Northers "come a-whistlin'" from beyond
    the neutral strip;
And the prairie dogs are sneezin', as if they had "The
    Grip";
Where the coyotes come a-howlin' 'round the ranches after
    dark,
And the mocking-birds are singin' to the lovely "medder
    lark";
Where the 'possum and the badger, and rattle-snakes
    abound,
And the monstrous stars are winkin' o'er a wilderness
    profound;
Where lonesome, tawny prairies melt into airy streams,
While the Double Mountains slumber, in heavenly kinds
    of dreams;
Where the antelope is grazin' and the lonely plovers call—
It was there that I attended "The Cowboys' Christmas
    Ball."

The town was Anson City, old Jones's county seat,
Where they raise Polled Angus cattle, and waving
    whiskered wheat;
Where the air is soft and "bammy," an' dry an' full of
    health,
And the prairies is explodin' with agricultural wealth;
Where they print the *Texas Western,* that Hec. McCann
    supplies,
With news and yarns and stories, uv most amazin' size;
Where Frank Smith "pulls the badger," on knowin'
    tenderfeet,
And Democracy's triumphant, and mighty hard to beat;

Where lives that good old hunter, John Milsap from
     Lamar,
Who "used to be the Sheriff, back East, in Paris, sah!"
'Twas there, I say, at Anson, with the lively "widder
     Wall,"
That I went to that reception, "The Cowboys' Christmas
     Ball."

The boys had left the ranches and come to town in piles;
The ladies—"kinder scatterin' "—had gathered in for
     miles.
And yet the place was crowded, as I remember well,
'Twas got for the occasion, at "The Morning Star Hotel."
The music was a fiddle an' a lively tambourine,
And a "viol came imported," by the stage from Abilene.
The room was togged out gorgeous—with mistletoe and
     shawls,
And candles flickered frescoes, around the airy walls.
The "wimmin folks" looked lovely—the boys looked
     kinder treed,
Till their leader commenced yellin': "Whoa! fellers, let's
     stampede,"
And the music started sighin', an' awailin' through the
     hall,
As a kind of introduction to "The Cowboys' Christmas
     Ball."

The leader was a feller that came from Swenson's Ranch,
They called him "Windy Billy," from "little Deadman's
     Branch."
His rig was "kinder keerless," big spurs and high-heeled
     boots;
He had the reputation that comes when "fellers shoots."
His voice was like a bugle upon the mountain's height;
His feet were animated, an' a *mighty, movin' sight,*
When he commenced to holler, "Neow fellers, stake yer
     pen!
"Lock horns ter all them heifers, an' russle 'em like men.
"Saloot yer lovely critters; neow swing an' let 'em go,
"Climb the grape vine 'round 'em—all hands do-ce-do!

"You Mavericks, jine the round-up—Jest skip her
    waterfall,"
Huh! hit wuz gettin' happy, "The Cowboys' Christmas
    Ball!"

The boys were tolerable skittish, the ladies powerful neat,
That old bass viol's music *just got there with both feet!*
That wailin', frisky fiddle, I never shall forget;
And Windy kept a singin'—I think I hear him yet—
"O Xes, chase your squirrels, an' cut 'em to one side,
"Spur Treadwell to the center, with Cross P Charley's
    bride,
"Doc. Hollis down the middle, an' twine the ladies' chain,
"Varn Andrews pen the fillies in big T Diamond's train.
"All pull yer freight tergether, neow swallow fork an'
    change,
" 'Big Boston' lead the trail herd, through little
    Pitchfork's range.
"Purr 'round yer gentle pussies, neow rope 'em! Balance
    all!"
Huh! hit wuz gettin' active—"The Cowboys' Christmas
    Ball!"

The dust riz fast an' furious, we all just galloped 'round,
Till the scenery got so giddy, that Z Bar Dick was downed.
We buckled to our partners, an' told 'em to hold on,
Then shook our hoofs like lightning, until the early
    dawn.
Don't tell me 'bout cotillions, or germans. No sir 'ee!
That whirl at Anson City just takes the cake with me.
I'm sick of lazy shufflin's, of them I've had my fill,
Give me a frontier break-down, backed up by Windy Bill.
McAllister ain't nowhar! when Windy leads the show,
I've seen 'em both in harness, and so I sorter know—
Oh, Bill, I shan't forget yer, and I'll oftentimes recall
That lively gaited sworray—"The Cowboys' Christmas
    Ball."

WILLIAM LAWRENCE "LARRY" CHITTENDEN

The Battle-Flag

It gleamed above our Old Brigade,
It led the deadly charge we made,
I saw it toss our Texan yell
Along the battle's maddest swell!

And when their pointed steel we met,
With swords unsheathed and bayonets set,
Against our storm of stifling rain
It swept our gallant riflemen!

Three times I felt it sink from sight,
Its bearer stricken in the fight;
But as one fell another came
To bear our burning oriflamme!

And still, with all its stars unrolled,
But blood on every glittering fold,
Above our worn, victorious lines
Its blended blue-and-scarlet shines!

(Away beneath the sloping West,
Small fingers shaped its glowing crest,
And, mindful of the coming strife,
Woke all its glorious stars to life!)

Oh, royal Flag! three forms are still
Who bore thee o'er yon bloody hill!
Woo vengeance to our battle-blades,
Thou leader of our bold brigades!

Wave high, O scarlet folds and blue,
Above the gallant and the true!
Shine out, O splendid stars, and light
Our thinning columns through the night!

MARY EVELYN MOORE DAVIS

Lasca

I want free life, and I want fresh air;
And I sigh for the canter after the cattle,
The crack of the whips like shots in battle,
The medley of hoofs and horns and heads
That wars and wrangles and scatters and spreads:
The green beneath and the blue above,
And dash and danger, and life and love—
And Lasca!
             Lasca used to ride
On a mouse-grey mustang close by my side,
With blue serape and bright-belled spur;
I laughed with joy as I looked at her!
Little knew she of books or creeds;
An Ave Maria sufficed her needs;
Little she cared save to be at my side.
To ride with me, and ever to ride,
From San Saba's shore to Lavaca's tide.
She was as bold as the billows that beat,
She was as wild as the breezes that blow:
From her little head to her little feet,
She was swayed in her suppleness to and fro
By each gust of passion; a sapling pine
That grows on the edge of a Kansas bluff
And wars with the wind when the weather is rough.
Is like this Lasca, this love of mine.

She would hunger that I might eat,
Would take the bitter and leave me the sweet;
But once, when I made her jealous for fun
At something I whispered or looked or done,
One Sunday, in San Antonio,
To a glorious girl in the Alamo,
She drew from her garter a little dagger,
And—sting of a wasp—it made me stagger!
An inch to the left, or an inch to the right,
And I shouldn't be maundering here tonight;
But she sobbed, and sobbing, so quickly bound

Her torn reboso about the wound
That I swiftly forgave her. Scratches don't count
        In Texas, down by the Rio Grande.

Her eye was brown—a deep, deep brown;
Her hair was darker than her eye;
And something in her smile and frown,
Curled crimson lip and instep high,
Showed that there ran in each blue vein,
Mixed with the milder Aztec strain,
The vigorous vintage of Old Spain.
She was alive in every limb
With feeling, to the finger tips;
And when the sun is like a fire,
And sky one shining, soft sapphire
One does not drink in little sips.

The air was heavy, the night was hot,
I sat by her side and forgot, forgot;
Forgot the herd that were taking their rest,
Forgot that the air was close oppressed,
That the Texas norther comes sudden and soon,
In the dead of the night or the blaze of the noon;
That, once let the herd at its breath take fright,
Nothing on earth can stop their flight;
And woe to the rider, and woe to the steed,
That falls in front of their mad stampede!

Was that thunder? I grasped the cord
Of my swift mustang without a word.
I sprang to the saddle, and she clung behind.
Away! on a hot chase down the wind!
But never was fox-hunt half so hard,
And never was steed so little spared.
For we rode for our lives. You shall hear how we fared
        In Texas, down by the Rio Grande.

The mustang flew, and we urged him on;
There was one chance left, and you have but one—
Halt, jump to the ground, and shoot your horse;

Crouch under his carcass, and take your chance:
And if the steers in their frantic course
Don't batter you both to pieces at once,
You may thank your star; if not, goodbye
To the quickening kiss and the long-drawn sigh,
And the open air and the open sky,
          In Texas, down by the Rio Grande.

The cattle gained on us, and just as I felt
For my old six-shooter behind in my belt,
Down came the mustang, and down came we,
Clinging together—and, what was the rest?
A body that spread itself on my breast,
Two arms that shielded my dizzy head,
Two lips that hard to my lips were prest;
Then came thunder in my ears,
As over us surged the sea of steers,
Blows that beat blood into my eyes,
And when I could rise—
Lasca was dead!

I gouged out a grave a few feet deep,
And there in the Earth's arms I laid her to sleep;
And there she is lying, and no one knows;
And the summer shines, and the winter snows;
For many a day the flowers have spread
A pall of petals over her head;
And the little grey hawk hangs aloft in the air,
And the sly coyote trots here and there,
And the black snake glides and glitters and slides
Into the rift of a cottonwood tree;
And the buzzard sails on,
And comes and is gone,
Stately and still, like a ship at sea.
And I wonder why I do not care
For the things that are, like the things that were.
Does half my heart lie buried there
          In Texas, down by the Rio Grande?

FRANK DESPREZ

The Cowboy's Lament

As I walked out in the streets of Laredo,
As I walked out in Laredo one day,
I spied a poor cowboy wrapped up in white linen,
Wrapped up in white linen as cold as the clay.

"Oh, beat the drum slowly and play the fife lowly,
Play the Dead March as you bear me along;
Take me to the graveyard, and lay the sod over me,
For I'm a young cowboy, and I know I've done
        wrong.

"I see by your outfit that you are a cowboy,"—
These words he did say as I boldly stepped by—
"Come, sit beside me and hear my sad story;
I was shot in the breast and I know I must die.

"Let sixteen gamblers come handle my coffin,
Let sixteen cowboys come sing me a song,
Take me to the graveyard and lay the sod over me,
For I'm a poor cowboy, and I know I've done wrong.

"My friends and relations they live in the Nation,
They know not where their boy has gone.
He first came to Texas and hired to a ranchman,
Oh, I'm a young cowboy, and I know I've done
        wrong.

"Go write a letter to my gray-haired mother,
And carry the same to my sister so dear;
But not a word shall you mention
When a crowd gathers round you my story to
        hear.

"There is another more dear than a sister,
She'll bitterly weep when she hears I am gone.
There is another who will win her affections,
For I'm a young cowboy, and they say I've done
        wrong.

"Go gather around you a crowd of young cowboys,
And tell them the story of this my sad fate;
Tell one and the other before they go further
To stop their wild roving before 't is too late.

"Oh, muffle your drums, then play your fifes merrily;
Play the Dead March as you bear me along.
And fire your guns right over my coffin;
There goes an unfortunate boy to his home.

"It was once in the saddle I used to go dashing,
It was once in the saddle I used to be gay;
First to the dram-house, then to the card-house:
Got shot in the breast, I am dying to-day.

"Get six jolly cowboys to carry my coffin;
Get six pretty maidens to bear up my pall;
Put bunches of roses all over my coffin,
Put roses to deaden the clods as they fall.

"Then swing your rope slowly and rattle your spurs
    lowly,
And give a wild whoop as you bear me along;
And in the grave throw me, and roll the sod over
    me,
For I'm a young cowboy, and I know I've done
    wrong.

"Go bring me a cup, a cup of cold water,
To cool my parched lips," the cowboy said;
Before I turned, the spirit had left him
And gone to its Giver—the cowboy was dead.

We beat the drum slowly and played the fife lowly,
And bitterly wept as we bore him along;
For we all loved our comrade, so brave, young, and
    handsome;
We all loved our comrade, although he'd done
    wrong.

ATTRIBUTED TO TROY HALE

Last Fall of the Alamo

"I am—
Excuse me, I was—the Alamo.
Ye who have tears to shed,
Shed.
Shades of Crockett, Bowie and the rest
Who in my sacred blood-stained walls were slain!
Shades of the fifty or sixty solitary survivors,
Each of whom alone escaped;
And shades of the dozen or so daughters,
Sisters, cousins and aunts of the Alamo,
Protest!
Against this foul indignity.
Ain't there enough jobs in the city
That need whitewashing
Without jumping on me?
Did I stand off 5000 Mexicans in '36
To be kalsomined and wall-papered
And fixed up with dados and pink mottoes
In '96?
Why don't you put bloomers on me at once,
And call me
The New Alamo?—
Tamaleville!
You make me tired.
I can stand a good deal yet,
So don't have any more chrysanthemum shows
In me.
If you do
I'll fall on you.
Sabe?"

                                        O. HENRY

Tamales

This is the Mexican
Don José Calderón
One of God's countrymen.
Land of the buzzard,
Cheap silver dollar, and
Cacti and murderers.
Why has he left his land
Land of the lazy man,
Land of the pulque
Land of the bull fight,
Fleas and revolution.

This is the reason,
Hark to the wherefore;
Listen and tremble.
One of his ancestors,
Ancient and garlicky,
Probably grandfather,
Died with his boots on.
Killed by the Texans,
Texans with big guns
At San Jacinto.
Died without benefit
Of priest or clergy;
Died full of Minié balls,
Mescal and pepper.

Don José Calderón
Heard of the tragedy.
Heard of it, thought of it,
Vowed a deep vengeance;
Vowed retribution
On the Americans,
Murderous gringos,
Especially Texans.
"Válgame Dios! qué
Ladrones, diablos,

Matadores, mentidores,
Carracos y perros,
Voy a matarles,
Con sólo mis manos,
Toditas sin falta."
Thus swore the Hidalgo
Don José Calderón.

He hied him to Austin.
Bought him a basket,
A barrel of pepper,
And another of garlic,
Also a rope he bought.
That was his stock in trade;
Nothing else had he.
Nor was he rated in
Dun or in Bradstreet,
Though he meant business,
Don José Calderón,
Champion of Mexico,
Don José Calderón
Seeker of vengeance.

With his stout lariat,
Then he caught swiftly
Tomcats and puppy dogs,
Caught them and cooked them,
Don José Calderón,
Vower of vengeance.
Now on the sidewalk
Sits the avenger
Selling Tamales to
Innocent purchasers.
Dire is thy vengeance,
Oh, José Calderón,
Pitiless Nemesis
Fearful Redresser
Of the wrongs done to thy
Sainted grandfather.

Now the doomed Texans,
Rashly hilarious,
Buy of the deadly wares,
Buy and devour.
Rounders at midnight,
Citizens solid,
Bankers and newsboys,
Bootblacks and preachers,
Rashly importunate,
Courting destruction,
Buy and devour.
Beautiful maidens
Buy and devour,
Gentle society youths
Buy and devour.

Buy and devour
This thing called Tamale;
Made of rat terrier,
Spitz dog and poodle,
Maltese cat, boarding house
Steak and red pepper,
Garlic and tallow,
Corn meal and shucks.
Buy without shame
Sit on store steps and eat,
Stand on the street and eat,
Ride on the cars and eat,
Strewing the shucks around
Over creation.

Dire is thy vengeance,
Don José Calderón,
For the slight thing we did
Killing thy grandfather.
What boots it if we killed
Only one greaser,
Don José Calderón?
This is your deep revenge,

You have greased all of us,
Greased a whole nation
With your Tamales,
Don José Calderón,
Santos Esperitos,
Vicente Camillo,
Quitana de Ríos,
De Rosa y Ribera.

O. HENRY

Riders of the Stars

Twenty abreast down the Golden Street ten thousand
  riders marched;
 Bow-legged boys in their swinging chaps, all clumsily
   keeping time;
And the Angel Host to the lone, last ghost their delicate
  eyebrows arched
 As the swaggering sons of the open range drew up to the
   Throne Sublime.

Gaunt and grizzled, a Texas man from out of the concourse
  strode,
 And doffed his hat with a rude, rough grace, then lifted
   his eagle head;
The sunlit air on his silvered hair and the bronze of his
  visage glowed;
 "Marster, the boys have a talk to make on the things
   up here," he said.

A hush ran over the waiting throng as the Cherubim
  replied:
 "He that readeth the hearts of men He deemeth your
   challenge strange,
Though He long hath known that ye crave your own, that
  ye would not walk but ride,
 Oh, restless sons of the ancient earth, ye men of the
   open range!"

Then warily spake the Texas man: "A petition and no
  complaint
 We here present, if the Law allows and the Marster He
   thinks it fit;
We-all agree to the things that be, but we're longing for
  things that ain't,
 So we took a vote and we made a plan and here is the
   plan we writ:—

" *'Give us a range and our horses and ropes; open the Pearly
  Gate,*

*And turn us loose in the unfenced blue riding the sunset
    rounds,*
*Hunting each stray in the Milky Way and running the
    Rancho straight;*
  *Not crowding the dogie stars too much on their way to the
    bedding-grounds.*

" 'Maverick comets that's running wild, we'll rope 'em and
    brand 'em fair,*
  *So they'll quit stampeding the starry herd and scaring the
    folks below,*
*And we'll save 'em prime for the round-up time and we
    riders'll all be there,*
  *Ready and willing to do our work as we did in the long
    ago.*

" 'We've studied the Ancient Landmarks, Sir; Taurus, the
    Bear, and Mars,*
  *And Venus a-smiling across the west as bright as a
    burning coal,*
*Plain to guide as we punchers ride night-herding the little
    stars,*
  *With Saturn's rings for our home corral and the Dipper
    our water-hole.*

" 'Here, we have nothing to do but yarn of the days that have
    long gone by,*
  *And our singing it doesn't fit in up here, though we tried it
    for old-time's sake;*
*Our hands are itching to swing a rope and our legs are stiff;
    that's why*
  *We ask you, Marster, to turn us loose—just give us an
    even break!' "*

Then the Lord He spake to the Cherubim, and this was
    His kindly word:
  "He that keepeth the threefold keys shall open and let
    them go;
Turn these men to their work again to ride with the starry
    herd;

My glory sings in the toil they crave; 't is their right.
    I would have it so."

Have you heard in the starlit dusk of eve when the lone
      coyotes roam,
  The *Yip! Yip! Yip!* of a hunting-cry, and the echo that
      shrilled afar,
As you listened still on a desert hill and gazed at the
      twinkling dome,
  And a viewless rider swept the sky on the trail of a
      shooting star?

HENRY HERBERT KNIBBS

The Daughter of Mendoza

O lend to me, sweet nightingale,
  Your music by the fountain,
And lend to me your cadences,
  O river of the mountain!
That I may sing my gay brunette,
A diamond spark in coral set,
Gem for a prince's coronet—
  The daughter of Mendoza.

How brilliant is the morning star,
  The evening star how tender,—
The light of both is in her eyes,
  Their softness and their splendor.
But for the lash that shades their light
They were too dazzling for the sight,
And when she shuts them, all is night—
  The daughter of Mendoza.

O ever bright and beauteous one,
  Bewildering and beguiling,

The lute is in thy silvery tone,
   The rainbow in thy smiling;
And thine is, too, o'er hill and dell,
The bounding of the young gazelle,
The arrow's flight and ocean's swell—
   Sweet daughter of Mendoza!

What though, perchance, we meet no more,
   What though too soon we sever?
Thy form will float like emerald light
   Before my vision ever.
For who can see and then forget
The glories of my gay brunette?
Thou art too bright a star to set,
   Sweet daughter of Mendoza!

MIRABEAU BUONAPARTE LAMAR

Texas

I went a-riding, a-riding,
Over a great long plain.
And the plain went a-sliding, a-sliding
Away from my bridle-rein.

Fields of cotton, and fields of wheat,
Thunder-blue gentians by a wire fence,
Standing cypress, red and tense,
Holding its flower rigid like a gun,
Dressed for parade by the running wheat,
By the little bouncing cotton. Terribly sweet
The cardinals sing in the live-oak trees,
And the long plain breeze,
The prairie breeze,
Blows across from swell to swell

With a ginger smell.
Just ahead, where the road curves round,
A long-eared rabbit makes a bound
Into a wheat-field, into a cotton-field,
His track glitters after him and goes still again
Over to the left of my bridle-rein.

But over to the right is a glare—glare—glare—
Of sharp glass windows.
A narrow square of brick jerks thickly up above the cotton
    plants,
A raucous mercantile thing flaring the sun from
    thirty-six windows,
Brazenly declaring itself to the lovely fields.
Tram-cars run like worms about the feet of this thing,
The coffins of cotton-bales feed it,
The threshed wheat is its golden blood.
But here it has no feet,
It has only the steep ironic grin of its thirty-six windows,
Only its basilisk eyes counting the fields,
Doing sums of how many buildings to a city, all day and
    all night.

Once they went a-riding, a-riding,
Over the great long plain.
Cowboys singing to their dogey steers,
Cowboys perched on forty-dollar saddles,
Riding to the North, six months to get there,
Six months to reach Wyoming.
"Hold up, paint horse, herd the little dogies,
Over the lone prairie."
Bones of dead steers,
Bones of dead cowboys,
Under the wheat, maybe.

The skyscraper sings another way,
A tune of steel, of wheels, of gold.
The ginger breeze blows, blows all day
Tanged with flowers and mold.

And the Texas sky whirls down, whirls down,
Taking long looks at the fussy town.
And old sky and a long plain
Beyond, beyond, my bridle-rein.

AMY LOWELL

The Defence of the Alamo

Santa Ana came storming, as a storm might come;
    There was rumble of cannon; there was rattle of blade;
There was cavalry, infantry, bugle and drum,—
    Full seven thousand in pomp and parade,
The chivalry, flower of Mexico;
And a gaunt two hundred in the Alamo!

And thirty lay sick, and some were shot through;
    For the siege had been bitter, and bloody, and long.
"Surrender or die!"—"Men, what will *you* do?"
    And Travis, great Travis, drew sword, quick and strong,
Drew a line at his feet . . . "Will you come? Will you go?
I die with my wounded, in the Alamo."

Then Bowie gasped, "Lead me over that line!"
    Then Crockett, one hand to the sick, one hand to his gun,
Crossed with him; then never a word or a sign
    Till all, sick or well, all, all save but one,
One man. Then a woman stepped, praying, and slow,
Across, to die at her post in the Alamo.

Then that one coward fled, in the night, in that night
    When all men silently prayed and thought
Of home; of to-morrow; of God and the right,
    Till dawn: and with dawn came Travis's cannon-shot,
In answer to insolent Mexico,
From the old bell-tower of the Alamo.

Then came Santa Ana, a crescent of flame!
  Then the red escalade; then the fight hand to hand;
Such an unequal fight as never had name
  Since the Persian hordes butchered that doomed Spartan band.
All day—all day and all night; and the morning? so slow,
Through the battle-smoke mantling the Alamo.

Now silence! Such silence! Two thousand lay dead
  In a crescent outside! And within? Not a breath
Save the gasp of a woman, with gory gashed head,
  All alone, all alone there, waiting for death;
And she but a nurse. Yet when shall we know
Another like this of the Alamo?

Shout "Victory, victory, victory ho!"
  I say 'tis not always to the hosts that win!
I say that the victory, high or low,
  Is given the hero who grapples with sin,
Or legion or single; just asking to know
When duty fronts death in his Alamo.

                                                JOAQUIN MILLER

Cattle

Other states were carved or born,
Texas grew from hide and horn.

Other states are long or wide,
Texas is a shaggy hide,

Dripping blood and crumpled hair;
Some fat giant flung it there,

Laid the head where valleys drain,
Stretched its rump along the plain.

Other soil is full of stones,
Texans plow up cattle-bones.

Herds are buried on the trail,
Underneath the powdered shale;

Herds that stiffened like the snow,
Where the icy northers go.

Other states have built their halls,
Humming tunes along the walls.

Texans watched the mortar stirred,
While they kept the lowing herd.

Stamped on Texan wall and roof
Gleams the sharp and crescent hoof.

High above the hum and stir
Jingle bridle-rein and spur.

Other states were made or born,
Texas grew from hide and horn.

                         BERTA HART NANCE

The Road to Texas

Beside the road to Texas
　　My father's mother lies,
With dust upon her bosom,
　　And dust upon her eyes.

Oh, cruel road to Texas,
　　How many hearts you broke
Before you gave to Texas
　　The rugged strength of oak.
　　　　　　BERTA HART NANCE

The Fight at San Jacinto

"Now for a brisk and a cheerful fight!"
　　Said Harman, big and droll,
As he coaxed his flint and steel for a light,
　　And puffed at his cold clay bowl;
"For we are a skulking lot," says he,
　　"Of land-thieves hereabout,
And the bold señores, two to one,
　　Have come to smoke us out."

Santa Ana and Castrillon,
　　Almontê brave and gay,
Portilla red from Goliad,
　　And Cos with his smart array.
Dulces and cigaritos,
　　And the light guitar, ting-tum!
Sant' Ana courts siesta—
　　And Sam Houston taps his drum. . . .

A soft, low tap, and a muffled tap,
　　And a roll not loud nor long—

We would not break Sant' Ana's nap,
  Nor spoil Almontê's song.
Saddles and knives and rifles!
  Lord! but the men were glad
When Deaf Smith muttered "Alamo!"
  And Karnes hissed "Goliad!"

The drummer tucked his sticks in his belt,
  And the fifer gripped his gun.
Oh, for one free, wild Texan yell,
  And we took the slope in a run!
But never a shout nor a shot we spent,
  Nor an oath nor a prayer that day,
Till we faced the bravos, eye to eye,
  And then we blazed away.

Then we knew the rapture of Ben Milam,
  And the glory that Travis made,
With Bowie's lunge and Crockett's shot,
  And Fannin's dancing blade;
And the heart of the fighter, bounding free
  In his joy so hot and mad—
When Millard charged for Alamo,
  Lamar for Goliad.

Deaf Smith rode straight, with reeking spur,
  Into the shock and rout:
"I've hacked and burned the bayou bridge,
  There's no sneak's back-way out!"
Muzzle or butt for Goliad,
  Pistol and blade and fist!
Oh, for the knife that never glanced,
  And the gun that never missed!

Dulces and cigaritos,
  Song and the mandolin!
That gory swamp was a gruesome grove
  To dance fandangoes in.

We bridged the bog with the sprawling herd
 That fell in that frantic rout;
We slew and slew till the sun set red,
 And the Texan star flashed out.

JOHN WILLIAMSON PALMER

Hymn of the Alamo

"Rise, man the wall, our clarion's blast
 Now sounds its final réveille;
This dawning morn must be the last
 Our faded band shall ever see.
To life, but not to hope, farewell!
 Yon trumpet's clang, and cannon's peal,
 And storming shout, and clash of steel,
Is ours, but not our country's knell!
Welcome the Spartan's death—
 'Tis no despairing strife—
We fall!—we die!—but our expiring breath
 Is Freedom's breath of life!"

"Here, on this new Thermopylae,
 Our monument shall tower on high,
And 'Alamo' hereafter be
 In bloodier fields the battle cry."
Thus Travis from the rampart cried;
 And when his warriors saw the foe
 Like whelming billows move below,
At once each dauntless heart replied,
"Welcome the Spartan's death—
 'Tis no despairing strife—
We fall!—we die!—but our expiring breath
 Is Freedom's breath of life!"

They come—like autumn leaves they fall,
   Yet, hordes on hordes, they onward rush;
With gory tramp they mount the wall
   Till numbers the defenders crush—
Till falls their flag when none remain!
    Well may the ruffians quake to tell
    How Travis and his hundred fell
Amid a thousand foemen slain!
They died the Spartan's death,
   But not in hopeless strife—
Like brothers died, and their expiring breath
   Was Freedom's breath of life!

REUBEN M. POTTER

The Men of the Alamo

To Houston at Gonzales town, ride, Ranger, for your
   life,
Nor stop to say good-bye to-day to home, or child, or
   wife;
But pass the word from ranch to ranch, to every Texan
   sword,
That fifty hundred Mexicans have crossed the Nueces
   ford,
With Castrillon and perjured Cos, Sesma and Almonte,
And Santa Anna ravenous for vengeance and for prey!
They smite the land with fire and sword; the grass
   shall never grow
Where northward sweeps that locust herd on San
   Antonio!
Now who will bar the foeman's path, to gain a breathing
   space,
Till Houston and his scattered men shall meet him
   face to face?
Who holds his life as less than naught when home and
   honor call,

And counts the guerdon full and fair for liberty to fall?
Oh, who but Barrett Travis, the bravest of them all!
With seven score of riflemen to play the rancher's
    game,
And feed a counter-fire to halt the sweeping prairie
    flame;
For Bowie of the broken blade is there to cheer them
    on,
With Evans of Concepcion, who conquered Castrillon,
And o'er their heads the Long Star flag defiant floats
    on high,
And no man thinks of yielding, and no man fears to
    die.

But ere the siege is held a week a cry is heard without,
A clash of arms, a rifle peal, the Ranger's ringing
    shout,
And two-and-thirty beardless boys have bravely hewed
    their way
To die with Travis if they must, to conquer if they
    may.

Was ever valor held so cheap in Glory's mart before
In all the days of chivalry, in all the deeds of war?
But once again the foemen gaze in wonderment and
    fear
To see a stranger break their lines and hear the Texans
    cheer.
God! how they cheered to welcome him, those spent
    and starving men!
For Davy Crockett by their side was worth an army
    then.
The wounded ones forgot their wounds; the dying
    drew a breath
To hail the king of border men, then turned to laugh
    at death.
For all knew Davy Crockett, blithe and generous as
    bold,
And strong and rugged as the quartz that hides its
    heart of gold.
His simple creed for word or deed true as the bullet
    sped,
And rung the target straight: "Be sure you're right,
    then go ahead!"

And were they right who fought the fight for Texas
    by his side?
They questioned not; they faltered not; they only
    fought and died.
Who hath an enemy like these, God's mercy slay him
    straight!—
A thousand Mexicans lay dead outside the convent
    gate,
And half a thousand more must die before the fortress
    falls,
And still the tide of war beats high around the
    leaguered walls.
At last the bloody breach is won; the weakened lines
    give way;
The wolves are swarming in the court; the lions stand
    at bay.

The leader meets them at the breach, and wins the
    soldier's prize;
A foeman's bosom sheathes his sword when gallant
    Travis dies.
Now let the victor feast at will until his crest be red—
We may not know what raptures fill the vulture with
    the dead.
Let Santa Anna's valiant sword right bravely hew and
    hack
The senseless corse; its hands are cold; they will not
    strike him back.
Let Bowie die, but 'ware the hand that wields his
    deadly knife;
Four went to slay and one comes back, so dear he sells
    his life.
And last of all let Crockett fall, too proud to sue for
    grace,
So grand in death the butcher dared not look upon his
    face.

But far on San Jacinto's field the Texan toils are set,
And Alamo's dread memory the Texan steel shall
    whet.
And Fame shall tell their deeds who fell till all the
    years be run.
"Thermopylae left one alive—the Alamo left none."

                      JAMES JEFFREY ROCHE

The Hell-Bound Train

A Texas cowboy on a barroom floor
Had drunk so much he could hold no more;
So he fell asleep with a troubled brain
To dream that he rode on the hell-bound train.

The engine with human blood was damp,
And the headlight was a brimstone lamp;
An imp for fuel was shoveling bones,
And the furnace roared with a thousand groans.

The tank was filled with lager beer,
The devil himself was engineer;
The passengers were a mixed-up crew—
Churchman, atheist, Baptist, Jew;

The rich in broadcloth, poor in rags,
Handsome girls and wrinkled hags;
Black men, yellow, red and white,
Chained together—fearful sight.

The train rushed on at an awful pace
And sulphur fumes burned hands and face;
Wilder and wilder the country grew,
Fast and faster the engine flew.

Loud and terrible thunder crashed.
Whiter, brighter lightning flashed;
Hotter still the air became
Till clothes were burned from each shrinking frame.

Then came a fearful ear-splitting yell,
Yelled Satan, "Gents, the next stop's hell!"
'Twas then the passengers shrieked with pain
And begged the devil to stop the train.

He shrieked and roared and grinned with glee,
And mocked and laughed at their misery,
"My friends, you've bought your seats on this road
I've got to go through with the complete load.

"You've bullied the weak, you've cheated the poor,
The starving tramp you've turned from the door,
You've laid up gold till your purses bust,
You've given play to your beastly lust.

"You've mocked at God in your hell-born pride.
You've killed and you've cheated; you've plundered
and lied,
You've double-crossed men and you've swore and
you've stole,
Not a one but has perjured his body and soul.

"So you've paid full fare and I'll carry you through;
If there's one don't belong, I'd like to know who,
And here's the time when I ain't no liar,
I'll land you all safe in the land of fire.

"There your flesh will scorch in the flames that roar,
You'll sizzle and scorch from rind to core."
Then the cowboy awoke with a thrilling cry,
His clothes were wet and his hair stood high.

And he prayed as he never until that hour
To be saved from hell and the devil's power.
His prayers and his vows were not in vain
And he paid no fare on the hell-bound train.

UNKNOWN

Hell in Texas

The devil, we're told, in hell was chained,
And a thousand years he there remained,
And he never complained, nor did he groan,
But determined to start a hell of his own
Where he could torment the souls of men
Without being chained to a prison pen.

So he asked the Lord if He had on hand
Anything left when He made the land.

The Lord said, "Yes, I had plenty on hand,
But I left it down on the Rio Grande.
The fact is, old boy, the stuff is so poor,
I don't think you could use it in hell any more."

But the devil went down to look at the truck,
And said if it came as a gift, he was stuck;
For after examining it careful and well
He concluded the place was too dry for hell.
So in order to get it off His hands
God promised the devil to water the lands.

For he had some water, or rather some dregs,
A regular cathartic that smelt like bad eggs.
Hence the deal was closed and the deed was given,
And the Lord went back to His place in Heaven.
And the devil said, "I have all that is needed
To make a good hell," and thus he succeeded.

He began to put thorns on all the trees,
And he mixed the sand with millions of fleas,
He scattered tarantulas along all the roads,
Put thorns on the cacti and horns on the toads;
He lengthened the horns of the Texas steers
And put an addition on jack rabbits' ears.

He put little devils in the broncho steed
And poisoned the feet of the centipede.
The rattlesnake bites you, the scorpion stings,
The mosquito delights you by buzzing his wings.
The sand burrs prevail, so do the ants,
And those that sit down need half soles on their pants.

The devil then said that throughout the land
He'd manage to keep up the devil's own brand,
And all would be mavericks unless they bore
The marks of scratches and bites by the score.
The heat in the summer is a hundred and ten,
Too hot for the devil and too hot for men.

The wild boar roams through the black chaparral,
It's a hell of a place he has for a hell;
The red pepper grows by the bank of the brook,
The Mexicans use it in all that they cook.
Just dine with a Greaser and then you will shout,
"I've a hell on the inside as well as without."

UNKNOWN

The Texas Rangers

Come all you Texas Rangers wherever you may be,
I'll tell you of some trouble which happened unto me.

My name 'tis nothing extra, the truth to you I'll tell,
Come all you jolly Rangers, I'm sure I wish you well.

It was the age of sixteen I joined the royal band,
We marched from San Antonio, unto the Rio Grande.

Our captain he informed us, perhaps he thought
    'twas right,
Before we reached the station, he was sure we would
    have to fight.

It was one morning early, our captain gave command,
"To arms, to arms," he shouted, "and by your horses
    stand."

We heard those Indians coming, we heard them give
    their yell,
My feelings at that moment no human tongue can tell.

We saw their smoke arising, it almost reached the
    sky,
My feelings at that moment, now is my time to die.

We saw those Indians coming, their arrows around us
   hailed,
My heart it sank within me, my courage almost failed.

We fought them full nine hours until the strife was
   o'er,
The like of dead and wounded, I never saw before.

Five hundred as noble Rangers as ever served the west,
We'll bury those noble Rangers, sweet peace shall be
   their rest.

I thought of my poor mother, those words she said
   to me,
"To you they are all strangers, you had better stay
   with me."

I thought she was old and childish, perhaps she did
   not know,
My mind was bent on roving and I was bound to go.

Perhaps you have a mother, likewise a sister too,
Perhaps you have a sweetheart to weep and mourn
   for you.

If this be your condition I advise you to never roam,
I advise you by experience you had better stay at
   home.

UNKNOWN

IV

California: The Golden Gate

San Francisco

The cable cars swing up the hill,
The cable cars swing down
And with them swings the roaring trade
Of San Francisco town.

A gull-gray city by the sea
The gray wall-sided warships win,
With sunlight on her windy hills,
And gray fog drifting in.

The tide goes up to Suisun,
The river fumbles at the Strait,
Westward the long Pacific swells
Slip sidling past the Golden Gate.

A green tide flows along the hills
And washes down into the sea,
The shadows of the waiting ships
Are darkly green as any tree.

And when the water lies at ease
And hills and sea melt into night,
With a slow sound the ferries pace
A milky way of light.

MARY AUSTIN

Winter in the Sierras

The pines are black on Sierra's slope,
And white are the curling snows,
The flowers are gone, the buckthorn bare,
And chilly the north wind blows;
The pine boughs creak,

And the pine trees speak
The language the north wind knows.

There's never a track leads in or out
Of the cave of the big brown bear,
The squirrels have hid in their deepest holes
And fastened the door with care;
The gaunt wolf howls,
And the red fox prowls,
As they hunt far down from the lair.

The eagle hangs on the wing all day
For the chance of a single kill,
And the little gray hawk hunts far and wide
Before he can get his fill.
The white flakes sift,
And the snow wreaths drift
To the cañons deep and still.

MARY AUSTIN

Ballad of the Hyde Street Grip

Oh, the rain is slanting sharply, and the Norther's blowing cold,
When the cable strands are loosened she is nasty hard to hold;
There's little time for sitting down and little time for gab,
For the bumper guards the crossing, and you'd best be keeping tab!
Two-and-twenty "let-go's" every double trip—
It takes a bit of doing on the Hyde Street Grip!

Throw her off at Powell street, let her go at Post,
Watch her well at Geary and at Sutter, when you coast,
Easy at the Power House, have a care at Clay,
Sacramento, Washington, Jackson, all the way!
Drop the rope at Union, never make a slip—
The lever keeps you busy on the Hyde Street Grip!

Foot-brake, wheel-brake, slot-brake and gong,
You've got to keep 'em working, or you'll be going wrong!
Rush her on the crossing, catch her on the rise,
Easy round the corners, when the dust is in your eyes!
And the bell will always stop you, if you hit her up a clip—
You are apt to earn your wages, on the Hyde Street Grip!

North Beach to Tenderloin, over Russian Hill,
The grades are something giddy and the curves are fit to kill!
All the way to Market Street, climbing up the slope,
Down upon the other side, hanging to the rope;
But the sight of San Francisco as you take the lurching dip!
There is plenty of excitement, on the Hyde Street Grip!

Oh, the lights are in the Mission and the ships are in the Bay;
And Tamalpais is looming from the Gate across the way;
The Presidio trees are waving and the hills are growing brown!
And the driving fog is harried from the Ocean to the town!
How the pulleys slap and rattle! How the cables hum and whip!
Oh, they sing a gallant chorus on the Hyde Street Grip!

When the Orpheum is closing and the crowd is on the way,
The conductor's punch is ringing and the dummy's light and gay;
But the wait upon the table by the Beach is dark and still—
Just the swashing of the surges on the shore below the mill;
And the flash of Angel Island breaks across the channel rip,
And the hush of midnight falls upon the Hyde Street Grip!

GELETT BURGESS

Shasta

The canyon is deep shade beneath
   And the tall pines rise out of it.
In the sun beyond, brilliant as death,
Is a mountain big with buried breath—
   Hark, I can hear the shout of it!

The engine, on the curve ahead,
   Turns into sight and busily
Sends up a spurt out of a bed
Of coal that lay for centuries dead
   But now recovers dizzily.

What shall I be, what shall I do
   In what divine experiment,
When, ready to be used anew,
I snap my nursing-bonds in two
   And fling away my cerement?

Shall my good hopes continue still
   And, gathering infinity,
Inhabit many a human will?—
An Indian in me, toward that hill,
   Conceives himself divinity.

                WITTER BYNNER

Land's End

(*Point Lobos, California*)

Here rage the furies that have shaped the world,
Here where a beaked old headland splits the sea
And white Niagaras of the surf are hurled
In crashing enmity
Against the rocks' worn giant filigree.
Above the thunder where the wave and shore
Merge and re-merge in fountain-bursts of spray,
The weird continual half-yelping roar
Of congregated seals rings out all day
From islets wet and gray.
And pelicans in heavy lines flap by,
And gulls skim low beneath the precipice,
And hunchback cypresses, limb-twisted, lie

On the blunt slopes and in the hoarse abyss,
And here and there a skeleton tree that stares,
Like agony petrified, with ashen bole
And boughs where life with all her struggles and cares
Incarnates her writhing soul.

Step to the gnarled cliff-edge; some Siren power
Will urge you, pull you doomward . . . down and down
There where in turquoise pools the kelp lies brown,
And where tall rollers charge in shower on shower
Of fierce erupting white, and the salt cascade
Drenching the misty shoals, and waterfalls
Replenished with every breaker, look on walls
Of inlets paved with jade.
Wild as the earth's beginning! Lone and grand
This universe of reef and cave and foam
As when scale-armored dragons clawed the sand
And the fish-lizard made the brine its home!
Hear! In each billow clamoring at the rock
Voices of masters throned aloof from man,
Lords of the deep for whom the great world-clock
Ticks not in years, but by a Cyclops' span
Of epochs and of eons. Hear the moan
Of time that stretches out to timelessness,
And power that trumpets of the shock and stress
Of planets forged in wars of storm and stone!

Ranging the headland's verge,
For but an hour I come, a transient thing,
Yet from this tumult and this beat and surge
Of elemental frenzies I shall bring
Back to the soberer world a brooding sense
Of some fresh wonder and magnificence,
The overtones of some age-hallowed glory,
When on this furrowed cypress promontory
Gods speak from the torn waves' droning eloquence.

STANTON A. COBLENTZ

From Russian Hill

Night, and the hill to me!
  Silence, no sound that jars;
Above, of stars a sea;
  Below, a sea of stars!

Trancéd in slumber's sway,
  The city at its feet.
A tang of salty spray
  Blends with the odors sweet

From garden-close and wall,
  Where the madroño stood,

And tangled chaparral,
  In the old solitude.

Here, from the Long Ago,
  Rezanov's sailors sleep;
There, the Presidio;
  Beyond, the pluméd steep;

The waters, mile on mile,
  Foam-fringed with feathery white;
The beaconed fortress isle,
  And Yerba Buena's light.

O hill of memories!
  Thy scroll so closely writ
With song, that bough and breeze
  And bird should utter it:

Hill of desire and dream,
  Youth's visions manifold,
That still in beauty gleam
  From the sweet days of old!

Ring out thy solemn tone,
  O far-off Mission bell!
I keep the tryst alone
  With one who loved me well.

A voice I may not hear!
  Face that I may not see,
Yet know a Presence near
  To watch the hour with me. . . .

How stately and serene
  The moon moves up the sky!
How silvery between
  The shores her footprints lie!

Peace, that no shadow mars!
  Night and the hill to me!
Below, a sea of stars!
  Above, of stars a sea!

INA COOLBRITH

Laguna Perdida

The stage-road runs on the sunrise plain
  To the north of the green lagoon
Where the wild ducks nest
And the ripples rest
And a lone man hides from a lonesome quest
  And the tulès are dark at noon.

The cowboys ride on the mottled plain
  To the west of the brown lagoon
Where the mustangs run,
And the dust-clouds spun
From their hammering hoofs rise up to the sun
  In the height of the blue-hot noon.

The outlaw rides on the sundown plain
  To the east of the gray lagoon
Where the buzzards wheel
And the far peaks reel
And the whirlwinds run like ghosts at his heel
  To the break in the bad-lands hewn.

The sheriff rides on the twilight plain
  To the south of the dry lagoon;
Through the silence grim,
Where the world grows dim
In a purple shadow from rim to rim
  Over sand-barrens, dune on dune.

Coyotés run on the moon-dim plain
  By the lip of the dead lagoon;
Where the shadows merge
Comes their shivering dirge
And the skull that lies by its salt-dry verge
  Gleams pale to the death-pale moon.

MAYNARD DIXON

Barriers Burned

(*A Rhyme of the San Francisco Breadline*)

It ain't such a terrible long time ago
  That Mrs. Van Bergen and me
Though livin' near by to each other, y' know,
  Was strangers, for all ye could see,
For she had a grand house an' horses to drive,
  An' a wee rented cottage was mine,
But now we need rations to keep us alive
  An' we're standin' together in line.

An' Mrs. Van Bergen she greets me these days
  With a smile an' a nod of the head;
"Ah, Mrs. McGinnis, how are you?" she says,
  "An' do you like Government bread?"
She fetches a bag made of crockydile skin
  An' I've got a sack when we meet,
But the same kind of coffee an' crackers goes in,
  An' it's all of it cooked in the street.

Sure, Mrs. Van Bergen is takin' it fine,
  Ye'd think she was used to the food;
We're gettin' acquainted, a-standin' in line,
  An' it's doin' the both of us good.

An' Mr. Van Bergen and Michael, my man,
(They've always been friendly, the men)
They're gettin' together and layin' a plan
For buildin' the city again!

CHARLES K. FIELD

Once by the Pacific

The shattered water made a misty din.
Great waves looked over others coming in,
And thought of doing something to the shore
That water never did to land before.
The clouds were low and hairy in the skies
Like locks blown forward in the gleam of eyes.
You could not tell, and yet it looked as if
The sand was lucky in being backed by cliff,
The cliff in being backed by continent.
It looked as if a night of dark intent
Was coming, and not only a night, an age.
Someone had better be prepared for rage.
There would be more than ocean water broken
Before God's last "Put out the light" was spoken.

ROBERT FROST

A Peck of Gold

Dust always blowing about the town
Except when sea fog laid it down.
And I was one of the children told
Some of the blowing dust was gold.

All the dust the wind blew high
Appeared like gold in the sunset sky.
But I was one of the children told
Some of the dust was really gold.

Such was life in the Golden Gate.
Gold dusted all we drank and ate.
And I was one of the children told
We all must eat our peck of gold.

ROBERT FROST

San Francisco From the Sea

Serene, indifferent of Fate,
Thou sittest at the Western Gate;
Upon thy heights so lately won
Still slant the banners of the sun;
Thou seest the white seas strike their tents,
O Warder of two Continents!
And scornful of the peace that flies
Thy angry winds and sullen skies,
Thou drawest all things, small or great,
To thee, beside the Western Gate.

O, lion's whelp, the hidest fast
In jungle growth of spire and mast,
I know thy cunning and thy greed,
Thy hard high lust and wilful deed,
And all thy glory loves to tell
Of specious gifts material.
Drop down, O fleecy Fog, and hide
Her skeptic sneer, and all her pride!
Wrap her, O Fog, in gown and hood
Of her Franciscan Brotherhood.
Hide me her faults, her sin and blame,

With thy grey mantle cloak her shame!
So shall she, cowléd, sit and pray
Till morning bears her sins away.
Then rise, O fleecy Fog, and raise
The glory of her coming days;
Be as the cloud that flecks the seas
Above her smoky argosies.
When forms familiar shall give place
To stranger speech and newer face;
When all her throes and anxious fears
Lie hushed in the repose of years;
When Art shall raise and Culture lift
The sensual joys and meaner thrift,
And all fulfilled the vision, we
Who watch and wait shall never see—
Who, in the morning of her race,
Toiled fair or meanly in our place—
But, yielding to the common lot,
Lie unrecorded and forgot.

BRET HARTE

What the Engines Said

Opening of the Pacific Railroad, May 12, 1869

What was it the Engines said,
Pilots touching,—head to head
Facing on the single track,
Half a world behind each back?
This is what the Engines said,
Unreported and unread.

With a prefatory screech,
In a florid Western speech,
Said the Engine from the WEST:

"I am from Sierra's crest;
And if altitude's a test,
Why, I reckon, it's confessed
That I've done my level best."

Said the Engine from the EAST:
"They who work best talk the least.
S'pose you whistle down your brakes;
What you've done is no great shakes,—
Pretty fair,—but let our meeting
Be a different kind of greeting.
Let these folks with champagne stuffing,
Not their Engines, do the *puffing*.

"Listen! Where Atlantic beats
Shores of snow and summer heats;
Where the Indian autumn skies
Paint the woods with wampum dyes,—
I have chased the flying sun,
Seeing all he looked upon,
Blessing all that he has blessed,
Nursing in my iron breast
All his vivifying heat,
All his clouds about my crest;
And before my flying feet
Every shadow must retreat."

Said the Western Engine, "Phew!"
And a long, low whistle blew.
"Come, now, really that's the oddest
Talk for one so very modest.
You brag of your East! *You* do?
Why, *I* bring the East to *you!*
All the Orient, all Cathay,
Find through me the shortest way;
And the sun you follow here
Rises in my hemisphere.
Really,—if one must be rude,—
Length, my friend, ain't longitude."

Said the Union: "Don't reflect, or
I'll run over some Director."
Said the Central: "I'm Pacific;
But, when riled, I'm quite terrific.
Yet to-day we shall not quarrel,
Just to show these folks this moral,
How two Engines—in their vision—
Once have met without collision."

This is what the Engines said,
Unreported and unread;
Spoken slightly through the nose,
With a whistle at the close.

BRET HARTE

Frisco's Defi

You may rock us, you may shock us,
  Taunt us, flaunt us, and take us for a jay—
But be danged if you can knock us,
        Frisco-by-the-Bay!

You may craze us, you may daze us,
  Smoke us, soak us and say we are too gay—
But be durned if you can feaze us,
        We're not built that way!

You may quake us, you may shake us,
  Roast us, toast us and grill us as you may
But be darned if you can make us
        Pack and move away!

You may jam us, you may slam us,
     Maim us, lame us and land on us to stay—
But be damned if you can damn us
          Frisco-by-the-Bay!

                                        H. S. HOOPER

A Ballad of the Gold Country

Deep in the hill the gold sand burned;
     The brook ran yellow with its gleams;
Close by, the seekers slept, and turned
     And tossed in restless dreams.

At dawn they waked. In friendly cheer
     Their dreams they told, by one, by one;
And each man laughed the dreams to hear,
     But sighed when they were done.

Visions of golden birds that flew,
     Of golden cloth piled fold on fold,
Of rain which shone and filtered through
     The air in showers of gold;

Visions of golden bells that rang,
     Of golden chariots that rolled,
Visions of girls that danced and sang,
     With hair and robes of gold;

Visions of golden stairs that led
     Down golden shafts of depths untold,
Visions of golden skies that shed
     Gold light on seas of gold.

"Comrades, your dreams have many shapes,"
     Said one who, thoughtful, sat apart:

"But I six nights have dreamed of grapes,
    One dream which fills my heart.

"A woman meets me crowned with vine;
    Great purple clusters fill her hands;
Her eyes divinely smile and shine,
    As beckoning she stands.

"I follow her a single pace;
    She vanishes, like light or sound,
And leaves me in a vine-walled place,
    Where grapes pile all the ground."

The comrades laughed: "We know thee by
    This fevered, drunken dream of thine."
"Ha, ha," cried he, "never have I
    So much as tasted wine!

"Now follow ye your luring shapes
    Of gold that climbs and gold that shines;
I shall await my maid of grapes,
    And plant her trees and vines."

All through the hills the gold sand burned;
    All through the lands ran yellow streams
To right, to left, the seekers turned,
    Led by the yellow gleams.

The ruddy hills were gulfed and strained;
    The rocky fields were torn and trenched;
The yellow streams were drained and drained,
    Until their sources quenched.

The gold came fast; the gold came free;
    The seekers shouted as they ran,
"Now let us turn aside and see
    How fares that husbandman!"

"No mine as yet, my friends, to sell;
    No bride to show," he smiling said:

"But here is water from my well,
   And here is wheaten bread."

"Is this thy tale?" they jeering cried;
   "Who was it followed luring shapes?
And who has won? It seems she lied,
   The maid of purple grapes!"

"When years have counted up to ten,"
   He answered gaily, smiling still,
"Come back once more, my merry men,
   And you shall have your fill

"Of purple grapes and sparkling wine,
  And figs and nectarines like flames,
And sweeter eyes than maid's shall shine
  In welcome at your names."

In scorn they heard; to scorn they laughed
  The water and the wheaten bread;
"We'll wait until a better draught
  For thy bride's health," they said.

* * * * * *

The years ran fast. The seekers went
  All up, all down the golden lands:
The streams grew pale; the hills were spent;
  Slow ran the golden sands.

And men were beggars in a day,
  For swift to come was swift to go;
What chance had got chance flung away
  On one more chance's throw.

And bleached and seamed and riven plains,
  And tossed and tortured rocks like ghosts,
And blackened lines and charred remains,
  And crumbling chimney posts,

For leagues their ghastly records spread
  Of youth and years and fortunes gone,
Like graveyards whose sad, living dead
  Had hopeless journeyed on.

* * * * * *

The years had counted up to ten:
  One night, as it grew chill and late,
The husbandman marked beggarmen
  Who leaned upon his gate.

"Ho here! good men," he eager cried,
  Before the wayfarers could speak;
"This is my vineyard. Far and wide
  For laborers I seek.

"This year has doubled on last year;
  The fruit breaks down my vines and trees;
Tarry and help till wine runs clear,
  And ask what price you please."

Purple and red, to left, to right,
  For miles the gorgeous vintage blazed;
And all day long and into night
  The vintage song was raised.

And wine ran free all thirst beyond,
  And no hand stinted bread or meat;
And maids were gay and men were fond,
  And hours were swift and sweet.

The beggarmen they worked with will;
  Their hands were thin, and lithe, and strong;
Each day they ate two good days' fill,
  They had been starved so long.

The vintage drew to end. New wine
  From thousand casks was dripping slow,
And bare and yellow fields gave sign
  For vintagers to go.

The beggarmen received their pay,
  Bright, yellow gold,—twice their demand;
The master, as they turned away,
  Held out his brawny hand,

And said: "Good men, this time next year
  My vintage will be bigger still;
Come back, if chance should bring you near,
  And it should suit your will."

The beggars nodded. But at night
  They said: "No more we go that way;
He did not know us then; he might
  Upon another day!"

HELEN HUNT JACKSON

Poppies on the Wheat

Along Ancona's hills the shimmering heat,
A tropic tide of air with ebb and flow
Bathes all the fields of wheat until they glow
Like flashing seas of green, which toss and beat
Around the vines. The poppies lithe and fleet
Seem running, fiery torchmen, to and fro
To mark the shore.
     The farmer does not know
That they are there. He walks with heavy feet,
Counting the bread and wine by autumn's gain,
But I,—I smile to think that days remain
Perhaps to me in which, though bread be sweet
No more, and red wine warm my blood in vain,
I shall be glad remembering how the fleet,
Lithe poppies ran like torchmen with the wheat.

        HELEN HUNT JACKSON

Just California

'Twixt the seas and the deserts,
 'Twixt the wastes and the waves,
Between the sands of buried lands
 And ocean's coral caves,
It lies nor East nor West,
 But like a scroll unfurled,
Where the hand of God hath hung it,
 Down the middle of the world.

It lies where God hath spread it
 In the gladness of His eyes,
Like a flame of jeweled tapestry
 Beneath His shining skies;

With the green of woven meadows,
   And the hills in golden chains,
The light of leaping rivers,
   And the flash of poppied plains.

Days rise that gleam in glory,
   Days die with sunset's breeze,
While from Cathay that was of old
   Sail countless argosies;
Morns break again in splendor
   O'er the giant New-born west,
But of all the lands God fashioned,
   'Tis this land is the best.

Sun and dews that kiss it,
   Balmy winds that blow,
The stars in clustered diadems
   Upon its peak of snow;
The mighty mountains o'er it,
   Below the white seas swirled—
Just California stretching down
   The middle of the world.

JOHN S. MCGROARTY

The King's Highway

"El Camino Real"

All in the golden weather, forth let us ride to-day,
You and I together, on the King's Highway,
The blue skies above us, and below the shining sea;
There's many a road to travel, but it's this road for me.

It's a long road and sunny, and the fairest in the world—
There are peaks that rise above it in their snowy mantles
   curled,

And it leads from the mountains through a hedge of chaparral,
Down to the waters where the sea gulls call.

It's a long road and sunny, it's a long road and old,
And the brown padres made it for the flocks of the fold;
They made it for the sandals of the sinner-folk that trod
From the fields in the open to the shelter-house of God.

They made it for the sandals of the sinner-folk of old;
Now the flocks they are scattered and death keeps the fold;
But you and I together we will take the road to-day,
With the breath in our nostrils, on the King's Highway.

We will take the road together through the morning's golden
    glow,
And we'll dream of those who trod it in the mellowed long
    ago;
We will stop at the Missions where the sleeping padres lay,
And we'll bend a knee above them for their souls' sake to
    pray.

We'll ride through the valleys where the blossom's on the
    tree,
Through the orchards and the meadows with the bird and
    the bee,
And we'll take the rising hills where the manzanitas grow,
Past the gray tails of waterfalls where blue violets blow.

Old Conquistadores, O brown priests and all,
Give us your ghosts for company when night begins to fall;
There's many a road to travel, but it's this road to-day,
With the breath of God about us on the King's Highway.

                                        JOHN S. MCGROARTY

San Francisco Falling

A groan of earth in labor pain,
Her ancient agony and strain;
A tremor of the granite floors—
A heave of seas, a wrench of shores,
A crash of walls, a moan of lips,
A terror on the towers and ships;
Blind streets where men and ghosts go by;
Whirled smoke mushrooming on the sky;
Roofs, turrets, domes, with one acclaim
Turned softly to a bloom of flame;
A thousand dreams of joy, of power,
Gone in the splendor of an hour.

EDWIN MARKHAM

San Francisco Arising

O hill-hung city of my West,
Where oft my heart goes home to rest,
There came an hour when all went by,
A cruel splendor on the sky.

Out of the Earth men saw advance
The front of Ruin and old Chance.
A groan of chaos shook your frame,
And a red wilderness of flame
Darkened the nations with your name.

Now, sons of the West, I see you rise,
The world's young courage in your eyes.
Sons of broad-shouldered Pioneers,
Seasoned by struggle and stern tears—
I see you rising, girt and strong,
To lay the new-squared beams in song.

Build greatly, men, for she must shine
With Athens of the singing Nine—
Build airily, for she must stand
With Shiraz of the rose-sweet land—
Build strongly, for her name must be
With Carthage of the sail-white sea.

EDWIN MARKHAM

Chinatown

A bit of East within a Chinese wall
Of magic, color, smell and sound—
Enclosed, and yet forever bound
Unto the west; an alien, bartering all
Its Asian mysteries in coin of trade;
Sharp, yet hidden as a sheathed blade.

A town of fantasy, pagoda hung;
Of flowered balconies with lanterns strung,
And slant eyes beckoning from balustrades.
A young town wrapped in dreams of dead decades;
A weaver making garment of the woof
Of commerce, wound with vision of Lao Tzu
The mystic; and the sad songs of Tu Fu;
And love of great Ming Huang, with souls aloof,
A town of sleeping homes, when day is through;
The Occident alone wakes up anew,
To eat and dance upon the Shanghai's roof,
Stamping its maudlin mirth with cloven hoof.

Here's teak from forests older than the T'ang
Silks, sandalwood and ivories displayed
Behind plate glass. Brass, cloisonné, cool jade.
A bell that once in Manchu temple rang
The Dragon and Republic in parade,

Firecrackers popping in toy cannonade.
Chop suey. Ginger. Nuts. One Doctor Chang,
Compounding wizard's brew of herb and fang.
The day's news on red paper on brick walls.
Shark's fins and octopus within a monger's stalls,
And, lone as Ishmael, upon a stone-paved street
A prisoned wildcat screaming in his cage
At greedy buyers, who would rend his meat
And grow to strength transmuted from his rage.

A withered man, with dimming eyes grown old,
But fingers delicate as any girl's,
Sits fashioning strange marvels from raw gold,
And jewels them with rubies and with pearls.
In houses of the Joss the sweet punks burn
To Buddha. At carved altars Ancients say
The Taoist prayers in poesy of fire;
While at Confucius' feet the sages learn;
To Him whose cross gleams whitely from the spire,
The incense rises, drifting higher, higher;
All earthly passions die, and tired hearts sing;
And hope is as the peach tree in the spring.

Small silk-swathed children, robin breasted, bright
And pert as sparrows, yet as strangely shy
As mountain quail in sudden flurried flight,
Flash out of alleys, cross curb, ever nigh
To death beneath some grinding juggernaut;
Then, tiring of life's fan-tan, so dear bought,
Turn unto other games, serene, alone,
Till dragged within doors by some gibbering crone.
Here, the Six Companies hold solemn meet;
There, reedy music and oboe calls
Unto the playhouse down the little street;
While ghosts of slain men stalk within the halls
And gape across the tables of the Tong;
The Piper pipes, and Death strikes his dull gong.

Some twenty posters ask for charity
For white man's need; the yellow will respond:

Of time, of gold, of self, equally free,
His spoken word good as a witnessed bond.

Within its Chinese wall, East goes its way;
And at the edge, upon each slippered day
The West crowds hard, lustful as sin—
Yet never wholly enters in.

ANNA BLAKE MEZQUIDA

Nostalgia

O, Frisco was a strumpet
With wind-blown locks astray,
Calling wild hearts to her
From half the world away,

Dancing by the waterfront,
Gold nuggets in both hands,
Luring with her painted lips
Men from distant lands.

San Francisco is a woman,
Mature but lovely still,
Smiling gracious welcome
To her mansion on the hill.

(But sometimes, in the evenings
When the fog comes from the sea,
The woman's laughter holds the lilt
Of the wench she used to be.)

GERTRUDE MILLARD

San Francisco Bay

How fair is San Francisco Bay
When golden stars consort and when
The moon pours silver paths for men,
And care walks by the other way!
Huge ships, black-bellied, lie below
Broad, yellow flags from silken Chind,
Round, blood-red banners from Nippon,
Like to her sun at sudden dawn—
Brave battleships as white as snow,
With bannered stars tossed to the wind,
Warm as a kiss when love is kind.

JOAQUIN MILLER

The Abalone Song

Oh! some folks boast of quail on toast
    Because they think it's toney;
But I'm content to owe my rent
    And live on abalone.

Oh! Mission Point's a friendly joint,
    Where every crab's a crony;
And true and kind you'll ever find
    The clinging abalone.

He wanders free beside the sea,
    Where'er the coast is stony;
He flaps his wings and madly sings—
    The plaintive abalone.

By Carmel bay, the people say,
    We feed the lazzaroni

On Boston beans and fresh sardines
  And toothsome abalone.

Some live on hope, and some on dope,
  And some on alimony;
But my tomcat, he lives on fat
  And tender abalone.

Oh! some drink rain and some champagne
  Or brandy by the pony;
But I will try a little rye
  With a dash of abalone.

Oh! some like jam, and some like ham,
  And some like macaroni;
But bring me in a pail of gin
  And a tub of abalone.

He hides in caves beneath the waves—
  His ancient patrimony;
And so 'tis shown that faith alone
  Reveals the abalone.

The more we take the more they make
  In deep-sea matrimony;
Race-suicide cannot betide
  The fertile abalone.

I telegraph my better half
  By Morse or by Marconi;
But if the need arise for speed,
  I send an abalone.

Oh! some think that the Lord is fat,
  And some that He is bony;
But as for me I think that He
  Is like an abalone.

GEORGE STERLING

The City by the Sea

At the end of our streets is sunrise;
At the end of our streets are spars;
At the end of our streets is sunset;
At the end of our streets—the stars.

Ever the winds of morning
Are cool from the flashing sea—
Flowing swift from our ocean,
Till the fog-dunes crumble and flee.

Slender spars in the offing,
Mast and yard in the slips—
How they tell on the Azure
Of the sea-contending ships!

Homeward into the sunset
Still unwearied we go,
Till the northern hills are misty
With the amber of afterglow.

Stars that sink to our ocean,
Winds that visit our strand,
The heavens are your pathway,
Where is a gladder land!

At the end our streets is sunrise;
At the end of our streets are spars;
At the end of our streets is sunset;
At the end of our streets—the stars.

GEORGE STERLING

The Cool, Grey City of Love

Tho I die on a distant strand,
And they give me a grave in that land,
Yet carry me back to my own city!
Carry me back to her grace and pity!
For I think I could not rest
Afar from her mighty breast.
She is fairer than others are
Whom they sing the beauty of.
Her heart is a song and a star—
My cool, grey city of love.

Tho they tear the rose from her brow,
To her is ever my vow;
Ever to her I give my duty—
First in rapture and first in beauty,
Wayward, passionate, brave,
Glad of the life God gave.
The sea-winds are her kiss,
And the sea-gull is her dove;
Cleanly and strong she is—
My cool, grey city of love.

The winds of the Future wait
At the iron walls of her Gate,
And the western ocean breaks in thunder,
And the western stars go slowly under,
And her gaze is ever West
In the dream of her young unrest.
Her sea is a voice that calls,
And her star a voice above,
And her wind a voice on her walls—
My cool, grey city of love.

Tho they stay her feet at the dance,
In her is the far romance.
Under the rain of winter falling,
Vine and rose will await recalling.

Tho the dark be cold and blind,
Yet her sea-fog's touch is kind,
And her mightier caress
Is joy and the pain thereof;
And great is thy tenderness,
O cool, grey city of love!

GEORGE STERLING

V

Cowboy Favorites

At a Cowboy Dance

Git yer little sage hens ready,
    Trot 'em out upon the floor—
Line up there, you cusses! Steady!
    Lively now! One couple more.
Shorty, shed that old sombrero;
    Bronco, douse that cigarette;
Stop that cussin', Casimero,
    'Fore the ladies! Now, all set!

S'lute yer ladies, all together!
    Ladies opposite the same—
Hit the lumber with yer leathers!
    Balance all, an' swing yer dame!
Bunch the heifers in the middle;
    Circle stags an' do-se-do!
Pay attention to the fiddle!
    Swing her round an' off you go!

First four forward! Back to places!
    Second follow—shuffle back!
Now you've got it down to cases—
    Swing 'em till their trotters crack!
Gents all right a-heel-and-toein'!
    Swing 'em, kiss 'em if you kin—
On to next an' keep a-goin'
    Till you hit yer pards ag'in!

Gents to center; ladies round 'em,
    Form a basket; balance all!
Whirl yer gals to where you found 'em!
    Promenade around the hall!
Balance to yer pards an' trot 'em
    Round the circle double quick!
Grab an' kiss 'em while you've got 'em—
    Hold 'em to it if they kick!

Ladies, left hand to yer sonnies!
    Alaman! Grand right an' left!

Balance all, an' swing yer honeys—
   Pick 'em up an' feel their heft!
Promenade like skeery cattle—
   Balance all an' swing yer sweets!
Shake yer spurs an' make 'em rattle!
   Keno! Promenade to seats!

JAMES BARTON ADAMS

The Cowboy's Life

The bawl of a steer,
To a cowboy's ear,
Is music of sweetest strain;
And the yelping notes
Of the gray coyotes
To him are a glad refrain.

And his jolly songs
Speed him along,
As he thinks of the little gal
With golden hair
Who is waiting there
At the bars of the home corral.

For a kingly crown
In the noisy town
His saddle he wouldn't change;
No life so free
As the life we see
Way out on the Yaso range.

His eyes are bright
And his heart as light
As the smoke of his cigarette;
There's never a care

For his soul to bear,
No trouble to make him fret.

The rapid beat
Of his bronco's feet
On the sod as he speeds along,
Keeps living time
To the ringing rhyme
Of his rollicking cowboy song.

Hike it, cowboys,
For the range away
On the back of a bronc' of steel,
With a careless flirt
Of the rawhide quirt
And a dig of a roweled heel!

The winds may blow
And the thunder growl
Or the breezes may safely moan;
A cowboy's life
Is a royal life,
His saddle his kingly throne.

Saddle up, boys,
For the work is play
When love's in the cowboy's eyes—
When his heart is light
As the clouds of white
That swim in the summer skies.

ATTRIBUTED TO JAMES BARTON ADAMS

The Stampede

The red sun breaks through muddy lakes of haze and rifted cloud,
And still and gray the prairies lay as motionless as the shroud.
But a distant roar was on the air, a rumble from afar,
And a dust cloud brown was sweeping down from the blue
    horizon's bar.

Above the line the great horns shine, beneath, the sharp
    hoofs speed,
And the solid ground shakes with the sound of a herd in
    full stampede.
And close to the lead is a coal-black steed, and a boy with a
    dashing bay,
Then a man with a roan who rides alone, whose hair is streaked
    with gray.

While the West still glowed they mounted and rode, and the
    reckless race began,
Through the dim starlight of the prairie night, and still they
    galloped on,
For life is cheap when men must keep these runaway brutes beside,
And until they stop, or the horses drop, it is ride and ride and ride.

The sun, from high in a murky sky, shines hot on the dusty track
Where two men ride by the great herd's side, still led by the
    fiery black;
An hour ago on the treacherous slough the gallant bay went down,
And a young voice clear rang out a cheer for the men who
    galloped on.

And now the black is falling back, panting, with low-hung head,
And shortening strides, though his dust-gray sides the spurs have
    marked with red.
He is out of the race, but into his place the gray-haired rider sweeps,
And foot by foot and inch by inch to the head of the herd he creeps.

And along the flank of the surging rank, over the trampling noise,
The echoes break as his pistols speak in sharp and threatening voice,

Till the danger is past, and they turn at last, with heavy,
    plunging tread,
Tired and blown, and the plucky roan swings slowly 'round ahead.

Give praise to the old gray veteran bold, who turned the
    maddened throng
Nor let it lack for the man with the black, who held the lead
    so long;
But what shall we add of the bare-faced lad, who knew that his race
    was done,
When, helpless, he lay by his fallen bay, but cheered his
    comrades on?

ARTHUR I. CALDWELL

Comin' to Town

The boys are comin' to town!—*Whoop la!*
  What does the marshal do?
He's gone and hid, that's what he did,
  Fer he knows a thing or two.
Fer he knows a thing or two,—*Yip, yip!*
  Fer he knows a thing or two.

The boys are comin' to town!—*Ker bang!*
  What does the dogs all do?
They hits the trail with a canine wail,
  Fer they know a thing or two.
Fer they know a thing or two,—*Ki yi!*
  Fer they know a thing or two.

The boys are comin' to town!—*Oh, my!*
  What does the old town do?
She goes to bed while they paint her red,
  Fer she knows a thing or two.
Fer she knows a thing or two,—*Wow, wow!*
  Fer she knows a thing or two.

ROBERT V. CARR

The Commission Man

Always happy, always bright,
Never changes, day or night;
Always askin' 'bout the folks,
Always knows the latest jokes.
Entertains you and the wife—
Shows and dinners—*bet your life!*
Nothin' swifter ever ran
Than that same commission man.
Comes out West stock-meetin' time;
Then the cuss is in his prime,
Passin' out his line of talk
To the shippers on the walk.
Scatters watch-charm souvenirs;
Claims that he kin sell your steers
Fer more money than the rest;
Swears his outfit is *the best*.
Then, before you know it, he
Makes you promise faithfully
That you'll ship to him next fall;
And, by Jup', you do—that's all.

ROBERT V. CARR

The Cowboy and the Stork

Bill Munson's wife was sick, you see;
Old Bill, he says that night to me:
"Go git a doctor on the run!"
And then I grabs that muckle-dun
Outlaw and jams him forty mile;
And then I gits a gray a while,
And leaves him at the Lazy T,
A-thinkin' some mean thoughts of me.

And then I gits a roan, and he
Was jes' a hoss I loves to see;
He jes' strings out and drags it down,
And soon we're siftin' into town.
The Doc drives back; and now old Bill
T'other day gives me a thrill—
The blamed old cuss, he did, *ho whee!*
He names that kidlet after me!

ROBERT V. CARR

Enlightenment

It seems the horse they furnished me
Was *rawther* rude; I could not see
Just what annoyed the brute, for he
Gave one long leap and shook me free;
And I descended to the earth
'Mid cruel shouts of ribald mirth.
"You cussed that bronk," the cowboys said,
"That's why he dumped you o'er his head;
Old Spot's *respectable* and he
Won't stand fer no profanity."

ROBERT V. CARR

Good-by, Steer

There you go, a four-year-old
Worth the fourth of a pound of gold;
Big and heavy and wild as sin,
The range will never see you ag'in.
Tenderloin fer the dude who shirks,
Neck and knuckles fer him who works;
Good-by, steer, the bull-board's down,
And you're on your way to Packin'town.

There you go, so long, old steer!
You made us sweat to git you here;
But loaded now with nineteen more,
Your days of runnin' the range are o'er.
Hide and taller, hoofs and horns,
Nothin' of you the packer scorns;
Good-by, steer, the bull-board's down,
And you're on your way to Packin'town.

ROBERT V. CARR

Home

Little old shack,
All tar-papered black,
Your chimney leans back
    From the north wind.
Your windows are few,
Your rooms only two,
But yet to my view
    You're a mansion.

Little old shack,
There's lots that you lack,
Yet still you've the knack
    To look home-like.
My hands builded you,
The wife helped me, too;
I guess you will do
    For our mansion.

ROBERT V. CARR

The Old Cowboy's Lament

The range's filled up with farmers and
        there's fences ev'rywhere,
    A painted house 'most ev'ry quarter mile;
They're raisin' blooded cattle and plantin'
        sorted seed,
    And puttin' on a painful lot o' style.

There hain't no grass to speak of and the
        water holes are gone,
    The wire of the farmer holds 'em tight;

There's little use to law 'em and little use
 to kick,
 And mighty sight less use there is to fight.

There's them coughin' separaters and their
  dirty, dusty crews,
 And wagons runnin' over with the grain;
With smoke a-driftin' upward and writin' on
  the air,
 A story that to me is mighty plain.

The wolves have left the country and the
  long-horns are no more,
 And all the game worth shootin' at is gone;
And it's time fer me to foller, 'cause I'm
  only in the way,
And I've got to be a-movin'—movin' on.

ROBERT V. CARR

The Roundup Cook

There's good cooks and there's bad ones—
 No harm in bein' frank;
But, speakin' gener'ly, I'll say,
 A roundup cook's a crank.
There's something aggravatin' in
 The dealin' out of chuck,
That makes a man not care fer jokes,
 And feel down on his luck.

If you should think to doubt my word,
 Jes' go and sass a cook;
And then fer some deep hole to hide,
 Go take a sudden look.

While goin's good, you'd better go
  Before the hash-knife falls,
Before the boss of pots and pans
  Your frame in anger crawls.

But yet we sort of like the cook,
  And love to hear him say:
"Oh, you'd better come and git it,
  Or I'll throw it all away!"
And to his face—tho', privately,
  We cuss him now and then—
We brag upon his chuck and act
  Like perfect gentlemen.

ROBERT V. CARR

Last Drift

I've sold the old ranch, stock and all,
  And let my cowboys go;
I'm driftin' into town this fall,
  'Long with the first deep snow;
I've stuck it out, the last cowman
  'Twixt here and Painted Stone;
For forty years—a healthy span—
  I've fought my fight alone.

I've fought the northers and the sheep,
  I've won, and lost, and won;
But every year, at spring's first peep,
  The old chuck wagon'd run;
Now it has vanished, with the rest—
  Its round-up days are o'er—
The range is gone—I s'pose it's best—
  And fate has closed the store.

Last night I dreamed of olden days,
    When cattle roamed the hills
And cowboys rode the prairie ways—
    No more their presence thrills—
I saw the moon shine through a rift,
    On him who stood night guard,
But woke to find that I must drift,
    Though driftin's hard, plumb hard!

ARTHUR CHAPMAN

The Legend of Boastful Bill

At a roundup on the Gily,
    One sweet mornin' long ago,
Ten of us was throwed right freely
    By a hawse from Idaho.
And we thought he'd go a-beggin'
    For a man to break his pride
'Til, a-hitchin' up one leggin',
    Boastful Bill cut loose and cried—

    "I'm a on'ry proposition for to hurt;
    I fulfill my earthly mission with a quirt;
    I kin ride the highest liver
    'Tween the Gulf and Powder River,
    And I'll break this thing as easy as I'd flirt."

So Bill climbed the Northern Fury
    And they mangled up the air
Till a native of Missouri
    Would have owned his brag was fair.
Though the plunges kep' him reelin'
    And the wind it flapped his shirt,
Loud above the hawse's squealin'
    We could hear our friend assert:

"I'm the one to take such rakin's as a joke.
Some one hand me up the makin's of a smoke!
If you think my fame needs bright'nin'
W'y I'll rope a streak of lightnin'
And I'll cinch 'im up and spur 'im till he's broke."

Then one caper of repulsion
  Broke that hawse's back in two.
Cinches snapped in the convulsion;
  Skyward man and saddle flew.
Up he mounted, never laggin',
  While we watched him through our tears,
And his last thin bit of braggin'
  Came a-droppin' to our ears:

"If you'd ever watched my habits very close
You would know I've broke such rabbits by the gross.
I have kep' my talent hidin';
I'm too good for earthly ridin'
And I'm off to bust the lightnin',—
Adios!"

Years have gone since that ascension.
  Boastful Bill ain't never lit,
So we reckon that he's wrenchin'
  Some celestial outlaw's bit.
When the night rain beats our slickers
  And the wind is swift and stout
And the lightnin' flares and flickers,
  We kin sometimes hear him shout:

"I'm a bronco-twistin' wonder on the fly;
I'm the ridin' son-of-thunder of the sky.
Hi! you earthlin's, shut your winders
While we're rippin' clouds to flinders.
If this blue-eyed darlin' kicks at you, you die!"

Stardust on his chaps and saddle,
  Scornful still of jar and jolt,

He'll come back some day, astraddle
   Of a bald-faced thunderbolt.
And the thin-skinned generation
   Of that dim and distant day
Sure will stare with admiration
   When they hear old Boastful say—

     "I was first, as old rawhiders all confessed.
     Now I'm last of all rough riders, and the best.
     Huh, you soft and dainty floaters,
     With your a'roplanes and motors—
     Huh! Are you the great grandchildren of the West!"

                    CHARLES BADGER CLARK, JR.

The Night Herder

I laughed when the dawn was a-peepin'
   And swore in the blaze of the noon,
But down from the stars is a-creepin'
   A softer, oneasier tune.
   Away, and away, and away,
     The whisperin' night seems to say
Though the trail-weary cattle are sleepin'
   And the desert dreams under the moon.

By day, if the roarin' herd scatters,
   My heart it is steady and set,
But now, when they're quiet, it patters
   Like the ball in a spinnin' roulette.
   Away, and away, and away
     To the rim where the heat lightnin's play—
Out there is the one trail that matters
   To the valley I never forget.

There's a pass where the black shadows
       shiver,

Then a desert all silvery blue,
A divide, and the breaks by the river,
    Then a light in the valley—and you!
    Away, and away, and away—
    'Tis a month till I see you by day,
But under the moon it's forever
    And the weary trail winds the world
        through.

The coyotes are laughin' out yonder,
    A happy owl whoops on the hill—
Oh, wild, lucky things that kin wander
    As far and as free as they will!
    Away, and away, and away,
    And I that am wilder than they
Must loll in my saddle and ponder
    Or sing for the cows to be still!

I see the dark river waves wrinkle;
    The valley trees droop in a swoon;
You're dreamin' where valley bells tinkle
    And half-asleep mockin'-birds croon.
    Away, and away, and away—
    Do your dainty dreams ever stray
To a camp where the desert stars twinkle
    And a lone rider sings to the moon?

CHARLES BADGER CLARK, JR.

Ridin'

There is some that like the city—
    Grass that's curried smooth and green,
Theayters and stranglin' collars,
    Wagons run by gasoline—
But for me it's hawse and saddle

Every day without a change,
And a desert sun a-blazin'
  On a hundred miles of range.

   Just a-ridin', a-ridin'—
     Desert ripplin' in the sun,
   Mountains blue along the skyline—
     I don't envy anyone
        When I'm ridin'.

When my feet is in the stirrups
  And my hawse is on the bust,
With his hoofs a-flashin' lightnin'
  From a cloud of golden dust,
And the bawlin' of the cattle
  Is a-comin' down the wind,
Then a finer life than ridin'
  Would be mighty hard to find.

   Just a-ridin', a-ridin'—
     Splittin' long cracks through the air,
   Stirrin' up a baby cyclone,
     Rippin' up the prickly pear
        As I'm ridin'.

I don't need no art exhibits
  When the sunset does her best,
Paintin' everlastin' glory
  On the mountains to the west;
And your opery looks foolish
  When the night bird starts his tune
And the desert's silver mounted
  By the touches of the moon.

   Just a-ridin', a-ridin',
     Who kin envy kings and czars
   When the coyotes down the valley
     Are a-singin' to the stars,
        If he's ridin'?

When my earthly trail is ended
    And my final bacon curled
And the last great roundup's finished
    At the Home Ranch of the world
I don't want no harps nor halos,
    Robes nor other dressed up things—
Let me ride the starry ranges
    On a pinto hawse with wings!

Just a-ridin', a-ridin'—
    Nothin' I'd like half so well
As a-roundin' up the sinners
    That have wandered out of hell,
        And a-ridin'.

CHARLES BADGER CLARK, JR.

Broncho Versus Bicycle

The first we saw of the high-tone tramp
War over thar at our Pecos camp;
He war comin' down the Santa Fe trail
Astride of a wheel with a crooked tail,
A-skinnin' along with a merry song,
An' ringin' a little warnin' gong.
He looked so outlandish, strange and queer
That all of us grinned from ear to ear,
An' every boy on the round-up swore
He had never seed sich a hoss afore.

Wal, up he rode, with a sunshine smile,
A-smokin' a cigarette, an' I'll
Be kicked in the neck if I ever seen
Sich a saddle as that on his queer machine.
Why, it made us laugh, for it wasn't half
Big enough for the back of a suckin' calf.

He tuk our fun in a keerless way.
A-venturin' only once to say
Thar wasn't a broncho about the place
Could down that wheel in a ten-mile race.

I'd a lightnin' broncho out in the herd
That could split the air like a flyin' bird,
An' I hinted round in an off-hand way
That, pervidin' the enterprise'd pay,
I thought as I might jest happen to light
On a hoss that'd leave 'im out o' sight.
In less'n a second we seed 'im yank
A roll o' greenbacks out of his flank,
An' he said, if we wanted to bet, to name
The limit, an' he would tackle the game.

Just a week afore we had all been down
On a jamboree to the nearest town,
An' the whiskey joints, an' the faro games,
An' shakin' our hoofs wi' the dance-house dames
Made a wholesale bust; an', pard, I'll be cussed
If a man in the outfit had any dust;
An' so I explained, but the youth replied
That he'd lay the money matter aside.

An' to show that his back didn't grow no moss
He'd bet his machine again' my hoss.
I tuk him up, and the bet war closed,
An' me a-chucklin', fur I supposed
I war playin' in dead sure winnin' luck,
In the softest snap I had ever struck;
An' the boys chipped in with a knowin' grin,
For they thought the fool had no chance to win.

An' so we agreed fur to run that day
To the Navajo Crossin' ten miles away—
As han'some a track as ever you seed
For testin' a hoss's purtiest speed,
Apache Johnson and Texas Ned

Saddled their horses and rode ahead
To station themselves ten miles away,
To act as judges and see fair play,
While Mexican Bart and Big Jim Hart
Stayed back for to give us an even start.

I got aboard of my broncho bird,
An' we came to the scratch an' got the word.
An' I laughed till my mouth spread from ear to ear
To see that tenderfoot drop to the rear.
The first three miles slipped away first-rate,
Then broncho began fur to lose his gait;
But I wa'n't oneasy, an' didn't mind,
With tenderfoot more'n a mile behind.
So I jogged along, with a cowboy song,
Till all of suddnt I heard that gong
A-ringin' a warnin' in my ear,
Ting! Ting! Ting! Ting! too infernal near,
An' lookin' back'ards I seed the chump
Of a tenderfoot gainin' every jump.

I hit ol' broncho a cut wi' the quirt,
An' once more got him to scratchin' dirt,
But his wind seemed weak, an' I tell you, boss,
I seed that he wasn't no ten-mile hoss.
Still the plucky brute took another shoot
An' pulled away from the wheel galoot.
But the animal couldn't hold his gait,
An' somehow the idee entered my pate
That if tenderfoot's legs didn't lose their grip
He'd own that hoss at the end o' the trip.

Close and closer come tenderfoot,
An' harder the whip to the hoss I put;
But the Eastern cuss, with a smile on his face,
Ran up to my side with his easy pace—
Rode up to my side, an', durn his hide,
Remarked 'twar a pleasant day fur a ride;
Then axed, onconsarned, if I had a match,

An' on his breeches give it a scratch,
Lit a cigarette, said he wished me good day,
An', as fresh as a daisy, scooted away.

Ahead he went—that infernal gong
A-ringin' "Good-by" as he flew along;
An' the smoke of his cigarette came back
Like a vapory snicker along the track.
On an' on he sped, gettin' further ahead,
His feet keepin' up that onceasable tread,
Till he faded away in the distance; an' when
I seed the condemned Eastern rooster again,
He war thar with the boys at the end of the race,
That same keerless, unconsarned smile on his face.

Now, pard, w'en a cowboy gits beat he don't sw'ar,
Nor kick, if the beatin' are done on the squar';
So I tuk that Easterner right by the hand,
An' told him that broncho awaited his brand.
Then I asked 'im his name, and whar from he came,
And how long he'd practised the wheel-rollin' game.
Tom Stevens, he said, war his name, an' he come
From a town they call Bosting, in ol' Yankeedom;
Then he jist paralyzed us by sayin' he'd whirled
That very identical wheel round the world.
Wal, pard, thar's the story o' how that smart chap
Done me up, w'en I thought I had sich a soft snap;
Done me up on a race with remarkable ease,
An' lowered my pride a good many degrees.

Did I give 'im the hoss? W'y, of course I did, boss,
An' I'll tell you it wa'n't no diminutive loss.
He writ me a letter from back in the East,
An' said He'd presented the neat, little beast
To a feller named Pope, who stands at the head
O' the ranch whar the cussed wheel horses ar' bred.

I've had other letters a-sayin' as how
Them crooked-tail wheels isn't in it, fur now
They're makin' a new-fangled sort of affair

With big rubber tires stuffed with nothing but air—
"Noomatics" they say is their name, an' they lay
Them high-up giraffe machines out o' the way;
An' as fur their speed, so the Stevens man writ,
"A streak o' greased lightnin' ain't in it a bit."
Thar's nothin', I'm thinkin', kin foller them things
In the way of surprisin' inventions but wings.

JOHN WALLACE CRAWFORD

The Cowboy's Dream

Last night as I lay on the prairie,
    A-watchin' the stars in the sky,
I wondered if I, a poor cowboy,
    Would go to that sweet by and by.

CHORUS:
Roll on, roll on;
    On little dogies, roll on, roll on.
Roll on, roll on:
    Roll on, little dogies, roll on.

The trail to that faraway region
    Is narrow and long they do say;
The wide one that leads to perdition
    Is staked out and blazed all the way.
    CHORUS

Some day we will be at the roundup,
    The cowboys like dogies will stand
For marking of them by the Judgment
    Who know every color and brand.
    CHORUS

There's many and many a cowboy
    Who'll not be seen at that last sale,

Who'll not be in them green pastures
   For missin' the long, narrow trail.
CHORUS

If only each bighearted cowboy
   Would watch for that great Judgment Day
And say to the boss of the Mighty Range
   "I'm ready, come drive me away."
CHORUS

For they, like the steers that are locoed,
   Stampede at the sight of a hand,
They're dragged with a rope to the marking place
   Or marked with some maverick brand.
CHORUS

I hope that I'll not be a strayed one,
   A maverick up there on high
Thrown in with a bunch of old rusties
   And scorned by the Great Boss's eye.
CHORUS

I've heard tell of some great big Owner
   Who'll never stock crowded, they say,
And always make room for the wanderer
   Who loses himself on the way.
CHORUS

It's said He'll never forget you,
   He knows every action and look,
So all of you cowboys get branded
   So your name's in the great Tally Book.
CHORUS

CHARLES J. FINGER

The High-Loping Cowboy

I been ridin' fer cattle the most of my life.
I ain't got no family, I ain't got no wife,
I ain't got no kith, I ain't got no kin,
I allus will finish what ere I begin.
I rode down in Texas where the cowboys are tall,
The State's pretty big but the hosses er small.
Fer singin' to cattle, I'm hard to outdo;
I'm a high-lopin' cowboy, an' a wild buckeroo.

I rode in Montana an' in Idaho;
I rode for Terasus in old Mexico.
I rope mountain lion an' grizzly bear,
I use cholla cactus fer combin' my hair.
I cross the dry desert, no water between,
I rode through Death Valley without no canteen.
At ridin' dry deserts I'm hard to outdo;
I'm a high-lopin' cowboy an' a wild buckeroo.

Why, I kin talk Spanish and Injun to boot,
I pack me a knife and a pistol to shoot.
I got no Señorita, an' I got no squaw,
I got no sweetheart, ner mother-in-law.
I never been tied to no apron strings,
I ain't no devil, but I got no wings.
At uh dodgin' the ladies, I'm hard to outdo;
I'm a high-lopin' cowboy, an' a wild buckeroo.

I drink red whiskey, an' I don't like beer,
I don't like mutton, but I do like steer.
I will let you alone if you leave me be,
But don't you get tough an' crawl on me.
I'll fight you now at the drop of a hat,
You'll think you're sacked up with a scratchin' wild cat.
At rough ready mixin' I'm hard to outdo;
I'm a high-lopin' cowboy, an' a wild buckeroo.

CURLEY W. FLETCHER

The Strawberry Roan

I'm a-layin' around, just spendin' muh time,
Out of a job an' ain't holdin' a dime,
When a feller steps up, an' sez, "I suppose
That you're uh bronk fighter by the looks
    uh yure clothes."

"Yuh figures me right—I'm a good one, I claim,
Do you happen tuh have any bad uns tuh
    tame?"
He sez he's got one, uh bad un tuh buck,
An' fur throwin' good riders, he's had lots uh
    luck.

He sez that this pony has never been rode,
That the boys that gets on 'im is bound tuh
    get throwed,
Well, I gets all excited an' asks what he pays,
Tuh ride that old pony uh couple uh days.

He offers uh ten spot. Sez I, "I'm yure man,
Cause the bronk never lived, that I couldn't fan;
The hoss never lived, he never drew breath,
That I couldn't ride till he starved plum tuh
    death.

"I don't like tuh brag, but I got this tuh say,
That I ain't been piled fur many uh day."
Sez he, "Get yure saddle, I'll give yuh uh
    chance."
So I gets in his buckboard an' drifts tuh
    his ranch.

I stays until mornin', an' right after chuck,
I steps out tuh see if that outlaw kin buck.
Down in the hoss corral, standin' alone,
Was this caballo, uh strawberry roan.

His laigs is all spavined an' he's got pigeon
    toes,
Little pig eyes an' uh big Roman nose,
Little pin ears that touch at the tip
An' uh double square iron stamped on his hip.

Yew necked an' old, with uh long lower jaw,
I kin see with one eye, he's uh reg'lar outlaw.
I puts on muh spurs—I'm sure feelin' fine—
Turns up muh hat, an' picks up muh twine.

I throws that loop on 'im, an' well I knows
    then,
That before he gets rode, I'll sure earn that
    ten.
I gets muh blinds on him, an' it sure was a fight,
Next comes muh saddle—I screws it down
    tight.

An' then I piles on 'im, an' raises the blind,
I'm right in his middle tuh see 'im unwind.
Well, he bows his old neck, an' I guess he
    unwound,
Fur he seems tuh quit livin' down on the
    ground.

He goes up t'ward the East, an' comes down
    t'ward the West,
Tuh stay in his middle, I'm doin' muh best,
He sure is frog walkin', he leaves uh big
    sigh,
He only lacks wings, fur tuh be on the fly.

He turns his old belly right up toward
    the sun,
He sure is uh sun-fishin' son-of-uh-gun,
He is the worst bucker I seen on the
    range,
He kin turn on uh nickle an' give yuh
    some change.

While he's uh-buckin' he squeals like
    uh shoat,
I tell yuh, that pony has sure got muh goat.
I claim that, no foolin', that bronk could
    sure step,
I'm still in muh saddle, uh-buildin' uh rep.

He hits on all fours, an' suns up his side,
I don't see how he keeps from sheddin'
    his hide.
I loses muh stirrups an' also muh hat,
I'm grabbin' the leather an' blind as uh bat.

With uh phenomenal jump, he goes up
    on high,
An' I'm settin' on nothin', way up in the sky,
An' then I turns over, I comes back tuh earth
An' lights in tuh cussin' the day of his birth.

Then I knows that the hosses I ain't able
    tuh ride
Is some of them livin'—they haven't all died,
But I bets all muh money they ain't no
    man alive,
Kin stay with that bronk when he makes
    that high dive.

CURLEY W. FLETCHER

The Six-Horse Limited Mail

We always ran out when we heard it come—
The chuck-a-luck of the coach and the thrum
Of hooves—barnboys, drummers, chambermaid—
For it was a sight as it swooped down the grade
At the end of the old Calapooia trail;
The yellow-wheeled stage of the Limited Mail,

Harness and buckles and doubletrees spun
Of silver and jet in the setting sun;
The three pairs of horses as galloping-white
As foam on a mountain torrent at night.
We could soon see the driver—he was belted to place
On the high rocking seat of the thoroughbrace—
Rising to give them the silk; heard him shout
As the length of his thirty-foot lash cracked out
Over withers and haunches! How the pebbles sprayed
From the pounding feet at the fusillade!
As if they were shod, not with iron, but with wings,
The leads skimmed the road, the lather-flecked swings
Pressing them close, and riding their hocks
The lumbering wheels striking fire from the rocks.
And always we cheered when they whirled through the gate
To the steps of the station with never a wait
Nor lessening of speed—the sudden stop peeling
Half moons in the sod, the brakeshoe squealing,
Barnboys already unhooking the traces
Before the passengers stepped from their places,
While the guard leapt off the boot with a gun
Packing the mailsacks and "dust" on the run,
The driver lighting a big black cigar,
Mustaches a-twirl, strode in to the bar
And the keeper with many a jovial sally
Boomed out a welcome to Umpqua valley.
Then the station door slammed to on the din—
The Six-Horse Limited Mail was in!

ETHEL ROMIG FULLER

Braggin' Bill's Fortytude

The days of yore—both good and ill
Was happy days for Braggin' Bill.

"In former times," said Bill, "a man
Jest had to be more subtile than
The sissified and sickly jays
Of these plumb tame, downtrodden days.
In sixty-nine," says he, "when I
Was young, adventuresome and spry
A feller had to be possess't
Of marv'lous fortytude out West.

"In sixty-nine or there about
When I was but a simple lout
I ran nine hundred steers—alone—
To Denver up from San Antone.
'Twas in the winter that I went
With that shebang of discontent
Through deserts bleak and blizzards bitter
And never lost a single critter.

"One night when I was thus engaged
While tempest howled and blizzard raged
A bothersome event occurred,
A thousand wolves attacked the herd.
But such a grim emergency
Was not a thing to baffle me,
Them days a feller was prepared
For such events, I wasn't scared.

"With courage modern herders lack
I charged into that savage pack
A flingin' snowballs left and right
At them fierce critters with all my might.
The blizzard raged so frigid thick
It wasn't hard to do the trick,
I ketched the snow a swirlin' round
Before it ever tetched the ground,

"And fashioned into balls them flakes
As hard as rocks—for goodness sakes—
And flung 'em with such deadly aim
I slew a thousand wolves with same.

And saved them critters' every gizzard
From ravin' beasts and ragin' blizzard,
Which wasn't toilsome, glory be,
For such a cunny coot as me."

No saddle yaps, I know, could fill
The noble boots of Braggin' Bill.

ATTRIBUTED TO C. WILES HALLOCK

The Lavender Cowboy

He was only a lavender cowboy,
    The hairs on his chest were two. . . .
He wished to follow the heroes
    Who fight as the he-men do.

Yet he was inwardly troubled
    By a dream that gave no rest;
When he read of heroes in action,
    He wanted more hair on his chest.

Herpicide, many hair-tonics
    Were rubbed in morning and night. . . .
Still, when he looked in the mirror
    No new hair grew in sight.

He battled for "Red Nell's" honor
    Then cleaned out a hold-up nest,
And died with his six-guns smoking. . . .
    But only two hairs on his chest.

HAROLD HERSEY

Boomer Johnson

Now Mr. Boomer Johnson was a gettin' old in spots,
But you don't expect a bad-man to go wrestlin' pans and pots;
But he'd done his share of killin' and his draw was gettin' slow,
So he quits a-punchin' cattle and he takes to punchin' dough.

Our foreman up and hires him, figurin' age had rode him tame,
But a snake don't get no sweeter just by changin' of its name.
Well, Old Boomer knowed his business—he could cook to make
    you smile,
But say, he wrangled fodder in a most peculiar style.

He never used no matches—left 'em layin' on the shelf;
Just some kerosene and cussin' and the kindlin' lit itself.
And, pardner, I'm allowin' it would give a man a jolt,
To see him stir *frijoles* with the barrel of his Colt.

Now killin' folks and cookin' ain't so awful far apart;
That must 'a' been why Boomer kept a-practicin' his art;
With the front sight of his pistol he would cut a pie-lid slick,
And he'd crimp her with the muzzle for to make the edges stick.

He built his doughnuts solid, and it sure would curl your hair,
To see him plug a doughnut as he tossed it in the air.
He bored the holes plumb center every time his pistol spoke,
Till the can was full of doughnuts and the shack was full of smoke.

We-all was gettin' jumpy—but he couldn't understand
Why his shootin' made us nervous when his cookin' was so grand.
He kept right on performin', and it weren't no big surprise,
When he took to markin' tombstones on the covers of his pies.

They didn't taste no better and they didn't taste no worse,
But a-settin' at that table was like ridin' in a hearse;
You didn't do no talkin' and you took just what you got,
So we et till we was foundered just to keep from gettin' shot.

Us at breakfast one bright mornin', I was feelin' kind of low,
When Old Boomer passed the doughnuts and I tells him plenty, "No!
All I takes this trip is coffee, for my stomach is a wreck,"
I could see the itch for killin' swell the wattles on his neck.

Scorn his grub? He strings some doughnuts on the muzzle of
    his gun,
And he shoves her in my gizzard and he says, "You're takin' one!"
He was set to start a graveyard, but for once he was mistook;
Me not wantin' any doughnuts, I just up and salts the cook.

Did they fire him? Listen, pardner, there was nothin' left to fire.
Just a row of smilin' faces and another cook to hire.
If he joined some other outfit and is cookin'—what I mean,
It's where they ain't no matches and they don't need kerosene.

                                        HENRY HERBERT KNIBBS

The Bosky Steer

Jake and Roany was a-chousin' along,
    And Jake was a-singin' what he called a song,
When up from a waller what should appear,
    But a moss-horned maverick, a bosky steer.

Jake he started with his hat pulled down,
    Built a blocker that would snare a town;
That steer he headed for the settin' sun,
    And believe me, neighbor, he could hump and run!

Roany he follered his pardner's deal,
    —Two ole waddies what could head and heel—
Both of 'em ridin' for the Chicken Coop,
    With a red-hot iron and a hungry loop.

The sun was a-shinin' in ole Jake's eyes,
  And he wasn't just lookin' for no real surprise,
When the steer gave a wiggle like his dress was tight,
  Busted through a juniper and dropped from sight.

Jake and his pony did the figure eight,
  But Jake did his addin' just a mite too late;
He left the saddle, and a-seein' red,
  He lit in the gravel of a river bed.

Now Roany's hoss was a good hoss, too,
  But he didn't understand just why Jake flew,
So he humped and started for the cavvyard,
  And left Roany settin' where the ground was hard.

Jake was lookin' at a swelled-up thumb,
  And he says, "I reckon we was goin' some!"
When Roany hollers, "Git a-movin' quick,
  Or you're sure goin' to tangle with that maverick!"

Roany clumb a-straddle of the juniper tree.
  "Ain't no more room up here," yells he.
So Jake he figured for hisself to save,
  By backin' in the openin' of a cut-bank cave.

The steer he prodded with his head one side,
  But he couldn't quite make it to ole Jake's hide;
Kep' snortin' and pawin' and proddin' stout,
  But every time he quit, why, Jake come out.

"You ole fool!" yips Roany, "Keep back out of sight!
  You act like you're *hankerin'* to make him fight!"
Then Jake he hollers kinda fierce and queer:
  "Back, hell, nothin'! There's a bear in here!"

HENRY HERBERT KNIBBS

Idaho Jack

Idaho Jack from the Salmon buttes
Grinned up at the buckaroos, workin' the chutes:
Feels of the cinch as he jerks up the slack
On the outlaw and mankiller, Red River Black:
Twists on the hackamore, tightens the noose,
Yells to the punchers, "All set, turn 'im loose."
Down goes the lever and bang goes the bell.
And out comes a cowboy a-ridin' for hell.

The crowd's up and screamin' with deafenin' cheers.
For they're sightin' a ride they'll remember for years.
Snake River Dugan leaps up and he bawls,
"Watch that bowlegged rider from Idaho Falls."
The outlaw's a killer who knows no defeat,
But the rider's still with him and holdin' his seat:
His spurs rake the stallion, who's sunfishin' back.
But he don't know the rider called Idaho Jack.

There's hazers and clowns with their trick ridin' mules:
Team ropers, pick-ups, and bull-doggin' fools;
Chuckeaters, ranch hands, and tenderfeet proud,
Of the kind you will meet in a rodeo crowd.
Pens full of cattle from the desert and range,
A-frightened and bawlin' at scenes new and strange;
Waddies and gamblers on dust-covered track
And the bets fifty-fifty on Idaho Jack.

There's yippin' and yellin' that reaches the skies,
But the cowboy don't hear for there's blood in his eyes.
On the mad fighting cayuse of sinew and bone
The rider from Idaho's holdin' his own.
When a roar and a shout bursts forth from the mob,
That starts with a cheer, and ends with a sob:
For the cinch breaks loose on Red River Black.
And down with the saddle comes Idaho Jack.

Like a flash, he's out from the hoofs below
As the stallion strikes with a killing blow,
Grazin' the saddle from horn to cinch.
And he gains his life by a half an inch.
The pick-ups are ready, and save his hide:
He rolls the "makin's" with mouth set wide;
Grins to the crowd, as he waddles back
And shakes his fist at Red River Black.

ATTRIBUTED TO JACK H. LEE

Ol' Dynamite

The outlaw stands with blindfold eyes,
   His feet set wide apart;
His coal-black hide gleams in the sun—
   Thar's killin' in his heart.

A puncher squats upon his heels,
   His saddle at his side;
He's sizin' up Ol' Dynamite,
   That he is booked to ride.

The cowboy rises, lifts his saddle—
   A little tune he's hummin'—
Walks catlike all around the hoss—
   "Hold him, boys, I'm comin'."

Now up above the outlaw's back
   He lifts the load of leather;
Then care-ful-lee he lets it down,
   Like the droppin' of a feather.

Ol' Dynamite he stands stock-still,
   Plumb like a gentled pony.
A leap, a yell! an' Buck's all set—
   "On with the cer-e-mo-nee."

The snubbers rip the blindfold off,
   The punchers yip and yell;
Ol' Dynamite gives one grand snort,
   Then starts his little hell.

He plunges forward on his feet,
   His hind heels in the air;
Then up and down he bucks and backs
   Like a loco rockin'-chair.

But now he stops—he spins around—
   He bawls, he bites, he kicks!
He r'ars straight up into the air,
   Then down on two steel sticks.

But look! "My Gawd!" The crowd screams out,
   "He's boltin' for the stand!"
Then just as quick he jerks up short—
   An' thar's Buck a-stickin' grand.

Buck leaps to earth, lifts his hat,
   Bows to the whirl of cheers—
Then turning slides his saddle off,
   An' quickly disappears.

PHIL LE NOIR

Cow-ponies

After we'd turned in they gathered round
Nosing our blankets and stepping about our
    feet
Carefully . . . Then they nosed
Their soft cool muzzles over the bags for
    something to eat,
And stood for a while, and dozed . . .

They switched their tails, remembering the
    long day
They'd carried us . . . and the flies . . .
They stared into the fire and rubbed their heads
    together—
Raised them with startled eyes
At the strange nicker far off in the sage—
                 Nostrils wide,
Bay heads, white noses tossed back from the
    dark.
The sound died . . . The fire licked out and died.

They drooped their ears and pawed, and nosed
The bags again, lipped a few scattered grains,
Then wandered away and dozed . . .
Watched each other in the moonlight,
    shuddered, and sighed,

And stood to sleep . . . The wind drifted their
  manes.

And we too turned to sleep, and all night long
We knew that they were round us while we
  slept,
And they—they knew it too . . .
                    Heads turned and tossed.
We swore across their dreams, they nosed in
  ours.
Above the corral the moon crept
And made a useless moon-dial of the snubbing
  post.

MAURICE LESEMANN

Run Little Dogies

As I looked out of my window
  I saw a cowboy come riding along,
His hat was shoved back and his spurs kept a-jingling
  And as he drew near he was singing this song.

  Hush, ciaola, little baby lie easy,
  Who's your real father may never be known.
  Oh, it's weeping, wailing, rocking the cradle,
  And tending a baby that's none of your own.

When spring comes along we round up the dogies,
  We stick on their brands and we bob off their tails,
Pick out the strays, then the herd is inspected,
  And then next day we go on the trail.

  Singing whoop pi-o-whoop, run along little dogies,
  For Montana will be your new home.
  Oh, it's whooping, swearing, driving the dogies,
  It's our misfortune we ever did roam.

Oh, it's worst in the night just after a round-up
   When dogies are grazing from the herd all around.
You have no idea of the trouble they give us
   To the cowboys who are holding them on the bed ground.

     Whoop pi-o-whoop, run along you little dogies,
     For Montana will be your new home.
     Oh, it's whooping, swearing, driving the dogies,
     It's our misfortune we ever did roam.

Oh, some think we go on trail for pleasure,
   But I can tell them that they are dead wrong,
If I ever got any fun out of trailing
   I'd have no reason for singing my song.

     Hush, ciaola, little baby lie easy,
     Who's your real father may never be known.
     Oh, it's weeping, wailing, rocking the cradle,
     And tending a baby that's none of your own.

RECORDED BY JOHN LOMAX FROM THE SINGING OF
FRANCIS SULLIVAN

The Stampede

We took our turn at the guard that night, just Sourdough Charlie
   and I,
And as we mounted our ponies, there were clouds in the
   western sky;
And we knew that before the morning the storm, by the north
   wind stirred,
Would scourge the plains with its furies fierce and madden the
   savage herd;
But we did not shrink the danger; we had ridden the plains
   for years,—
The crash of the storm and the cattle's cry were music in our ears.

We drove the herd to a circle, for the winds were calm, and
    we knew
That somewhere near to the midnight shift the storm-fiends
    would be due.
We rode the rounds unceasingly, and we worked with an
    anxious will
Until the cattle were lying down and the mighty herd was still,
And only the musical breathing of the bedded beasts arose
As we rounded the living circle and guarded their light repose.

Then the storm came in in anger; the winds of a sudden turned,
The lightnings flamed through the seething skies, and the prairies
    blazed and burned;
The thunders rolled like an avalanche, and they shook the
    rocking world,
That trembling quaked as the storm so wild its banners of
    blaze unfurled;
The fires flew over the frightened herd and leaped from horn to horn
Till horrible clamors rose and fell in chaos of fear forlorn.

The herd awoke in a minute; but we rode through the flashing ways
And sang with a will the olden songs we learned in our
    childhood days;
The human voice has a wondrous power, and the wildest beast
    that moans
Forgets its fear in a dream of peace at the sound of its tender tones;
And on through the blinding flashes and on through the dark
    and the light,
We rode with the old songs ringing, and we prayed for the
    death of night.

I never could tell how it happened; there came a tremendous crash.
A wolf jumped out of the chaparral—and the herd was off in
    a flash!
And Charlie was riding before them; then I saw him draw his gun
And fire at the plunging leaders, till he turned them one by one;
Then the darkness fell, I could not see, and then in the
    blinding light
My pard went down, and the maddened herd swept on through the
    savage night!

Him I found where the cattle rushed in the wild of their wandering,
Broken and beaten by scores of hoofs, a crushed and a
    mangled thing!
And his pony lay with a broken leg, as dead as a rotten log,
Where its foot had slipped in the hidden hole of a worthless
    prairie-dog.
We buried him there—you can see the stones—and whether we
    die or live,
We gave him the best of a funeral that a cowboy camp can give.

His name? It was Sourdough Charlie, sir; and whether a
    good or bad,
We called him that for a score of years—it was all the name
    he had!
I found a locket above his heart, with a picture there of grace
That showed a girl with a curly head and a most uncommon face;
Hero, you say! Well, maybe so; for I know it is oft confessed
That he's the kind of a man it takes for the work here in the West.

FREEMAN E. MILLER

Vaquero

His broad-brimm'd hat push'd back with
    careless air,
The proud vaquero sits his steed as free
As winds that toss his black abundant hair.
No rover ever swept a lawless sea
With such a haught and heedless air as he
Who scorns the path, and bounds with swift
    disdain
Away, a peon born, yet born to be
A splendid king; behold him ride, and reign.

How brave he takes his herds in branding days,
On timber'd hills that belt about the plain;

He climbs, he wheels, he shouts through winding
       ways
Of hiding ferns and hanging fir; the rein
Is loose, the rattling spur drives swift; the mane
Blows free; the bullocks rush in storms before;
They turn with lifted heads, they rush again,
Then sudden plunge from out the wood, and
       pour
A cloud upon the plain with one terrific roar.

   Now sweeps the tawny man on stormy steed,
His gaudy trappings toss'd about and blown
About the limbs as lithe as any reed;
The swift long lasso twirl'd above is thrown
From flying hand; the fall, the fearful groan
Of bullock toil'd and tumbled in the dust—
The black herds onward sweep, and all disown
The fallen, struggling monarch that has thrust
His tongue in rage and roll'd his red eyes in
       disgust.

                      JOAQUIN MILLER

The Hired Man on Horseback

(With apologies to G. K. Chesterton and Don Juan of Austria)

The typical cowboy is . . . simply a riding farmhand.—James
Stephens, *International Book Review*

The cowboy, after all, was never anything more than a hired man
on horseback.—Editorial Page, *Minneapolis Tribune, San Francisco
Chronicle*

Harp and flute and violin, throbbing through the night,
Merry eyes and tender eyes, dark head and bright;
Moon shadow on the sun dial to mark the moments fleet,

The magic and enchanted hours where moonlight lovers
    meet;
 And the harp notes come all brokenly by night winds
    stirred—
But the hired man on horseback is singing to the herd!
  (Whoopie-ti-yo-o-o! Hi yo-o, my little dogies!)
  Doggerel upon his lips and valor in his heart,
  Not to flinch and not to fail, not to shirk his part;
  Wearily and wearily he sees the stars wheel by,
  And he knows his guard is nearly done by the great
    clock in the sky.

  He hears the Last Guard coming and he hears their
    songs begun,
  A foolish song he will forget when he forgets the sun.
    (Whoopie ti-yo-o-o! Hi yo-o, my little dogies!)
  "We got 'em now, you sleepy men, so pull your
    freight to bed
  And pound your ear an hour or two before the east is
    red."
  If to his dreams a face may come? Ah, turn your eyes
    away,
  Nor guess that face may come by dream that never
    comes by day.
  Red dawn breaking through the desert murk;
  The hired man on horseback goes laughing to his
    work.

The broker's in his office before the stroke of ten,
He buys and smiles and he sells and smiles at the word of
    other men;
But he gets his little commission flat, whether they buy or
    sell,
So be it drouth or storm or flood, the broker's crops do well.
They are short of Katy Common, they are long on Zinc
    Preferred—
But the hired man on horseback is swimming with the herd!
  White horns gleaming where the flood rolls brown,
  Lefty fighting the lower point as the current sweeps
    them down,

Lefty fighting the stubborn steers that will not turn
    or slow,
They press beside him, they swim below him—"Come
    out and let them go!"
But Lefty does not leave them and Lefty tries once
    more,
He is swinging the wild leaders in toward the northern
    shore;
"He'll do to ride the river with!" (Bridging the years
    between,
Men shall use those words again—and wonder what
    they mean.)
He is back to turn the stragglers in to follow the
    leaders through,
When a cottonwood snag comes twisting down and
    cuts the herd in two;
When a whirling snag comes twisting down with
    long arms lashing hate,
On wearied horse and wearied man—and they see it
    come, too late!
—A brown hand lifted in the splashing spray;
Sun upon a golden head that never will be gray;
A low mound bare until new grass is grown—
But the Palo Pinto trail herd has crossed the
    Cimarron!

A little midnight supper when the play is done,
Glancing lights and sparkling eyes—the night is just
    begun.
Beauteous night, O night of love!—Youth and joy are met.
Shine on our enchantment still! "Sweet, your eyes are wet."
"Dear, they sing for us alone!" Such the lover's creed.
—But the hired man on horseback is off with the
    stampede!

There is no star in the pit-dark night, there is none
    to know or blame,
And a hundred yards to left or right, there is safety
    there—and shame!

A stone throw out on either side, with none to guess
    or tell—
But the hired man on horseback has raised the
    rebel yell!
He has turned to loosen his saddle strings, he has
    fumbled his slicker free,
He whirls it high and he snaps it wide wherever the
    foremost be,
He slaps it onto a longhorn's eyes till he falters in
    his stride—
An oath and a shot, a laugh and a shot, and his wild
    mates race beside;
A pony stumbles—no, he is up, unhurt and
    running still;
"Turn 'em, turn 'em, turn 'em, Charlie!
    Good boy, Bill!"
They are crashing through the cactus flats where the
    badger holes are thick;
Day is breaking, clouds are lifting, leaders turn to
    mill—
"Hold 'em, cowboys! Turn 'em, Charlie!—God!
    Where's Bill!"

The proud Young Intellectuals, a cultured folk are these,
They scorn the lowly Babbitts and their hearts are
    overseas;
They turn their backs upon us, and if we ask them why
They smile like jesting Pilate, and they stay for no reply;
They smile at faith and honor, and they smile at shame
    and crime—
But the old Palo Pinto man is calling for his time.
    For he heard old voices and he heard hoofs beat,
    Songs that long ago were gay to time with drumming
    feet;
    Bent back straightens and dim eyes grow bright—
    The last man on horseback rides on into the night!
    Cossack and Saracen
    Shout their wild welcome then,
    Ragged proud Conquistadores claim him kind and
    kin,

And the wild Beggars of the Sea leap up to swell
  the din:
And Hector leans upon the wall, and David bends to
  scan
This new brown comrade for the old brown clan,
The great hearted gentlemen who guard the outer
  wall
Black with sin and stained with blood—and faithful
  through it all;
Still wearing for all ornament the scars they won
  below—
And the Lord God of Out-of-Doors, He cannot let
  them go!
They have halted the hired horseman beyond the
  outer gate,
But the gentlemen adventurers cry shame that he
  should wait;
And the sour saints soften, with a puzzled grin,
As Esau and Ishmael press to let their brother in.
Hat tip-tilted and his head held high,
Brave spurs jingling as he passes by—
Gray hair tousled and his lips a-quirk—
"To the Master of the Workmen, with the tally of
  his work!"

EUGENE MANLOVE RHODES

Breakers of Broncos

So! breakers of broncos! With miles of jagged wire,
You seek to break the spirit of this range;
With lariat of barbed-wire fence, you hope
To tame its heart, and with your iron heel,
Hot from the desert, to sear upon its hip
Your molten brand—as wranglers at a round up,
With bit and spur and lasso, strive to curb
And brand an outlaw fresh from winter range.

O breaker of broncos, listen! Can't you hear
The northwind snickering at you? The coyote
Upon the mesa, jeering? The waterfall
Chuckling among the rocks? The croaking magpie,
The hooting owl, the crane, the curlew? Look!
The chokecherry blossom, the sage, the bitterroot,
Bending with mirth, wag their heads, and laugh
At you! Why, even the broomtail cayuse kicks
His heels against the mountain sky, and snorts!

O breakers of broncos, we fling you on the wind
This handful of dust, this bitter alkali!—
As well attempt to rope the bucking stars,
Or burn your bars upon the flank of the moon!
When will you whirl your lasso at the sun?
Or bridle it? Or straddle the lightning-flash?

LEW SARETT

Bucking Bronco

My love is a rider, wild broncos he breaks,
Though he's promised to quit it, just for my sake.
He ties up one foot, the saddle puts on,
With a swing and a jump he is mounted and gone.

The first time I met him, 't was early one spring,
Riding a bronco, a high-headed thing.
He tipped me a wink as he gayly did go,
For he wished me to look at his bucking bronco.

The next time I saw him, 't was late in the fall,
Swinging the girls at Tomlinson's ball:
He laughed and he talked as we danced to and
    fro,—
Promised never to ride on another bronco.

He made me some presents, among them a ring;
The return that I made him was a far better thing;
'T was a young maiden's heart, I'd have you all
    know
He'd won it by riding his bucking bronco.

Now, all you young maidens, where'er you reside,
Beware of the cowboy who swings the rawhide,
He'll court you and pet you and leave you and go
In the spring up the trail on his bucking bronco.

BELLE STARR

Night-herding Song

Oh, slow up, dogies, quit your roving round,
You have wandered and tramped all over the ground;
Oh, graze along, dogies, and feed kinda slow,
And don't forever be on the go—
Oh, move slow, dogies, move slow.

I have circle-herded, trail-herded, night-herded, too,
But to keep you together, that's what I can't do;
My horse is leg-weary and I'm awful tired,
But if I let you get away I'm sure to get fired—
Bunch up, little dogies, bunch up.

Oh, say, little dogies, when you goin' to lay down
And quit this forever siftin' around?
My limbs are weary, my seat is sore;
Oh, lay down, dogies, like you've laid before—
Lay down, little dogies, lay down.

Oh, lay still, dogies, since you have laid down,
Stretch away out on the big open ground;

Snore loud, little dogies, and drown the wild sound
That will all go away when the day rolls round—
Lay still, little dogies, lay still.

HARRY STEPHENS

Ten Thousand Cattle

Ten thousand cattle straying,
They quit my range and travel'd away,
And it's sons-of-guns is what I say,
I am dead broke, dead broke this day.

    CHORUS:
Dead broke! In gambling hells delaying,
Dead broke! Ten thousand cattle straying,
And it's sons-of-guns is what I say,
They've rustled my pile, my pile away.

My girl she has gone straying,
She's quit me too and travel'd away,
With a son-of-a-gun from I-o-way,
I'm a lone man, lone man this day.
    CHORUS

So I've took to card playing,
I handle decks but it don't seem to pay,
And it's son-of-a-gunner I get each day,
They've rustled my pile, my pile away.
    CHORUS

Tho' all my luck's gone straying,
Tho' I make no strike by night or day,
It is sons-of-guns I still will say,
I'm in the game to stay, to stay.
    CHORUS

OWEN WISTER

As I Walked Out

As I walked out one morning for pleasure
   I met a cowpuncher a jogging along.
His hat was thrown back and his spurs was a jingling
   And as he advanced he was singing this song.

    CHORUS:
Sing hooplio, get along my little dogies
For Wyoming shall be your new home,
It's hooping and yelling and cursing those dogies
To our misfortune but none of your own.

In the springtime we round up the dogies,
   Slap on the brands and bob off their tails,
Then we cut and the herd is inspected
   And then we throw them onto the trail.
    CHORUS

In the evening we round in the dogies
   As they are grazing from herd all around,
You have no idee the trouble they give us
   As we are holding them on the bedground.
    CHORUS

In the morning we throw off the bedground
   Aiming to graze them an hour or two,
When they are full you think you can drive them
   On the trail, but be damned if you do.
    CHORUS

Some fellows go on the trail for pleasure
   But they have got this thing down wrong,
If it hadn't been for these troublesome dogies,
   I never would thought of writing this song.
    CHORUS

UNKNOWN

Bill and Parson Sim

Bill Riley was a cowboy and a quicker shot than him
There wasn't in the country, exceptin' Parson Sim.
And I reckon you could ride the trail from Texas to the line
And braver men than Bill and Sim I'll bet you couldn't find.
Bill, he was tall and lanky with black and piercing eyes
That seemed to flash like lightnin' when storm is in the skies.

His voice was soft and solemn-like, his heart was kind and true,
But he could paint the town as red as any man I knew.
Sim, he was mighty near as tall, with sunny eyes of blue
That seemed to laugh and sparkle, as eyes will sometimes do.
The boys they called him Parson, he owed it to his hair,
And to the classic language he'd use when he would swear.

They chummed as boys together and learned to shoot and ride,
Worked for the same cow out-fits, and grew up side by side.
One bed it always done for both, they used the same war sack,
Stuck up for one another, and all their money'd whack.
Well, Bill and Sim one winter, 'twas back in eighty-nine,
Were batchin' near a tradin' post up north close to the line—

And they was havin' rafts of fun and spendin' lots of coin
Between the little tradin' post and Old Fort Assenboin.
But one night they took in a dance and there they met a gal,
'Twas old Bucky Berry's daughter, his oldest daughter Val.
Her right name was Valentine, they called her Val for short,
She was as fine a little rose as bloomed in that resort.

Her hair was kinder yaller and shined like placer gold,
And on the hearts of Bill and Sim she got an awful hold.
So when she danced with other men, well, Bill he'd hit the rag,
And when Sim couldn't get her smiles he, too, would want a jag.
Waltz, quadrille, and polka was danced till break of day,
And both the fiddlers got so drunk the darn chumps wouldn't play.

Old Berry he was loaded too and pulled his forty-five,
And worked upon one musician like bees upon their hive.

But ne'er a tune could Berry with all his labor get,
The women folks put on their wraps and dancin' had to quit.
'Twas then the bloody fight was fit, the worst I ever saw,
And I have seen some red hot scraps come off without a flaw.

You see, Bill was stalking 'round, intoxicated quite,
On Love and Injun whiskey, and itchin' for a fight.
While Parson Sim he, too, had on a pretty decent load
And tackled Val to take her home in language *a la mode*.
But just as he was askin' her and she got up to go
Bill he came up to where they was a walkin' kind of slow.

And with a sort of stately bow he turned his back on Sim
And asked Val if she wouldn't take the homeward ride with him.
Well, 'twas over in a second, a few cuss words was said,
Sim he was grazed along the cheek and Bill's was through his head.
And there poor Bill lay bleedin', a-gaspin' hard for breath,
With Sim a-standin' over him, his face as white as death.

A look of horror crossed his face and sorrow filled his eyes
As Bill's brave spirit left the clay and started for the skies.
I reckon that he thought of how in all those happy years
They both had been like brothers and shared their joys and fears.
Then moanin'-like he took the gal and started for the door,
For she had fainted dead away when Bill dropped to the floor.

And with a yell some pulled their guns and made a sudden rush,
They tho't they held a winnin' hand, but Sim he had a flush.
Fer now his fightin' blood was up, and layin' Val aside
To get her out of danger, he let the bullets slide.
Old Buck he got his gal away, then he came back to fight,
But everything was over and he saw an awful sight.

The punchers they was lyin' round, a dozen men or more,
Looked like the field of Gettysburg, so many strewed the floor,
And Parson Sim was dyin' with his arms around poor Bill
His head a-lyin' on the breast that now was cold and still.
He'd won the fight, though wounded, then kneelin' by the spot
Where Bill was lyin' cold in death he fired the fatal shot

That let him follow after Bill, he died without a groan,
And with Bill restin' in his arms he sought the great unknown.
We laid them on a sunny hill, they're sleepin' side by side
Beneath the western prairie soil where once they used to ride.
And Val she never married, and sometimes comes to weep
And wet the flowers with her tears where both her lovers sleep.

UNKNOWN

Buckaroo Sandman

It's the Buckaroo Sandman
On his lullaby pony,
Riding over the stardust trail
To rock-a-bye land.

All the Buckaroo cowhands
Bronco pillows are ridin',
Poundin' leather to Sleepy-town
Over Dream Land sand.

At the Baby Land rodeo, to and fro,
Swingin' in the saddle of Dad's elbow.
Giddy-up, giddy-up,
Get a dogie in your dream lasso.

When the daylight is breakin'
Over valley and plain,
In your little corral
Asleep with mother again.

UNKNOWN

The Cowboy

Oh, a man there lives on the Western plains,
With a ton of fight and an ounce of brains,
Who herds the cows as he robs the trains
And goes by the name of cowboy.

He laughs at death and scoffs at life;
He feels unwell unless in some strife.
He fights with a pistol, a rifle, or knife,
This reckless, rollicking cowboy.

He sets up drinks when he hasn't a cent;
He'll fight like hell with any young gent.
When he makes love, he goes it hell-bent,
Oh, he's some lover, this cowboy.

He shoots out lights in a dancing hall;
He gets shot up in a drunken brawl.
Some coroner's jury then ends it all,
And that's the last of the cowboy.

UNKNOWN

Curly Joe

A mile below Blue Canyon on the lonely Pinon trail,
Near the little town of Sanctos, nestled in a quiet dale,
Is the grave of a young cowboy whose name is now unknown
Save by a few frontiersmen who call the spot their own.

He was as fine a rider as ever forked a steed,
He was brave and kind and generous, never did a dirty deed,
Curly Joe, the name he went by, was enough, none cared to know
If he ever had another, so they called him Curly Joe.

'Bout a mile from the Sanctos village lived an ex-grandee of Spain
And his daughter, bonny Enza, called the White Rose of the Plain.
Curly loved this high-born lassie since that time so long ago
When he found her on the mountains, lost and blinded by the snow.

But coquettish was fair Enza, 'tis a woman's foolish trait
That has blasted many a manhood like the harsh decrees of fate.
When pressed in earnest language, not flowery but sincere,
For an answer to his question she smiled and shed a tear.

When she answered, "Really, Joe boy, quite wearisome you grow.
Your sister, sir, forever, but your wife, no never, Joe."
Not another word was spoken, in a week poor Joe was dead,
Killed by a bucking bronco, or at least that's what they said.

For many a year the tombstone that marked this cowboy's grave
In quaint and curious language this prophetic warning gave:
"Never hope to win the daughter of the boss that owns the brand,
For I tried it and changed ranges to a far and better land."

UNKNOWN

Doney-gal

Traveling up the lonesome trail
Where man and his horse seldom ever fail;
Rain and hail, sleet and snow,
Me and my Doney-gal a-bound to go.

Sogging along through fog and dew,
Wishing for sunny days and you;
Rain and hail, sleet and snow,
Me and my Doney-gal a-bound to go.

Over the prairies lean and brown,
On through the wastes where stands no town;
Rain and hail, sleet and snow,
Me and my Doney-gal a-bound to go.

Swimming the rivers across our way,
We fight on forward day end on day;
Rain and hail, sleet and snow,
Me and my Doney-gal a-bound to go.

Bedding the cattle, singing a song,
We ride the night-herd all night long;
Rain and hail, sleet and snow,
Me and my Doney-gal a-bound to go.

When the storm breaks on the quiet mead,
We follow the cattle on their wild stampede;
Rain and hail, sleet and snow,
Me and my Doney-gal a-bound to go.

Trailing the herd through mountains green,
We pen the cattle in Abilene.
Rain and hail, sleet and snow,
Me and my Doney-gal a-bound to go.

Round the camp-fire's flickering glow,
We sing the songs of long ago.
Rain and hail, sleet and snow,
Me and my Doney-gal a-bound to go.

UNKNOWN

Empty Saddles

Empty saddles in the old corral,
Where do ya ride tonight?
Are you roundin' up the dogies,
    The strays of long ago?
    Are ya on the trail of buffalo?

Empty saddles in the old corral,
Where do ya ride tonight?
Are there rustlers on the border,
    Or a band of Navajo?
    Are ya heading for the Alamo?

Empty boots covered with dust,
Where do ya ride tonight?
Empty guns, covered with rust,
Where do you talk tonight?

Empty saddles in the old corral,
My tears will be dried tonight
If you'll only say I'm lonely,
    As ya carry my old pal,
    Empty saddles in the old corral.

UNKNOWN

The Gal I Left Behind Me

A Cowboy Version

I struck the trail in seventy-nine,
The herd strung out behind me;
As I jogged along my mind ran back
To the gal I left behind me.
    That sweet little gal, that true little gal,
    The gal I left behind me!

If ever I get off the trail
And the Indians they don't find me,
I'll make my way straight back again
To the gal I left behind me.
    That sweet little gal, that true little gal,
    The gal I left behind me!

When the night was dark and the cattle run,
With the boys coming on behind me,
My mind run back at my pistol's crack
To the gal I left behind me.
    That sweet little gal, that true little gal,
    The gal I left behind me!

The wind did blow, the rain did flow,
The hail did fall and blind me;
I thought of that gal, that sweet little gal,
That gal I'd left behind me!
    That sweet little gal, that true little gal,
    The gal I left behind me!

She wrote ahead to the place I said,
I was always glad to find it.
She says, "I'm true, when you get through
Ride back and you will find me."
    That sweet little gal, that true little gal,
    The gal I left behind me!

When we sold out I took the train,
I knew where I would find her;
When I got back we had a smack,
And that was no gol-darned liar.
    That sweet little gal, that true little gal,
    The gal I left behind me!

UNKNOWN

Git Along Little Dogies

As I was a-walkin', one mornin' for pleasure,
    I spied a young cowboy a-lopin' along:
His hat was throw'd back, and his spurs was a-jingle,
    And as he rid by he was singin' this song.

    Tip-pee ti-yi-yo, git along little dogies;
    It's your misfortune and none o' my own,
    Yip-pee ti-yi-yo, git along little dogies,
    The plains o' Wyoming will be your new home.

First thing in the spring we round-up all the dogies;
    We ear-mark, and brand 'em, and bob off their tails;
Then wrangle our hosses, load up the chuck wagon,
    And throw the wild snuffy bunch on the North trail.

Some boys ride the long North trail just for the pleasure,
    But soon find they figgered most terrible wrong;
Them dogies are kinky, and try for to scatter
    All over the plains, as we roll 'em along.

    It's whoo-pee, and yip-pee, whilest drivin' the dogies;
    Oh how I wish that they'd ramble alone.
    It's punchin', and yippin', "Git on little dogies,"
    For you know Wyoming will soon be your home.

Your maws was all raised-up away down in Texas,
    Whar sandburrs, and cacti, and jimpson-weed grow.
We'll fill you on prick'y-pear, catclaw, and *cholla,*
    Then roll you along the trail for Idaho.

Oh, you'll soon be soup for ol' Uncle Sam's Injuns,
    It's "Beef, heap good beef," I hear 'em all cry.
So git along, ramble on, roll little dogies,
    You'll all be beef-stew in the sweet by and by.

UNKNOWN

Old Paint

REFRAIN:
Good-bye, Old Paint, I'm a-leavin' Cheyenne.
Good-bye, Old Paint, I'm a-leavin' Cheyenne.

My foot in the stirrup, my pony won't stand;
Good-bye, Old Paint, I'm a-leavin' Cheyenne.
    REFRAIN

I'm a-leavin' Cheyenne, I'm off for Montan';
Good-bye, Old Paint, I'm a-leavin' Cheyenne.
    REFRAIN

I'm a-ridin' Old Paint, I'm a-leadin' Old Fan;
Good-bye, Old Paint, I'm a-leavin' Cheyenne.
    REFRAIN

With my feet in the stirrups, my bridle in my hand;
Good-bye, little Annie, I'm off for Cheyenne.
    REFRAIN

Old Paint's a good pony, he paces when he can;
Good-bye, little Annie, I'm off for Cheyenne.
    REFRAIN

Oh hitch up your horses and feed 'em some hay,
And seat yourself by me so long as you stay.
REFRAIN

My horses ain't hungry, they'll not eat your hay
My wagon is loaded and rolling away.
REFRAIN

My foot in my stirrup, my reins in my hand;
Good-morning, young lady, my horses won't stand.

Good-bye, Old Paint, I'm a-leavin' Cheyenne,
Good-bye, Old Paint, I'm a-leavin' Cheyenne.

UNKNOWN

The Great Round-up

When I think of the last great round-up
On the eve of eternity's dawn,
I think of the past of the cowboys
Who have been with us here and are gone.
And I wonder if any will greet me
On the sands of the evergreen shore
With a hearty, "God bless you, old fellow,"
That I've met with so often before.

I think of the big-hearted fellows
Who will divide with you blanket and bread,
With a piece of stray beef well roasted,
And charge for it never a red.
I often look upward and wonder
If the green fields will seem half so fair,
If any the wrong trail have taken
And fail to "be in" over there.

For the trail that leads down to perdition
Is paved all the way with good deeds,
But in the great round-up of ages,
Dear boys, this won't answer your needs.
But the way to the green pastures, though narrow,
Leads straight to the home in the sky,
And Jesus will give you the passports
To the land of the sweet by-and-by.

For the Savior has taken the contract
To deliver all those who believe,
At the headquarters ranch of his Father,
In the great range where none can deceive.
The Inspector will stand at the gateway
And the herd, one by one, will go by—
The round-up by the angels in judgment
Must pass 'neath his all-seeing eye.

No maverick or slick will be tallied
In the great book of life in his home,
For he knows all the brands and the earmarks
That down through the ages have come.
But, along with the tailings and sleepers,
The strays must turn from the gate;
No road brand to gain them admission,
But the awful sad cry "Too late."

Yet I trust in the last great round-up
When the rider shall cut the big herd,
That the cowboys shall be represented
In the earmark and brand of the Lord,
To be shipped to the bright, mystic regions
Over there in green pastures to lie,
And led by the crystal still waters
In that home of the sweet by-and-by.

                                        UNKNOWN

I Want to Be a Cowboy

I want to be a cowboy and with the cowboys stand,
Big spurs upon my bootheels and a lasso in my hand;
My hat broad brimmed and belted upon my head
    I'll place,
And wear my chaparajos with elegance and grace.

The first bright beam of sunlight that paints the east
    with red
Would call me forth to breakfast on bacon, beans,
    and bread;
And then upon my broncho so festive and so bold
I'd rope the frisky heifer and chase the three year old.

And when my work is over to Cheyenne then I'll head,
Fill up on beer and whiskey and paint the damn town
    red.
I'll gallop through the front streets with many a
    frightfull yell;
I'll rope the slant old heathen and yank them straight
    to hell.

                                        UNKNOWN

Little Joe, the Wrangler

Little Joe, the wrangler, will never wrangle more;
    His days with the "remuda"—they are done.
'Twas a year ago last April he joined the outfit here,
    A little "Texas stray" and all alone.

'Twas long late in the evening he rode up to the herd
    On a little old brown pony he called Chow;
With his brogan shoes and overalls a harder-looking kid,
    You never in your life had seen before.

His saddle 'twas a Southern kack built many years ago,
    An O. K. spur on one foot idly hung,
While his "hot roll" in a cotton sack was loosely tied
    behind
    And a canteen from the saddle horn he'd slung.

He said he had to leave his home, his daddy'd married
    twice,
    And his new ma beat him every day or two;
So he saddled up old Chow one night and "lit a shuck"
    this way—
    Thought he'd try and paddle now his own canoe.

Said he'd try and do the best he could if we'd only give
    him work,
    Though he didn't know "straight" up about a cow;
So the boss he cut him out a mount and kinder put him on,
    For he sorter liked the little stray somehow.

Taught him how to herd the horses and learn to know
    them all,
    To round 'em up by daylight; if he could
To follow the chuck-wagon and to always hitch the team
    And help the "cocinero" rustle wood.

We'd driven to Red River and the weather had been fine;
    We were camped down on the south side in a bend,
When a norther commenced blowing and we doubled
    up our guards,
    For it took all hands to hold the cattle then.

Little Joe, the wrangler, was called out with the rest,
    And scarcely had the kid got to the herd,
When the cattle they stampeded; like a hailstorm, long
    they flew,
    And all of us were riding for the lead.

'Tween the streaks of lightning we could see a horse far
    out ahead—
    'Twas little Joe, the wrangler, in the lead;

He was riding "Old Blue Rocket" with his slicker 'bove
    his head,
    Trying to check the leaders in their speed.

At last we got them milling and kinder quieted down,
    And the extra guard back to the camp did go;
But one of them was missin', and we all knew at a glance
    'Twas our little Texas stray—poor Wrangler Joe.

Next morning just at sunup we found where Rocket fell,
    Down in a washout twenty feet below;
Beneath his horse, mashed to a pulp, his spurs had rung
    the knell
    For our little Texas stray—poor Wrangler Joe.

UNKNOWN

The Old Chisholm Trail

Come along, boys, and listen to my tale,
I'll tell you of my troubles on the old Chisholm trail.

    CHORUS:
Coma ti yi youpy, youpy yea, youpy yea,
Coma ti yi youpy, youpy yea.

I started up the trail October twenty-third,
I started up the trail with the 2-U herd.

Oh, a ten-dollar hoss and a forty-dollar saddle,
And I'm goin' to punchin' Texas cattle.

I woke up one morning on the old Chisholm trail,
Rope in my hand and a cow by the tail.

I'm up in the mornin' afore daylight
And afore I sleep the moon shines bright.

Old Ben Bolt was a blamed good boss,
But he'd go to see the girls on a sore-backed hoss.

Old Ben Bolt was a fine old man
And you'd know there was whisky wherever he'd land.

My hoss throwed me off at the creek called Mud,
My hoss throwed me off round the 2-U herd.

Last time I saw him he was going 'cross the level
A-kicking up his heels and a-running like the devil.

It's cloudy in the west, a-looking like rain,
And my damned old slicker's in the wagon again.

No chaps and no slicker, and it's pouring down rain,
And I swear, by God, that I'll never night-herd again.

Crippled my hoss, I don't know how,
Ropin' at the horns of a 2-U cow.

We hit Caldwell and we hit her on the fly,
We bedded down the cattle on the hill close by.

Feet in the stirrups and seat in the saddle,
I hung and rattled them longhorn cattle.

Last night I was on guard and the leader broke the ranks,
I hit my horse down the shoulders and I spurred him in the flanks.

The wind commenced to blow, and the rain began to fall,
Hit looked, by grab, like we was goin' to lose 'em all.

My slicker's in the wagon and I'm gittin' mighty cold,
And these longhorn sons-o'-guns are gittin' hard to hold.

Saddle up, boys, and saddle up well,
For I think these cattle have scattered to hell.

I jumped in the saddle and grabbed holt the horn,
Best blamed cow-puncher ever was born.

I hit my pony and he gave a little rack,
And damned big luck if we ever git back.

With my blanket and my gun and my rawhide rope,
I'm a-slidin' down the trail in a long, keen lope.

I popped my foot in the stirrup and gave a little yell,
The tail cattle broke and the leaders went to hell.

I don't give a damn if they never do stop;
I'll ride as long as an eight-day clock.

Foot in the stirrup and hand on the horn,
Best damned cowboy ever was born.

I herded and I hollered and I done very well,
Till the boss said, "Boys, just let 'em go to hell."

I and old Blue Dog arrived on the spot
And we put them to milling like the boiling of a pot.

Stray in the herd and the boss said kill it,
So I shot him in the rump with the handle of the skillet.

We rounded 'em up and put 'em on the cars,
And that was the last of the old Two Bars.

Oh, it's bacon and beans most every day—
I'd as soon be a-eatin' prairie hay.

I'm on my best horse and I'm goin' at a run,
I'm the quickest-shootin' cowboy that ever pulled a gun.

I went to the wagon to get my roll,
To come back to Texas, dad-burn my soul.

Well, I met a little gal and I offered her a quarter,
She says, "Young man, I'm a gentleman's daughter."

I went to the boss to draw my roll,
He had it figgered out I was nine dollars in the hole.

I'll sell my outfit just as soon as I can,
I won't punch cattle for no damned man.

I'll sell my horse and I'll sell my saddle;
You can go to hell with your longhorn cattle.

Goin' back to town to draw my money,
Goin' back to town to see my honey.

With my knees in the saddle and my seat in the sky,
I'll quit punching cows in the sweet by-and-by.

Fare you well, old trail-boss, I don't wish you any harm,
I'm quittin' this business to go on the farm.

No more cow-puncher to sleep at my ease,
'Mid the crawlin' of the lice and the bitin' of the fleas.

It's round up your cavvy, and it's rope out your pack,
And strap your old kak well fast on his back;

Your foot in the stirrup and your hand on the horn,
You're the best durned cowboy that ever was born;

You land in the saddle and give a loud yell,
For the longhorn cattle have got to take the hill.

You round up a bunch of dogies and take down the trail,
But the first thing you know you land in jail.

But the sheriff's an old puncher and he fixes your bail,
It's a durned poor country with a cowboy in jail.

So round up your foreman and hit him for your roll,
You're goin' to town and act a little bold.

You strap on your chaps, your spurs and your gun,
For you're going to town to have a little fun.

You ride a big bronc' that will buck and prance,
And you pull out your gun and make the tenderfoot dance.

You go into the gamblin' house looking kinda funny
For you got every pocket just chuck-full o' money.

You play cards with a gambler who's got a marked pack;
You walk back to the ranch with your saddle on your back.

Now I've punched cattle from Texas to Maine,
And I've known some cowboys by their right name.

No matter though whatever they claim,
You'll find every dirty cuss exactly the same.

So, dig in your spurs and peel your eyes to heaven,
And never overlook a calf with Eleven Slash Eleven.

 CHORUS:
Singing hi yi yippi, hi yippi yea,
Singing hi yi yippi, yippi yea yea.

I went to the bar and called for a drink,
The bartender said I was a gink.

 CHORUS:
Tum-a-ti-yi-yippi-yippi-ya-ya,
Tum-a-ti-yippi-yippi-ya.

He knew these words would likely cause a fight,
An' he went for his hip like a streak of light.

I beat him to the draw and hit him on the ear,
And down he went like an old beef steer.

Oh, the peckerwood's a-peckin' an' the children are a-cryin',
The old folks a-fightin' an' the hogs are a-dyin'.

I met her in the road but she wouldn't tell her name;
I thought, by gosh, what a fine-lookin' dame!

I'm a-goin' to the boss an' git my roll,
I'm a-goin' downtown an' take a little stroll.

I went up to the boss and we had a little chat,
I slapped him in the face with my big slouch hat.

Oh, the boss says to me, "I'll fire you,
Not only you, but the whole damn crew."

Oh, my roll's on my saddle an' my head's in the sky,
An' it's all day long on the old XY.

After we got through, we put them on the cars,
And that was the last of the old Two Bars.

I hit the first train, it was the Cannon Ball,
I went rockin' home right early in the fall.

I hadn't been home but two days or three,
Till I put off my gal for to see.

"If you've made up your mind to quit the cowboy life,
I have fully decided to be your little wife."

Farewell, old Blue Dog, I wish you no harm,
I have quit the business to go on the farm.

Good-by, old Blue Dog, on you I could rely,
I shall always love you until the day I die.

Good-by, old Blue Dog, you've been a good friend,
Around the night herds on you I could depend.

With lightning in his eye and thunder in his heels,
He went spinning 'round like a hoop on a reel.

I'll sell my saddle and I'll buy me a plow,
And I'll swear, begod, I'll never rope another cow.

UNKNOWN

The Trail Herd

Clouded sun on coolin' morn,
 Squeakin' taps and spurs a-rattle,
Loungin' 'cross my saddle horn,
 Trailin' dull-eyed bawlin' cattle.
Chokin' dust clouds in the air,
 Off across the range a-driftin',
Punchers cussin' stragglers there
 As the mornin' mist is liftin'.

Wild-eyed mavericks on the prod,
 Plungin' ponies, buckin', snortin',
On across the sun baked sod
 Full o' ginger, a-cavortin'.
Ol' chuck wagon on ahead
 Fer to get the grub pile ready,
Sun a-blazin' fiery red,
 Calves a-wobblin' or unsteady.

Summer day a-growin' old
  As the crimson sun is sinkin',
River sparklin' just like gold
  Where the thirsty herd is drinkin'.
Cook a-yellin', "Grub pile, boys!"
  Cups on ol' tin plates a-rattle,
Punchers makin' lots o' noise
  On the bed ground with the cattle.

Silence on the midnight air,
  Me on night herd slowly moggin'
Round the bedded cattle there,
  Singin' to 'em as I'm joggin'.
Camp fire twinklin' down below,
  River sort o' lullabyin'
To the sleepers soft an' low
  On their blanket beds a-lyin'.

Second watch a-rollin' out,
  Sleepy-eyed with grimy faces,
At the foreman's lusty shout,
  Saddlin' up to take our places.
Me a-drowsin' off to rest
  With the starry sky above me,
Thoughts of you within my breast,
  Dreamin', dreamin' that you love me.

UNKNOWN

The Trail to Mexico

It was in the merry month of May
When I started for Texas far away,
I left my darling girl behind;
She said her heart was only mine.

O, it was when I embraced her in my arms,
I thought she had ten thousand charms;
Her caresses were soft, her kisses were sweet,
Saying, "We'll get married next time we meet."

It was in the year of 'eighty-three
That A. J. Stinson hired me;
He says, "Young man, I want you to go
And follow this herd into Mexico."

Well, it was early in the year
When I started out to drive those steers;
Through sleet and snow 'twas a lonesome go
As the herd rolled on into Mexico.

When I arrived in Mexico,
I wanted to see my girl but I could not go;
So I wrote a letter to my dear
But not a word for years did I hear.

Well, I started back to my once-loved home,
Inquired for the girl I had called my own;
They said she had married a richer life,
Therefore, wild cowboy, seek another wife.

"O buddie, O buddie, please stay at home,
Don't forever be on the roam.
There is many a girl more true than I,
So pray don't go where the bullets fly."

"Oh, curse your gold and your silver, too.
God pity a girl that won't prove true.
I'll travel west where the bullets fly.
I'll stay on the trail till the day I die."

UNKNOWN

When the Work's All Done This Fall

A group of jolly cowboys, discussing plans at ease,
Says one, "I'll tell you something, boys, if you will
   listen, please.
I am an old cowpuncher and hyer I'm dressed in rags,
I used to be a tough one and go on great big jags.
But I have got a home, boys, a good one, you all know,
Although I have not seen it since long, long ago.
I'm going back to Dixie once more to see them all,
Yes, I'm going to see my mother when the work's all
   done this fall.

"After the roundup's over and after the shipping's
   done,
I am going right straight home, boys, ere all my money
   is gone.
I have changed my ways, boys, no more will I fall;
And I am going home, boys, when the work's all done
   this fall.
When I left home, boys, my mother for me cried,
Begged me not go, boys, for me she would have died;
My mother's heart is breaking, breaking for me, that's
   all,
And with God's help I'll see her when the work's all
   done this fall."

That very night this cowboy went out to stand his
   guard;
The night was dark and cloudy and storming very
   hard;
The cattle they got frightened and rushed in wild
   stampede,
The cowboy tried to head them, riding at full speed.
While riding in the darkness so loudly did he shout,
Trying his best to head them and turn the herd about,
His saddle horse did stumble and on him did fall,
The poor boy won't see his mother when the work's
   all done this fall.

His body was so mangled the boys all thought him
  dead,
They picked him up so gently and laid him on a bed;
He opened wide his blue eyes and looking all around
He motioned to his comrades to sit near him on the
  ground.
"Boys, send my mother my wages, the wages I have
  earned,
For I am afraid, boys, my last steer I have turned.
I'm going to a new range, I hear my Master's call,
And I'll not see my mother when the work's all done
  this fall.

"Bill, you may have my saddle; George, you may
  take my bed;
Jack may have my pistol, after I am dead.
Boys, think of me kindly when you look upon them all,
For I'll not see my mother when the work's all done
  this fall."
Poor Charlie was buried at sunrise, no tombstone at
  his head,
Nothing but a little board and this is what it said,
"Charlie died at daybreak, he died from a fall,
The boy won't see his mother when the work's all
  done this fall."

                                        UNKNOWN

VI

Heroes and Villains

Fine!

Judge Bean's court, knowed near and far,
Was post office, billiard hall, and bar.
Law and justice, whiskey, and wine—
All was noted upon his sign,
And all was dealt with a high old hand
Over this west-of-the-Pecos land.
But Bean, as he swallered his ol' red-eye,
Allowed that expenses was doggoned high,
And so, for impudence, killin', theft,
He laid on fines both right and left.

Once ol' Bart, his right-hand man,
Gallops in as hard as he can,
Bringin' the news of a man shot dead
Down by the Pecos' sandy bed.
"By gobs, Bart, though it's kinder fur,
I reckon I'll go as the coroner!"
Sixteen miles the judge goes lopin',
Sets on the body and says: "Court's open!"
Searches a pocket and finds a gun,
And twenty bucks in another one.

"By gobs, boys, this coroner's court
Finds 'twas an accident cut him short.
And now, as the court of law and order,
West of the Pecos and down to the border.
I fine this corpse, for totin' a gun,
Twenty bucks! And the case is done!"

Under the shade of his spreadin' sign,
Doin' his duty and likin' it *fine,*
Ol' Judge Bean, with all his snortin',
Made his court plumb self-supportin'!

S. OMAR BARKER

The Law West of the Pecos

Judge Roy Bean of Vinegarroon
Held high court in his own saloon.
Fer a killin' or thievin' or other sech fracas,
Bean was the law out west of the Pecos.
Set on a keg an' allowed no foolin',
Closed ever' case with "That's my rulin'!"
A gun butt thump an' a judgy snort
Announced to the boys he was openin' court;
And every once in a while or less,
He'd thump with his gun fer a short recess,
Step to the bar like a spry ol' lynx
An' call all present to buy some drinks.
Juryman, witness, thirsty or dry,
Stepped right up fer their ol' red-eye.

Once on a jury a man called Hanks
Set where he wuz an' says, "No, thanks!"
"Now by gobs!" wuz Judge Bean's snort,
"I fine yuh ten fer contempt of court!"

Hanks he hemmed an' Hanks he hawed,
But finally out of his pants he drawed
A bill fer twenty, an' paid his fine.
"Ten bucks change," he says, "is mine."

"Change?" roars the law of the Pecos Range.
"This here court don't make no change!"
Judge Bean smiled his sixgun smile:
"I raise yuh ten an' take your pile!
An' now, by gobs, without no foolin',
Wet up your whistles, fer that's my rulin'!"

Oh, out in the West when the range wuz raw,
West of the Pecos law was law!

S. OMAR BARKER

The Sheep Beezness

"I'm tell j'you what, these sheeps beezness,"
   Thus spoke Borrego Joe,
"It take wise feller like myself
   For savvy make heem go!

"One feller dat make plenty fail
   He's my fr'en' Pancho Pete.
I steal from heem one t'ousand sheeps!
   I'm t'ink he's got for queet!"

Beside his campfire that same night
   Said Pancho Pete to me:
"I'm tell you, Meester Guarda-Bosq',
   One theeng is plain for see:

"Borrego Joe, she's vamos soon
   Away from thees *buen pais!*
I speak you true the reason now—
   I'm not for tell you lies!

"In sheep beezness she's broke for sure!
   Eet make you laugh for hear!
I'm make the steal from my fr'en' Joe
   Twelve hundred sheeps thees year!"

                        S. OMAR BARKER

When Billy the Kid Rides Again

High are the mountains and low is the plain,
Where Billy the Kid comes a-ridin' again.

Old Juánico sees him—black on the moon,
And two haggard horsemen come following soon.

Now topping the rim-rock, now hid in a vale,
Four ghostly white riders press close on his trail.

No thudding of hoofbeats, no sound anywhere,
But nine silent dead men are racing the air.

Beyond the old courthouse and following fast,
The tenth pale pursuer springs out of the past.

Old Juánico sees them—no other eye can,
The galloping Kid and his strange caravan.

Fort Sumner to White Oaks, Tularosa to Bent—
Gaunt horsemen await him at each settlement.

For blood's in the moonmist, as two dozen dead
Swoop down the dim trails where their killer has fled.

Gray in the mountains and white on the plain,
At moon haunted midnight they're riding again.

Time shadows the silence in old Lincoln town—
Look! Billy the Kid comes a-galloping down!

S. OMAR BARKER

Jesse James

Among our country's outlaws
There are some lusty names,
But many a voice would make a choice
Of Jesse Woodson James.

No wishy-washy man was he
Of milk and *aqua pura*.
He shook the ground for miles around
His native soil, Mizzoura.

"Allow me!" said his brother,
His helpful partner, Frank.
Then out they'd sail to rob the mail
Or polish off a bank.

The sheriffs found, unlike the hound,
His bite worse than his bark.
He shot as well as William Tell
Though apples weren't his mark.

And those who came to spoil his game
Found people sometimes coy.
For lots would say, "It's Jesse's way,
He's just a home-town boy.

"They done him wrong when he was young.
Perhaps he should have borne it.
But we have found it is not sound
To step upon a hornet."

He robbed and looted banks and trains.
He took what wasn't his'n.
He thumbed his nose at all of those
Who sadly muttered, "Prison!"

A price was put upon his head.
His luck began to crack.
Two of his men turned traitor then
And shot him in the back.

Jesse died at thirty-five,
Frank lived to threescore-ten.
Of their kind you will not find
Two more daring men.

Some call Jess Missouri's pride,
Some say he's her shame,
All we can say is, anyway
He earned his outlaw fame.

ROSEMARY & STEPHEN BENÉT

Jesse James

Jesse James was a two-gun man,
     (*Roll on, Missouri!*)
Strong-arm chief of an outlaw clan,
     (*From Kansas to Illinois!*)
He twirled an old Colt forty-five;
     (*Roll on, Missouri!*)
They never took Jesse James alive.
     (*Roll, Missouri, roll!*)

Jesse James was King of the Wes';
     (*Cataracts in the Missouri!*)
He'd a di'mon' heart in his lef' breas';
     (*Brown Missouri rolls!*)
He'd a fire in his heart no hurt could stifle;
     (*Thunder, Missouri!*)
Lion eyes an' a Winchester rifle.
     (*Missouri, roll down!*)

Jesse James rode a pinto hawse;
Come at night to a water-cawse;
Tetched with the rowel that pinto's flank;
She sprung the torrent from bank to bank.

Jesse rode through a sleepin' town;
Looked the moonlit street both up an' down;
Crack-crack-crack, the street ran flames
An' a great voice cried, "I'm Jesse James!"

Hawse an' afoot they're after Jess!
     (*Roll on, Missouri!*)
Spurrin' an' spurrin'—but he's gone Wes'.
     (*Brown Missouri rolls!*)
He was ten foot tall when he stood in his boots;
     (*Lightnin' like the Missouri!*)
More'n a match fer sich galoots.
     (*Roll, Missouri, roll!*)

Jesse James rode outa the sage;
Roun' the rocks come the swayin' stage;
Straddlin' the road a giant stan's
An' a great voice bellers, "Throw up yer han's!"

Jesse raked in the di'mon' rings,
The big gold watches an' the yuther things;
Jesse divvied 'em then an' thar
With a cryin' child had lost her mar.

They're creepin'; they're crawlin'; they're stalkin' Jess;
    (Roll on, Missouri!)
They's a rumor he's gone much further Wes';
    (Roll, Missouri, roll!)
They's word of a cayuse hitched to the bars
    (Ruddy clouds on Missouri!)
Of a golden sunset that busts into stars.
    (Missouri, roll down!)

Jesse James rode hell fer leather;
He was a hawse an' a man together;
In a cave in a mountain high up in air
He lived with a rattlesnake, a wolf, an' a bear.

Jesse's heart was as sof' as a woman;
Fer guts an' stren'th he was sooper-human;
He could put six shots through a woodpecker's eye
And take in one swaller a gallon o' rye.

They sought him here an' they sought him there,
    (Roll on, Missouri!)
But he strides by night through the ways of the air;
    (Brown Missouri rolls!)
They say he was took an' they say he is dead,
    (Thunder, Missouri!)
But he ain't—he's a sunset overhead!
    (Missouri down to the sea!)

Jesse James was a Hercules.
When he went through the woods he tore up the trees.

When he went on the plains he smoked the groun'
An' the hull lan' shuddered fer miles aroun'.

Jesse James wore a red bandanner
That waved on the breeze like the Star Spangled Banner;
In seven states he cut up dadoes.
He's gone with the buffler an' the desperadoes.

Yes, Jesse James was a two-gun man
　　　(*Roll on, Missouri!*)
The same as when this song began;
　　　(*From Kansas to Illinois!*)
An' when you see a sunset bust into flames
　　　(*Lightnin' like the Missouri!*)
Or a thunderstorm blaze—that's Jesse James!
　　　(*Hear that Missouri roll!*)

WILLIAM ROSE BENÉT

"Black Bart, P08"

Welcome, good friend; as you have served your term,
　　And found the joy of crime to be a fiction,
I hope you'll hold your present faith, stand firm
　　And not again be open to conviction.

Your sins, though scarlet once, are now as wool:
　　You've made atonement for all past offenses,
And conjugated—'twas an awful pull!—
　　The verb "to pay" in all its moods and tenses.

You were a dreadful criminal—by Heaven,
　　I think there never was a man so sinful!
We've all a pinch or two of Satan's leaven,
　　But you appeared to have an even skinful.

Earth shuddered with aversion at your name;
   Rivers fled backward, gravitation scorning;
The sea and sky, from thinking on your shame,
   Grew lobster-red at eve and in the morning.

But still red-handed at your horrid trade
   You wrought, to reason deaf, and to compassion.
But now with gods and men your peace is made
   I beg you to be good and in the fashion.

What's that?—you "ne'er again will rob a stage"?
   What! did you do so? Faith, I didn't know it.
Was *that* what threw poor Themis in a rage?
   I thought you were convicted as a poet!

I own it was a comfort to my soul,
   And soothed it better than the deepest curses,
To think they'd got one poet in a hole
   Where, though he wrote, he could not print, his
      verses.

I thought that Welcker, Plunkett, Brooks, and all
   The ghastly crew who always are begriming
With villain couplets every page and wall,
   Might be arrested and "run in" for rhyming.

And then Parnassus would be left to me,
   And Pegasus should bear me up it gaily,
Nor down a steep place run into the sea,
   As now he must be tempted to do daily.

Well, grab the lyre-strings, hearties, and begin:
   Bawl your harsh souls all out upon the gravel.
I must endure you, for you'll never sin
   By robbing coaches, until dead men travel.

                  AMBROSE BIERCE

The Convicts' Ball

San Quentin was brilliant. Within the halls
Of the noble pile with the frowning walls
(God knows they've enough to make them frown,
With a Governor trying to break them down!)
Was a blaze of light. 'Twas the natal day
Of his nibs the popular John S. Gray,
And many observers considered his birth
The primary cause of his moral worth.
"The ball is free!" cried Black Bart, and they all
Said a ball with no chain was a novel ball;
"And I never have seed," said Jimmy Hope,
"Sech a lightsome dance withouten a rope."
Chinamen, Indians, Portuguese, Blacks,
Russians, Italians, Kanucks and Kanaks,
Chilenos, Peruvians, Mexicans—all
Greased with their presence that notable ball.
None were excluded excepting, perhaps,
The Rev. Morrison's churchly chaps,
Whom, to prevent a religious debate,
The Warden had banished outside of the gate.
The fiddler, fiddling his hardest the while,
"Called off" in the regular foot-hill style:
"Circle to the left!" and "Forward and back!"
And "Hellum to port for the stabbard tack!"
(This great *virtuoso,* it would appear,
Was Mate of the *Gatherer* many a year.)

"Ally man left!"—to a painful degree
His French was unlike to the French of Paree,
As heard from our countrymen lately abroad,
And his *"doe cee doe"* was the gem of the fraud.
But what can you hope from a gentleman barred
From circles of culture by dogs in the yard?
'Twas a glorious dance, though, all the same,
The Jardin Mabille in the days of its fame
Never saw legs perform such springs—
The cold-chisel's magic had given them wings.

They footed it neatly, those ladies and gents:
Dull care (said Long Moll) had a helly go-hence!

'Twas a very aristocratic affair:
The *crème de la crème* and *élite* were there—
Rank, beauty and wealth from the highest sets,
And Hubert Howe Bancroft sent his regrets.

AMBROSE BIERCE

Pete's Error

There's a new grave up on Boot Hill, where we've
    planted Rowdy Pete;
He died one evenin', sudden, with his leather on his feet;
He was Cactus Center's terror with that work of art, the
    Colt,
But somehow, without warnin', he up and missed his holt.

His fav'rite trick in shootin' was to grab his victim's right,
Then draw his own revolver—and the rest was jest
    "Good-night";
He worked it in succession on nine stout and well-armed
    men,
But a sickly-lookin' stranger made Pete's feet slip up at
    ten.

Pete had follered out his programme and had passed the
    fightin' word;
He grabbed the stranger's right hand, when a funny thing
    occurred;
The stranger was left-handed, which Pete hadn't figgered
    out,
And, afore he fixed his error, Pete was dead beyond all
    doubt.

ARTHUR CHAPMAN

The Sheriff's Report

We jest went out to git him, and we did—
    We trailed him from the sagebrush to the pine;
We seen the long-dead ashes where he'd hid
    And where he'd cooked his bit of bacon rine.

We found the hoss, where it had fell and died,
    But he'd gone on—a tough nut, yes, that's true—
We seen the blood where he had stopped and tied
    His coat-sleeve round his worn and busted shoe.

We heard his lead, a-singin' past our ears,
    Where he stood pat, 'way up a lonely draw;
We smelt his powder, yet it brung no fears,
    'Cause wasn't we the Majesty of Law?

We seen his face, his black eyes blazin' hate,
    We heard him fall, and in plain view he slid;
The world's some better off, I calkilate—
    We jest went out to git him, and we did.

                                        ARTHUR CHAPMAN

Cash In

O life is a game of poker
And I've played it straight to the end;
But the last chip's down on the table
And I'm done with the game, my friend.

The fire in my blood it flickers
Like a guttering candle light,
When the tallow beads in greasy tears
And the wind whips in from the night.

The deck was stacked by the Dealer
Before He would let me in;
The cards were marked, and I knew it—
There was never a chance to win.

But I bluffed the game to a finish—
Till He nodded and called my hand—
Palms empty and crossed—but the lips
    still smile—
And the Dealer will understand.

SHARLOT M. HALL

Plain Language from Truthful James

Which I wish to remark,
    And my language is plain,
That for ways that are dark
    And for tricks that are vain,
The heathen Chinee is peculiar,
    Which the same I would rise to explain.

Ah Sin was his name;
  And I shall not deny,
In regard to the same,
  What that name might imply;
But his smile it was pensive and childlike,
  As I frequent remarked to Bill Nye.

It was August the third,
  And quite soft was the skies;
Which it might be inferred
  That Ah Sin was likewise;
Yet he played it that day upon William
  And me in a way I despise.

Which we had a small game,
  And Ah Sin took a hand:
It was Euchre. The same
  He did not understand;
But he smiled as he sat by the table,
  With the smile that was childlike and bland.

Yet the cards they were stocked
  In a way that I grieve,
And my feelings were shocked
  At the state of Nye's sleeve,
Which was stuffed full of aces and bowers,
  And the same with intent to deceive.

But the hands that were played
  By that heathen Chinee,
And the points that he made,
  Were quite frightful to see,—
Till at last he put down a right bower,
  Which the same Nye had dealt unto me.

Then I looked up at Nye,
  And he gazed upon me;
And he rose with a sigh,
  And said, "Can this be?

We are ruined by Chinese cheap labor,"—
    And he went for that heathen Chinee.

In the scene that ensued
    I did not take a hand,
But the floor it was strewed
    Like the leaves on the strand
With the cards that Ah Sin had been hiding,
    In the game "he did not understand."

In his sleeves, which were long,
    He had twenty-four jacks,—
Which was coming it strong,
    Yet I state but the facts;
And we found on his nails, which were taper,
    What is frequent in tapers,—that's wax.

Which is why I remark,
    And my language is plain,
That for ways that are dark
    And for tricks that are vain,
The heathen Chinee is peculiar,—
    Which the same I am free to maintain.

                  BRET HARTE

Pizen Pete's Mistake

It was in the Yellow Dog Saloon one sultry summer night,
Old "Pizen Pete" was on the prod and looking for a fight.
With a forty-five in either hand, red whiskers and long hair,
'Twas enough to make a man turn pale to see him standing there.

And then there came into the room, as the swinging doors
   swung wide,
A young lad of scarce twenty years, with a gun on either side.

He did not look to right or left as he walked up to the bar,
And leaning there he calmly said, "A big drink of Three Star."

He raised the whiskey to his lips; Pizen Pete stepped back
    with a sneer;
His six-gun roared and, as it did, the glass seemed to disappear.
The stranger slowly turned around, and I saw his face turn red.
"Do that again, old timer, and I'll burn yuh down!" he said.

"Go ahead and draw," said Pete, with a grin. His own gun was
    in hand.
"Just make a move for your six-gun, an' I'll kill yuh where
    yuh stand!"
The youngster quickly jumped aside, and his guns began to roar.
And when the smoke had cleared away, Pizen Pete lay on the floor.

"Say, stranger, what's your name?" I asked. "It seems like I've
    seen your face."
He didn't turn or answer, but quickly left the place.
He went out and mounted his pony; I heard him as he did,
And then his voice came drifting back: "My name is Billy the Kid."

ATTRIBUTED TO MERRILL HONEY

Indigo Pete's J. B.

I was leavin' the Blue Dog on the run
When *pop* goes a deputy sheriff's gun,
And he must a-been talkin' to me at that,
For off goes my ol' gray Stetson hat;
She hit on her edge and she rolled along,
For the wind was a-blowin' loud and strong.
So I took after my ol' J. B.
The same as the sheriff took after me.

I pitched the rein to my ol' cayuse,
Stood in the stirrups and turned him loose,

But my hat kept gainin', it hopped, it flew,
It run on the rim for a mile or two,
Got snagged in the sage and almost stopped,
Then up in the air it flipped and flopped,
Turnin' and turnin' away up high,
And takin' it easy—like eagles fly,
Then divin' down quick like an eagle drops,
Only that ol' hat she never stops;
Thinks I, "I savvy the whole durn show,
That hat is a-headin' for Mexico!"
So I took after my ol' J. B.
The same as the sheriff took after me.

Then all of a sudden the stars came out,
But the wind kept whistlin' wild and stout,
And I plum lost sight of my ol' gray hat
But I kept on foggin' across the flat,
Figurin' as how in the mornin' sun,
I'd find her fresh for another run.
And sure enough, when the mornin' came,
There was my ol' J. B., the same
Spinnin' along with a bounce and jump
Like a wheel turned loose on a down-hill hump;
Past Alamogordo on the fly,
Then Deming and Lordsburg shootin' by,
A-tryin' to ketch my ol' J. B.
The same as the sheriff took after me.

When the Rio Grande hove in sight,
Thinks I, "It's a case of ol' hat, good night!"
But she riz on a gust and she sailed across,
And I follered her trail on a played-out hoss,
Till we struck a bar and we pulled out slow,
And me and my hat was in Mexico.

Thinks I, "Ol' hat, we have come a stretch,
You are hard to beat and you're hard to ketch,
You been whipped by brush and rolled
    and stomped,

You been set on, stood on, squeezed
   and tromped,
You been soaked by rain and scorched
   by fire,
And squashed plum flat by a wagon tire,
You been used for whippin' broncos' ears,
And slapped in the face of ornery steers,
Or packin' water or fannin' flame,
Or stoppin' a hole in a window frame,
And you're goin' yet—the same as me."
So I stuck my head in my ol' J. B.
Then I waved for the sheriff to go to hell,
And I headed South for a breathin' spell.

HENRY "HARRY" KIBBS

The Ballad of Billy the Kid

No man in the West ever won such renown
As young Billy Bonney of Santa Fe town,
And of all the wild outlaws that met a bad end,
None so quick with a pistol or true to a friend.

It was in Silver City his first trouble came,
A man called Billy's mother a very foul name;
Billy swore to get even, his chance it came soon,
When he stabbed that young man in Joe Dyer's saloon.

He kissed his poor mother and fled from the scene,
A bold desperado and not yet fifteen;
He hid in a sheep-camp but short was his stay,
For he stole an old pony and rode far away.

At monte and faro he next took a hand,
And lived in Tucson on the fat of the land;
But the game was too easy, the life was too slow,
So he drifted alone into Old Mexico.

It was not very long before Billy came back.
With a notch in his gun and some gold in a sack;
He struck for the Pecos his comrades to see,
And they all rode to Lincoln and went on a spree.

There he met his friend Tunstall and hired as a hand
To fight with the braves of the Jingle-Bob brand;
Then Tunstall was murdered and left in his gore;
To avenge that foul murder Young Billy he swore.

First Morton and Baker he swiftly did kill,
Then he slaughtered Bill Roberts at Blazer's sawmill;
Sheriff Brady and Hindman in Lincoln he slew,
Then he rode to John Chisum's along with his crew.

There he stood off a posse and drove them away,
In McSween's house in Lincoln he made his next play;
Surrounded he fought till the house was burned down,
But he dashed through the flames and escaped from the town.

Young Billy rode north and Young Billy rode south,
He plundered and killed with a smile on his mouth,
But he always came back to Fort Sumner again
For his Mexican sweetheart was living there then.

His trackers were many, they followed him fast,
At *Arroyo Tiván* he was captured at last;
He was taken to Lincoln and put under guard,
And sentenced to hang in the old court-house yard.

J. Bell and Bob Ollinger watched day and night,
And Bob told Young Billy he'd made his last fight.
Young Billy gave Ollinger scarcely a glance,
But sat very still and awaited his chance.

One day he played cards with J. Bell in the room,
Who had no idea how close was his doom;
Billy slipped off a handcuff, hit Bell on the head,
Then he snatched for the pistol and shot him down dead.

Bob Ollinger heard and he ran to the spot
To see what had happened and who had been shot;
Young Billy looked down from a window and fired,
Bob Ollinger sank to the ground and expired.

Then Young Billy escaped on a horse that was near,
As he rode forth from Lincoln he let out a cheer;
Though his foes they were many he feared not a one,
So long as a cartridge remained in his gun.

But his comrades were dead or had fled from the land,
It was up to Young Billy to play a lone hand;
And Sheriff Pat Garrett he searched far and wide,
Never thinking the Kid in Fort Sumner would hide.

But when Garrett heard Billy was hiding in town,
He went to Pete Maxwell's when the sun had gone down;
The door was wide open, the night it was hot,
So Pat Garrett walked in and sat down by Pete's cot.

Young Billy had gone for to cut him some meat,
No hat on his head and no boots on his feet;
When he saw two strange men on the porch in the gloom,
He pulled his gun quick and backed into the room.

Billy said, Who is that? and he spoke Maxwell's name,
Then from Pat Garrett's pistol the answer it came—
The swift, cruel bullet went true to its mark,
And Young Billy fell dead on the floor in the dark.

So Young Billy Bonney he came to his end,
Shot down by Pat Garrett who once was his friend;
Though for coolness and courage both gunmen ranked high,
It was Fate that decided Young Billy should die.

Each year of his life was a notch in his gun,
For in twenty-one years he had slain twenty-one.
His grave is unmarked and by desert sands hid,
And so ends the true story of Billy the Kid.

HENRY HERBERT KNIBBS

The Shallows of the Ford

Did you ever wait for daylight when the stars along the
    river
  Floated thick and white as snowflakes in the water deep
    and strange,
Till a whisper through the aspens made the current break
    and shiver
  As the frosty edge of morning seemed to melt and spread
    and change?

Once I waited, almost wishing that the dawn would never
    find me;
  Saw the sun roll up the ranges like the glory of the Lord;
Was about to wake my partner who was sleeping close
    behind me,
  When I saw the man we wanted spur his pony to the
    ford.

Saw the ripples of the shallows and the muddy streaks that
    followed,
  As the pony stumbled toward me in the narrows of the
    bend;
Saw the face I used to welcome, wild and watchful, lined
    and hollowed;
  And God knows I wished to warn him, for I once had
    called him friend.

But an oath had come between us—I was paid by Law
    and Order;
  He was outlaw, rustler, killer—so the border whisper ran;
Left his word in Caliente that he'd cross the Rio border . . .
  Call me coward? But I hailed him. . . . "Riding close
    to daylight, Dan!"

Just a hair and he'd have got me, but my voice, and not
    the warning,
  Caught his hand and held him steady; then he nodded,
    spoke my name,

Reined his pony round and fanned it in the bright and
    silent morning,
  Back across the sunlit Rio up the trail on which he came.

He had passed his word to cross it—I had passed my
    word to get him—
  We broke even and we knew it; 't was a case of give-
    and-take
For old times. I could have killed him from the brush;
    instead, I let him
  Ride his trail. . . . I turned . . . my partner flung his arm
    and stretched awake;

Saw me standing in the open; pulled his gun and came be-
    side me;
  Asked a question with his shoulder as his left hand
    pointed toward
Muddy streaks that thinned and vanished . . . not a word,
    but hard he eyed me
  As the water cleared and sparkled in the shallows of the
    ford.

HENRY HERBERT KNIBBS

Waring of Sonora-town

The heat acrost the desert was a-swimmin' in the sun,
  When Waring of Sonora-town,
  Jim Waring of Sonora-town,
From Salvador come ridin' down, a-rollin' of his gun.

He was singin' low an' easy to his pony's steady feet,
  But his eye was live an' driftin'
  Round the scenery an' siftin'
All the crawlin' shadows shiftin' in the tremblin' gray mesquite.

Eyes was watchin' from a hollow where a outlaw Chola lay:
   Two black, snaky eyes, a-yearnin'
   For Jim's hoss to make the turnin',
Then—to loose a bullet burnin' through his back—the Chola way.

Jim Waring's gaze, a-rovin' free an' easy as he rode,
   Settled quick—without him seemin'
   To get wise an' quit his dreamin'—
On a shiny ring a-gleamin' where no ring had ever growed.

But the lightnin' don't give warnin'—just a lick, an' she is through.
   Waring set his gun to smokin',
   Playful-like—like he was jokin',
An'—a Chola lay a-chokin', an' a buzzard cut the blue.

HENRY HERBERT KNIBBS

Kit Carson's Ride

Room! room to turn around in, to breathe and be
     free,
To grow to be giant, to sail as at sea
With the speed of the wind on a steed with his
     mane
To the wind, without pathway or route or a rein.
Room! room to be free where the white border'd
     sea
Blows a kiss to a brother as boundless as he;
Where the buffalo come like a cloud on the plain,
Pouring on like the tide of a storm-driven main,
And the lodge of the hunter to friend or to foe
Offers rest; and unquestion'd you come or you
     go.
My plains of America! Seas of wild lands!
From a land in the seas in a raiment of foam,

That has reached to a stranger the welcome of
      home,
I turn to you, lean to you, lift you my hands.

Run? Run? See this flank, sir, and I do love
      him so!
But he's blind, badger blind. Whoa, Pache, boy,
      whoa.
No, you wouldn't believe it to look at his eyes,
But he's blind, badger blind, and it happen'd this
      wise:

"We lay in the grass and the sunburnt clover
That spread on the ground like a great brown
      cover
Northward and southward, and west and away
To the Brazos, where our lodges lay,
One broad and unbroken level of brown.
We were waiting the curtains of night to come
      down
To cover us trio and conceal our flight
With my brown bride, won from an Indian town
That lay in the rear the full ride of a night.

"We lounged in the grass—her eyes were in
      mine,
And her hands on my knee, and her hair was as
      wine
In its wealth and its flood, pouring on and all
      over
Her bosom wine red, and press'd never by one.
Her touch was as warm as the tinge of the clover
Burnt brown as it reach'd to the kiss of the sun.
Her words they were low as the lute-throated
      dove,
And as laden with love as the heart when it
      beats
In its hot, eager answer to earliest love,
Or the bee hurried home by its burthen of sweets.

"We lay low in the grass on the broad plain
     levels,
Old Revels and I, and my stolen brown bride;
'Forty full miles if a foot to ride!
Forty full miles if a foot, and the devils
Of red Comanches are hot on the track
When once they strike it. Let the sun go down
Soon, very soon,' muttered bearded old Revels
As he peer'd at the sun, lying low on his back,
Holding fast to his lasso. Then he jerk'd at his
     steed
And he sprang to his feet, and glanced swiftly
     around,
And then dropp'd, as if shot, with an ear to the
     ground;
Then again to his feet, and to me, to my bride,
While his eyes were like flame, his face like a
     shroud,
His form like a king, and his beard like a cloud,
And his voice loud and shrill, as both trumpet
     and reed,—
'Pull, pull in your lassoes, and bridle to steed,
And speed you if ever for life you would speed.
Aye, ride for your lives, for your lives you must
     ride!
For the plain is aflame, the prairie on fire,
And the feet of wild horses hard flying before
I heard like a sea breaking high on the shore,
While the buffalo come like a surge of the sea,
Driven far by the flame, driving fast on us three
As a hurricane comes, crushing palms in his ire.'

"We drew in the lassoes, seized saddle and
     rein,
Threw them on, cinched them on, cinched them
     over again,
And again drew the girth; and spring we to
     horse,
With head to the Brazos, with a sound in the
     air

Like the surge of a sea, with a flash in the eye,
From that red wall of flame reaching up to the
   sky;
A red wall of flame and a black rolling sea
Rushing fast upon us, as the wind sweeping
   free
And afar from the desert blown hollow and hoarse.

"Not a word, not a wail from a lip was let fall,
We broke not a whisper, we breathed not a
   prayer,
There was work to be done, there was death in
   the air,
And the chance was as one to a thousand for all.

"Twenty miles! . . . thirty miles! . . . a
   dim distant speck . . .
Then a long reaching line, and the Brazos in
   sight!
And I rose in my seat with a shout of delight.
I stood in my stirrup, and look'd to my right—
But Revels was gone; I glanced by my shoulder
And saw his horse stagger; I saw his head
   drooping
Hard down on his breast, and his naked breast
   stooping
Low down to the mane, as so swifter and bolder
Ran reaching out for us the red-footed fire.
He rode neck to neck with a buffalo bull,
That made the earth shake where he came in his
   course,
The monarch of millions, with shaggy mane full
Of smoke and of dust, and it shook with desire
Of battle, with rage and with bellowings hoarse.
His keen, crooked horns, through the storm of
   his mane,
Like black lances lifted and lifted again;
And I looked but this once, for the fire licked
   through,
And Revels was gone, as we rode two and two.

"I look'd to my left then—and nose, neck, and
       shoulder
Sank slowly, sank surely, till back to my thighs,
And up through the black blowing veil of her
       hair
Did beam full in mine her two marvelous eyes,
With a longing and love yet a look of despair
And of pity for me, as she felt the smoke fold
       her,
And flames leaping far for her glorious hair.
Her sinking horse falter'd, plunged, fell and was
       gone
As I reach'd through the flame and I bore her
       still on.
On! into the Brazos, she, Pache and I—
Poor, burnt, blinded Pache. I love him . . .
       That's why."

                                        JOAQUIN MILLER

Death Rode a Pinto Pony

Death rode a pinto pony
       Along the Rio Grande,
Beside the trail his shadow
       Was riding on the sand.

The look upon his youthful face
       Was sinister and dark,
And the pistol in his scabbard
       Had never missed its mark.

The moonlight on the river
       Was bright as molten ore,
The ripples broke in whispers
       Along the sandy shore.

The breath of prairie flowers
    Had made the night-wind sweet,
And a mockingbird made merry
    In a lacy-leafed mesquite.

Death looked toward the river,
    He looked toward the land,
He took his broad sombrero off
    And held it in his hand,
And Death felt something touch him
    He could not understand.

The lights at Madden's ranch house
    Were brighter than the moon,
The girls came tripping in like deer,
    The fiddles were in tune,

And Death saw through the window
    The man he came to kill,
And he that did not hesitate
    Sat hesitating still.

A cloud came over the moon,
    The moon came out and smiled,
A coyote howled upon the hill,
    The mockingbird went wild.

Death drew his hand across his brow
    As if to move a stain,
Then slowly turned his pinto horse
    And rode away again.

WHITNEY MONTGOMERY

Custer

(June 25, 1876)

What! shall that sudden blade
    Leap out no more?
No more thy hand be laid
Upon the sword-hilt smiting sore?
    O for another such
    The charger's rein to clutch,—
One equal voice to summon victory,
    Sounding thy battle-cry,
Brave darling of the soldiers' choice!
    Would there were one more voice!

    O gallant charge, too bold!
    O fierce, imperious greed
To pierce the clouds that in their darkness
      hold
Slaughter of man and steed!
    Now, stark and cold,
Among thy fallen braves thou liest,
And even with thy blood defiest
    The wolfish foe:
    But ah, thou liest low,
And all our birthday song is hushed indeed!

    Young lion of the plain,
    Thou of the tawny mane!
Hotly the soldiers' hearts shall beat,
    Their mouths thy death repeat,
Their vengeance seek the trail again
    Where thy red doomsmen be;
But on the charge no more shall stream
Thy hair,—no more thy sabre gleam,—
    No more ring out thy battle-shout,
    Thy cry of victory!

Not when a hero falls
The sound a world appalls:

For while we plant his cross
There is a glory, even in the loss:
  But when some craven heart
  From honor dares to part,
Then, then, the groan, the blanching cheek,
  And men in whispers speak,
Nor kith nor country dare reclaim
  From the black depths his name.

  Thou, wild young warrior, rest,
By all the prairie winds caressed!
  Swift was thy dying pang;
  Even as the war-cry rang
Thy deathless spirit mounted high
  And sought Columbia's sky:—

There, to the northward far,
   Shines a new star,
And from it blazes down
The light of thy renown!

EDMUND CLARENCE STEDMAN

Billy the Kid

or

William H. Bonney

Bustin' down the canyon,
Horses on the run,
Posse just behind them,
'T was June first, seventy-one.

Saddle guns in scabbards,
Pistols on saddle bow,
The boys were ridin' for their lives—
The Kid en Alias Joe.

Thirty miles west of the Gila
They bade the posse good-bye,
For they couldn't keep up with the
    lightweight Kids,
No matter how hard they'd try.

From the land of the Montezuma,
Past the hills of the Mogollons,
By night en day they made their way
Till they landed in Tombstone.

Those were frontier towns, old pardner;
'T was a game of take en give,

And the one who could draw the fastest
Was the only one who'd live.

Whiskey en women en poker,
Monte en Faro en Stud,
Just a short wild race, who'd keep the pace
Would land in a river of blood.

Fightin' en drinkin' en gamblin',
Nigger en Mex en White;
'T was a riot of sin, let the best man win;
'T was drink, when called, or fight.

En every one claimed a woman,
Though none of their claims would stand
'Gainst the Kid, who was quicker'n lightning
With a gun in either hand.

Believing that John H. Tunstall
Was the man who was in the right,
He offered him his services
In the Lincoln County fight.

The Kid rode with Brewer's posse
Who avenged John Tunstall's loss,
Killing William Morton, en Baker
Roberts en Joe Ross.

Locked in the Dolan house in Lincoln,
Then used as a county jail,
Handcuffed en with a double guard,
Trailing a ball en chain,

He killed his guards, Bell en Olinger,
In the jail yard in daylight,
Stole the horse of the probate clerk
En on him made his flight.

Caught a-napping at last in Sumner,
In Pete Maxwell's room one night,

Not knowing he was waylaid,
Not knowing with whom to fight;

A chance shot fired by Garrett,
A chance shot that found its mark;
'T was lucky for Pat the Kid showed plain,
While Garrett was hid in the dark.

If Garrett was game, I don't know it;
He never appeared so to me;
If any of you fellows think so,
I'll refer you to Oliver Lee.

                              N. HOWARD THORP

Fandango

They beat the tom-tom, they plucked the guitar,
The mandolin twanged for Dolores Salazar—
For her flashing teeth, for her midnight hair,
For her tiny shoes and brown legs bare,
Whirling red petticoat and thin white blouse—
The beauty and the terror of the Vale of Taos.

Young Dick Wooton was a mountain man,
A strappin' trapper with a skin of tan;
He stooped as he swung through the six-foot door,
His moccasins shuffled on the hard dirt floor:
"Look out, pelados, fur I'm on my spree!
This here fandango belongs to me!"

Then he saw Dolores smiling slow,
And he stopped like a gut-shot buffalo.
From Belly River to the Rio Grande
Grizzlies and Indians he had shot offhand;
But her eyes cut deeper than he'd ever been hurt—

Deeper than the scars beneath his buckskin shirt—
So he drank (for she scared him worse than death)
Three gourds of whisky 'fore he caught his breath.

Then he grabbed Dolores like an angry bear,
He pranced and shuffled and he smelled her hair,
While the whisky ran and the trappers howled,
And her Mexican lovers sulked and scowled,
She smiled at his chin and she smiled in his chest,
What he said she savvied, or else she guessed,
Until Dick, a-floating on a wave of bliss,
Lifted her up and gave her a kiss.

Then Don Cornelio began the fray—
His knife blade glittered in a wicked way—
And Dick, all paralyzed with fright,
Was happy again, for he loved a fight.
He yelped a war whoop, let Dolores fall,
He bashed Cornelio against the wall:
"Come on, pelados! Jine the spree,
Fur this fandango belongs to me!"

'Twas six to a hundred or thereabout—
Fists were flying and knives were out—
Kit Carson caught up the drummer's chair,
Gripped each leg and broke it off square,
Yelled as he handed them round to each one,
"Give 'em Green River!" and began the fun.
The women screamed and choked up the door;
Pelados were lying all over the floor;
The music stopped and the lights blinked out;
Kit and his comrades raised a shout,
Felled the men who blocked their path,
And left a trail like the day of wrath.

Back in the house where their rifles stood
They laughed and swore and wiped off the blood,
Jeered at the Prefect and the mob outside,
Paid blood-money for the man who had died,
Tipped the priest for the masses said

For the soul of the stabber who now lay dead,
Posted a sentry at either door,
Spread out blankets and lay down to snore.

But little thought Dick Wooton gave
To the broken heads and the new-made grave.
Melancholy as a bull in spring,
What to him could sunup bring
But a lonely ride on the trails afar
And dreams of the lovely Salazar?
For well he knew that her folks would ban
A match with a gringo mountain man.

The chill gray dawn was over all—
Mountain and meadow and 'dobe wall—
When Kit and his comrades took their way
Out of the town of Taos next day.
The streets were lined with a sullen throng,
Jealous, and smarting with sense of wrong;
But nobody stirred to do them harm,
For each one rode with rifle on arm.

Dolores stood by her father's house,
Quieter since last night's carouse;
But under her gay rebozo's fold
Her heart was pounding, her eyes were bold,
Though brothers and lovers on either side,
Bitter and scowling, watched Dick ride.

Kit saw what ailed Dick Wooton's heart;
Kit slapped him on the back right smart:
"Ho, Dick! Are you wantin' to trap a squaw?
Bent's Fort's a-waitin' on Arkansaw—
Hyar's the gal, and yonder's the trail,
If you ain't scairt of the Prefect's jail."

Dick stooped from his saddle to say good-by,
Whispered her ear and looked in her eye;
She flashed him a smile like the break of morn,
Reached her hand to his saddle horn,

Placed her foot on his moccasin—
He caught her, and struck his spurs well in.

Her mother squealed, and her father swore,
Her lovers rushed past the open door—
But Kit rode there with his rifle, grim,
And nobody wanted to tackle him.

Dick and Dolores waved farewell
To her people crowding the streets pell-mell:
"Adios, pelados, fur I've had my spree,
And this here beauty belongs to me!"

                              STANLEY VESTAL

Oliver Wiggins

'Twas at the Cimarron Crossing
On the trail to Santy Fee,
Kit Carson met up with a caravan
That was a sight to see.

The teamsters were all greenhorns,
The wagon master a coward;
Their wagon wheels were warped and shrunk,
Their guns were all smooth-bored.

"No, ye don't!" says the wagon master,
"You'll go on to Santy Fee;
I've told Kit's men to leave us now—
Tonight you sleep with me!"

Kit Carson made his camp that night
A mile from the wagon park;
He sent Sol Silver to Oliver Wiggins
A little after dark.

"Would ye like to be one o' the Carson men
And travel along o' Kit?
He got his start on a mule like yourn
With a rope for bridle and bit.

"Wait till the greenhorns are all asleep
And you see Kit's campfire flare;
Then slip away from the wagon train—
Come dawn, we'll be far from hyar."

The wolves were howling loud and long,
The wagon master snored,
When Oliver Wiggins slipped away
To where Kit's campfire roared.

Said Kit, "My boy, I like your spunk;
I'll make a man of you;
I'll give you a rifle for that popgun,
And buckskins for your coat of blue.

"Shoot straight and tell the truth," Kit said,
"Shoot straight, fight hard to win;
The Carson men are all like that—
They die, but don't give in."

The only man in the outfit
That had a speck of gall
Was a boy named Oliver Wiggins—
Fifteen, and six foot tall.

He was a-herdin' the cavvy,
Ridin' a sore-backed mule,
Totin' a pistol long as your arm—
A runaway from school!

The Kiowas come charging
To lift the teamsters' hair,
Kit and his men from the wagons then
Met the reds and stopped them there.

"Mount and after 'em, boys!" yelled Kit
As the redskins turned around;
At every bullet the trappers fired
Some Injun bit the ground.

The Carson men rode swift as the wind,
The Kiowas fled from harm;
In the front of the charge rode Oliver, poppin'
A pistol—long as your arm!

The wagon master told the boy,
"You acted like a fool!
Them redskins might have took your hair,
And I'd ha' lost a mule!"

Oliver said, "I want my pay—
I'm through with the wagon train;
I'm going to Taos with the Carson men—
I'll not work for *you* again!"

For twelve long years young Oliver
Served Carson true as steel;
The Indians caught the wagon master
And burned him on a wagon wheel.

STANLEY VESTAL

Custer's Last Charge

(*June 25, 1876*)

Dead! Is it possible? He, the bold rider,
    Custer, our hero, the first in the fight,
Charming the bullets of yore to fly wider,
    Far from our battle-king's ringlets of light!
Dead, our young chieftain, and dead, all
        forsaken!

No one to tell us the way of his fall!
Slain in the desert, and never to waken,
  Never, not even to victory's call!

Proud for his fame that last day that he met
    them!
  All the night long he had been on their
    track,
Scorning their traps and the men that had set
    them,
  Wild for a charge that should never give
    back.
There on the hilltop he halted and saw them,—
  Lodges all loosened and ready to fly;
Hurrying scouts with the tidings to awe them,
  Told of his coming before he was nigh.

All the wide valley was full of their forces,
  Gathered to cover the lodges' retreat!—
Warriors running in haste to their horses,
  Thousands of enemies close to his feet!
Down in the valleys the ages had hollowed,
  There lay the Sitting Bull's camp for a prey!
Numbers! What recked he? What recked
    those who followed—
  Men who had fought ten to one ere that
    day?

Out swept the squadrons, the fated three
    hundred,
  Into the battle-line steady and full;
Then down the hillside exultingly thundered,
  Into the hordes of the old Sitting Bull!
Wild Ogalallah, Arapahoe, Cheyenne,
  Wild Horse's braves, and the rest of their
    crew,
Shrank from that charge like a herd from a
    lion,—
  Then closed around, the grim horde of wild
    Sioux!

Right to their centre he charged, and then
     facing—
  Hark to those yells! and around them, O
     see!
Over the hilltops the Indians come racing,
  Coming as fast as the waves of the sea!
Red was the circle of fire around them;
  No hope of victory, no ray of light,
Shot through that terrible black cloud
     without them,
  Brooding in death over Custer's last fight.

Then did he blench? Did he die like a craven,
  Begging those torturing fiends for his life?
Was there a soldier who carried the Seven
  Flinched like a coward or fled from the
     strife?
No, by the blood of our Custer, no quailing!
  There in the midst of the Indians they
     close,
Hemmed in by thousands, but ever assailing,
  Fighting like tigers, all 'bayed amid foes!

Thicker and thicker the bullets came singing;
  Down go the horses and riders and all;
Swiftly the warriors round them were ringing,
  Circling like buzzards awaiting their fall.
See the wild steeds of the mountain and
     prairie,
  Savage eyes gleaming from forests of mane;
Quivering lances with pennons so airy,
  War-painted warriors charging amain.

Backward, again and again, they were driven,
  Shrinking to close with the lost little band;
Never a cap that had worn the bright Seven
  Bowed till its wearer was dead on the
     strand.
Closer and closer the death circle growing,
  Ever the leader's voice, clarion clear,

Rang out his words of encouragement
        glowing,
    "We can but die once, boys,—we'll sell
        our lives dear!"

Dearly they sold them like Berserkers raging,
    Facing the death that encircled them round;
Death's bitter pangs by their vengeance
        assuaging,
    Marking their tracks by their dead on the
        ground.
Comrades, our children shall yet tell their
        story,—
    Custer's last charge on the old Sitting
        Bull;
And ages shall swear that the cup of his
        glory
    Needed but that death to render it full.

FREDERICK WHITTAKER

The Smugglers

By the sands of Rio Bravo,
        Races with the law they ran,
Through Chihuahua to Sonora,
        Down the trail to Mazatlán.

But the law rode fast and caught them,
        Booty, burro, horse, and man;
Pepe, Luis, Coyotito,
        Ended not as they began.

OWEN WISTER

Belle Starr

A cowboy hat, and underneath
Two weapons flashing from a sheath
Of knitted brows, brows that are clear
Of storm or wrath. Perhaps once a year
A woman, she, and with such eyes
Like watch dogs kenneled in her brain,
   Woe to the fool who gropes,
Likewise to him who views her with disdain.

A queen self-crowned by self-reliance,
The laws, she holds them in defiance,
Laughs long and loud at sheriff's writ,
And somehow that's the last of it.
But who is she? So indiscreet
Who over-rides you on the street
   Not caring whoever you are
   That's Belle Starr.

Brunette with raven hair is she,
And calls herself a Cherokee,
But who would dare dispute her claim
Or even question whence she came?
   The timid press reporter
Sneaks closer and closer to her gown;
   She turns abruptly, seldom speaks,
But always checks him with a frown
Which plainly means, "Down, Pompey, down!"

Arrest her! Oh, you try that game?
   In Dallas many years ago
The county sheriff tried the same.
   One rapid shot, the rest you know;
Still Belle loves to give her name:
   "Please let me have your best cigar,
   I'm Belle Starr."

We knew her when her fingers strayed on ivory keys,
　How well she played in Texas, nights long ago,
　But things have changed since then, you know,
　Once when we sought her out one day,
　She laughed full fifty miles away,
　At Dallas fashions and the fools
　Who followed after social rules.

To see her mounted, and with speed
　Ride far into the setting sun,
Meant simply this, a daring deed
　Scarce thought of ere the deed was done,
With lawless men the most at ease,
She bets and gambles, but you'll please
　Observe she never goes too far—
　That's Belle Starr.

Who says she never loved? He lies!
A woman's heart in such disguise
Must surely be the wreck that hides
When love drifts outwards with the tides.
Alas for those who lived to feel,
The months and years around them reel,
And crumble into space with still
The same old yearning to fulfill.

Be merciful—condemn her not—
By scornful words or evil thoughts,
For should you strike her mountain glen
Where only hide the roughest men,
And tap the door some stormy night,
A voice might bid you to alight—
　"Come in, I care not who you are,
　I'm Belle Starr."

UNKNOWN

Billy the Kid

Version 1

Billy was a bad man
And carried a big gun,
He was always after Greasers
And kept 'em on the run.

He shot one every morning,
For to make his morning meal.
And let a white man sass him,
He was shore to feel his steel.

He kept folks in hot water,
And he stole from many a stage;
And when he was full of liquor
He was always in a rage.

He kept things boilin' over,
He stayed out in the brush,
And when he was full of dead eye,
T'other folkses better hush.

But one day he met a man
Who was a whole lot badder.
And now he's dead,
And we ain't none the sadder.

UNKNOWN

Billy the Kid

Version 2

I'll sing you a true song of Billy the Kid,
I'll sing of the desperate deeds that he did,

Way out in New Mexico long, long ago,
When a man's only chance was his own 44.

When Billy the Kid was a very young lad,
In the old Silver City he went to the bad;
Way out in the West with a gun in his hand
At the age of twelve years he first killed his man.

Fair Mexican maidens play guitars and sing
A song about Billy, their boy bandit king,
How ere his young manhood had reached its sad end
He'd a notch on his pistol for twenty-one men.

'Twas on the same night when poor Billy died
He said to his friends: "I am not satisfied;
There are twenty-one men I have put bullets through,
And Sheriff Pat Garrett must make twenty-two."

Now this is how Billy the Kid met his fate:
The bright moon was shining, the hour was late,
Shot down by Pat Garrett, who once was his friend,
The young outlaw's life had now come to its end.

There's many a man with a face fine and fair
Who starts out in life with a chance to be square,
But just like poor Billy he wanders astray
And loses his life in the very same way.

UNKNOWN

Black Bart

Black Bart held up the Cow Creek stage in his manner so polite:
"Ladies and gentlemen," he said, "be pleased now to alight.

"Your money and your jewelry I'm aimin' to collect,
To aid a worthy purpose that I trust you will respect."

They lined up with their hands high and Bart he passed the hat.
They filled it and he grinned at 'em for he was standing pat.

The driver was a brave man, too gallant for his health,
And he had swore that with his life he'd guard the express wealth.

He tried to draw his peg leg but Black Bart saw the move,
He shot the driver through the head, his marksmanship to prove.

He spoke to all the passengers, "Now take it in good part.
It's really quite an honor to be held up by Black Bart."

UNKNOWN

Bonnie Black Bess

A Cowboy's Song

When fortune's blind goddess
Had fled my abode,
And friends proved unfaithful
I took to the road;
To plunder the wealthy
And relieve my distress,
I bought you to aid me,
My Bonnie Black Bess.

No vile whip nor spur
Did your sides ever gall,
For none did you need,
You would bound at my call;
And for each act of kindness
You would me caress.
Thou art never unfaithful,
My Bonnie Black Bess.

When dark, sable midnight
Her mantle had thrown
O'er the bright face of nature,
How oft we have gone
To the famed Hounslow heath,
Though an unwelcome guest
To the minions of fortune,
My Bonnie Black Bess!

How silent you stood
When the carriage I stopped!
The gold and the jewels
Its inmates would drop.
No poor man I plundered
Nor e'er did oppress
The widows or orphans,
My Bonnie Black Bess.

When Argus-eyed justice
Did me hot pursue,
From York town to London
Like lightning we flew.
No toll bars could stop you,
The waters did breast,
And in twelve hours we made it,
My Bonnie Black Bess.

But hate darkens o'er me,
Despair is my lot,
And the law does pursue me
For the many I've shot;
To save me, poor brute,
Thou hast done thy best,
Thou art worn out and weary,
My Bonnie Black Bess.

Hark! they never shall have
A beast like thee;
So noble and gentle
And brave, thou must die,
My dumb friend,
Though it does me distress.
There! There! I have shot thee,
My Bonnie Black Bess.

In after years
When I am dead and gone,
This story will be handed
From father to son;
My fate some will pity,
And some will confess
'Twas through kindness I killed thee,
My Bonnie Black Bess.

No one can e'er say
That ingratitude dwelt
In the bosom of Turpin—
'Twas a vice never felt.

I will die like a man
And soon be at rest;
Now, farewell forever,
My Bonnie Black Bess.

UNKNOWN

The Raven Visits Rawhide

It was meetin' night in Rawhide Town,
And the congregation was settlin' down
To hear the sermon of Parson Brown,
    When hell broke loose again.
Next door in Hank's Café Paree,
The boss was off on his weekly spree,
And settin' 'em up to the cowmen free
    From a barrel of nigger gin.

The parson strained his lungs to shout,
But Hank's rejoicin' drowned him out,
The devil was winnin' without a doubt
    And heaven's hopes looked slim.
The parson paused, then shouted, "Men,
The time's at last appointed when
We'll beard the devil in his den,
    And have it out with him."

Out of the church with his little flock,
The parson paraded down the block,
Lifted the latch without a knock,
    And entered the hall of sin.
The music ended, the laughter died,
Tongues went speechless and eyes grew wide,
As the parson calmly stepped inside,
    And the others followed in.

For an instant no one dared to speak,
Even the parson's knees were weak.
He'd forgot the vengeance he'd planned to wreak,
   And Hank looked on with a frown.
But Hank was not so easily downed,
He grabbed a glass and held his ground
And ordered the boys to drink a round
   To the parson of Rawhide Town.

"It's the bottoms up!" the barkeeper cried,
"We'll drink to hell where we'll all be fried,
Where we'll cast our souls that are crimson-dyed,
   In the tears our women shed."
The toast was drunk, then Hank stepped up,
Offered the parson a brimmin' cup,
And said, "Drink up, you prayin' pup,
   And trot on home to bed."

Hank laughed when suddenly out on the floor,
A stranger stepped with a forty-four—
And Hank was looking into the bore,
   And wond'ring what to do.
The stranger was lean and hard and small,
And he spoke words with a lazy drawl,
He said, "Now, boys, now listen all,
   And I'll have a word with you.

"I ain't the kind to be buttin' in,
And I'll prob'ly never be here again,
But, boys, I'm mad—I'm mad as sin,
   And I'm going to have my say.
Take my advice and don't get rough.
I'm called the Raven, and boys, I'm tough.
If you think I ain't, jes' call my bluff,
   Now, pray, you buzzards, pray."

Down in the dirt on the rum-soaked floor,
The cowmen knelt till their knees were sore.
And they prayed as they'd never prayed before,
   To save their souls from hell.

And when the parson said amen,
They followed him out of the devil's den,
And they swore they'd be different men,
   But they crossed their fingers well.

The Raven and Hank were left alone,
And the Raven spoke in a gentle tone.
He said, "I'm sorry you pulled that bone,
   For your technique sure is bad!
My sole intentions in comin' here
Was merely to buy a round of beer,
And lift your roll, but now I fear
   I've run things in a ditch.

"So open your poke and spill the dough,
And I'm beggin' your pardon as I go
That I had to spoil your little show,
   'Cause our ideas didn't hitch."

Hank looked twice at the forty-four
And decided he'd better act before
His guest became a trifle sore,
   So he shoved the roll across the floor.
The Raven bid him a soft good night,
Lifted his gun and blinked the light,
Slammed the door and was off in flight,
   Ridin' the parson's horse.

                      UNKNOWN

Roy Bean

Cowboys, come and hear a story of Roy Bean in all his
   glory,
"All the law West of the Pecos," was his line:

You must let our ponies take us, to a town on Lower
    Pecos
Where the High Bridge spans the canon thin and fine.

He was born one day near Toyah where he learned to
    be a lawyer
And a teacher and a barber for his fare,
He was cook and old shoe mender, sometimes preacher
    and bar-tender:
It cost two bits to have him cut your hair.

He was certain sure a hustler and considerable a
    rustler
And at mixing up an egg nog he was grand.
He was lively, he was merry, he could drink a Tom and
    Jerry,
On occasion at a round-up took a hand.

You may find the story funny, but once he had no
    money
Which for him was not so very strange and rare,
And he went to help Pap Wyndid but he got so
    absent-minded
Then he put his RB brand on old Pap's steer.

Now Pap was right smart angry so Roy Bean went
    down to Langtry
Where he opened up an office and a store.
There he'd sell you drinks or buttons or another
    rancher's muttons,
Though the latter made the other feller sore.

Once there came from Austin city a young dude
    reputed witty,
Out of Bean he thought he'd quickly take a rise:
And he got frisky as he up and called for whiskey
And he said to Bean, "Now hurry, damn your eyes."

On the counter threw ten dollars and it very quickly
    follers

That the bar-keep took full nine and gave back one,
Then the stranger give a holler as he viewed his single
    dollar,
And at that commenced the merriment and fun.

For the dude he slammed the table just as hard as he
    was able,
That the price of whiskey was too high he swore.
Said Roy Bean, "Cause of your fussin' and your most
    outrageous cussin'
You are fined the other dollar by the law.

"On this place I own a lease, sir, I'm the justice of the
    peace, sir,
And the Law west of the Pecos all is here,
For you've acted very badly," then the stranger went
    off sadly
While down his cheek there rolled a bitter tear.

Then one day they found a dead man who had been in
    life a Red man
So it's doubtless he was nothing else than bad.
Called on Bean to view the body, so he took a drink of
    toddy,
Then he listed all the things the dead man had.

Now the find it was quite rare, oh, for he'd been a
    "cocinero"
And his pay day hadn't been so far away,
He'd a bran' new fine white Stetson and a dandy Smith
    and Wesson
And a bag of forty dollars jingled gay.

Said Roy Bean, "You'll learn a lesson for I see a Smith
    and Wesson
And to carry implements of war is wrong,
So I fine you forty dollar," and the man gave ne'er a
    holler
Which concludes this very interesting song.

UNKNOWN

Whiskey Bill,—A Fragment

A-down the road and gun in hand
Comes Whiskey Bill, mad Whiskey Bill;
A-lookin' for some place to land
Comes Whiskey Bill.
An' everybody'd like to be
Ten miles away behind a tree
When on his joyous, aching spree
Starts Whiskey Bill.

The times have changed since you made love,
O Whiskey Bill, O Whiskey Bill!
The happy sun grinned up above
At Whiskey Bill.
And down the middle of the street
The sheriff comes on toe and feet
A-wishin' for one fretful peek
At Whiskey Bill.

The cows go grazing o'er the lea,—
Poor Whiskey Bill! Poor Whiskey Bill!
An' aching thoughts pour in on me
Of Whiskey Bill.
The sheriff up and found his stride;
Bill's soul went shootin' down the slide,—
How are things on the Great Divide,
O Whiskey Bill?

UNKNOWN

The Wrangler Kid

The grass fire swooped like a red wolf pack,
On the wings of a west wind dry.

Its red race left the scorched plains black
   'Neath a sullen, smoky sky.

And the wagon boss of the Bar-Y-Cross
   He rallied his roisterous crew.
"Boys, shoot some steers, and hang the loss,
   An' split them smack in two!"

They split six steers, with the blood side down,
   They dragged them to and fro.
But the grass fire laughed like a demon clown
   At a devil's three-ringed show.

The flame draft drove like a wind from hell,
   Across the drags they drew.
"It's no use boys!" came the foreman's yell.
   "She's roarin' right on through."

They scattered, then, from the headfire's path,
   To close in from the sides,
And some stayed on to fight its wrath,
   Some fled to save their hides.

Now one who stayed was the Wrangler Kid,
   His whisker fuzz scorched black,
And he battled hard, as the others did,
   But the fire still pushed them back.

It pushed them back as the wind veered round,
   Till trapped, they faced its sweep,
At the edge of a gully that split the ground,
   Too wide for a horse to leap.

'Twas down from the saddle dropped boss and men,
   And into the gully they fled.
Safe now the men, but their horses then
   Were left to the grass fire's hell.

What! lives there a man who loves life less
   Than the dumb-brute horse he rides?

The Wrangler Kid stayed shelterless
   On the bank at the horses' side.

And he cut them free from the drags they drew,
   Through the flames he spurred alone.
To-day the Kid bears scars, 'tis true,
   Brands of the Red God's own.

UNKNOWN

VII

Desert Songs

Desert Bloom

A glow of purples at set of sun;
   A creep of shadows when day is done;
A spot of blue sky showing still
   Away beyond the sheltering hill;
Rocky ridges toward the west
   Like sentinels standing on a crest.
The lure of the desert written there
   For all who feel its beauty rare.

Does life seem barren and hard to you?
   Go look on the desert's promise true.
Think you there are places that "God forgot"?
   Behold such scenes and believe it not.
God watches o'er every hill and plain,
   And in due time He gives His rain.
"There is no desert, no death, no gloom."
   That is the message of "Desert Bloom."

GERTRUDE THOMAS ARNOLD

In Old Tucson

Within a 'dobe wall,
In yonder desert, sere and bare,
While purple shadows of the night
Were falling everywhere,
And on the air, so soft and warm,
Faintly came the night-bird's call,
I left her standing there,
Amid the flowers, within a 'dobe wall
In Old Tucson.

Her eyes were dark as pools
In shaded desert wells;
Her words were like the tones
Of far-off mission bells;
The jet-black hue of night
Was on her glorious hair,
And still within that garden
I seem to see her—there
In Old Tucson.

And often in my dreams
She stands within a patio
In Old Tucson, where 'dobe walls
Were builded low;
And in a garden rare the hollyhocks
Grow straight and tall,
Within a 'dobe wall,
Where purple shadows slanting fall—
In Old Tucson.

CHARLES BEGHTOL

Back to Arizona

Take me back to Arizona as it was in early days,
Ere the cowboy on the ranges had the moving-picture
    craze.
Let me see the festive puncher, with his bronco on the
    run,
Coming into town and shooting up the landscape with his
    gun.
Let me see the chuckawalla and the Gila monster, too,
Of the murderous Apache let me get a fleeting view;
Let me see a frontier squabble as it was in days of yore,
When the "bad man" of the border waded in a sea of
    gore.

Take me back to Arizona and the plains of alkali,
On the cactus-covered mesa in the desert let me lie.
Let me hear the rattler rattling as he crawls about the
    sand,
And the restive cattle bawling as they feel the red-hot
    brand.
Let me see the city marshal make a gun-play in the street,
And a victim later buried with his boots upon his feet!
Take me back to Arizona—let me see a poker game
As in days when it was prudent not to ask a stranger's
    name.

Take me back to Arizona, where they "sized" a fellow,
    not
By the boodle which he carried, but the skill with which
    he shot!
Where the towns were short on water, but all-fired long
    on gin,
And there never was much mourning when a fellow-man
    "cashed in."
Take me back among the ki-yotes and the centipedes and
    such,
Where a brand-iron was respected and a "rustler" hated
    much!
Take me back to Arizona when it lived a wild career,
And they had a man for breakfast every morning in the
    year!

Take me back to Arizona—Arizona rough and wild,
Where the days were dry and dusty and the whisky
    wasn't mild!
Let me live again those stirring frontier days when all
    was new,
When the faro banks were frequent—but the churches
    mighty few!
Let me join a sheriff's posse and get on a horse-thief's
    track,
Where a hanging-bee was likely if they brought the fellow
    back!

Take me back to Arizona in the palmy days I saw,
When high boot-heels were in fashion, and a six-gun was
    the law!

E. A. BRINISTOOL

The History of Arizona: How It Was Made and Who Made It

The devil was given permission one day
To select him a land for his special sway,
So he hunted around for a month or more
And fussed and fumed and terribly swore;
But at last was delighted a country to view,
Where the prickly pear and the mesquite grew.
With a survey brief, without further excuse,
He took his stand near the Santa Cruz.

He saw there was some improvement to make,
For he felt his own reputation at stake.
An idea struck him, and he swore by his horns
To make a complete vegetation of thorns.
He studded the land with the prickly pear,
And scattered the cactus everywhere;
The Spanish dagger, sharp-pointed and tall,
And last the cholla—the worst of all.

He imported the Apaches direct from hell,
And, the ranks of the sweet-scented train to swell,
A legion of skunks, whose loud, loud smell
Perfumed the country he loved so well.
And then for his life he could not see why
The river should any more water supply;
And he swore if he gave it another drop
You might take his head and horns for a mop.

He filled the river with sand till 'twas almost dry,
And poisoned the land with alkali;
And promised himself on its slimy brink
The control of all who from it should drink.
He saw there was one more improvement to make—
He imported the tarantula and rattlesnake,
That all who might come to this country to dwell
Would be sure to think it was almost hell.

He fixed the heat at one hundred and seven,
And banished forever the dew from heaven;
But remarked as he heard his furnace roar,
That the heat might reach five hundred or more.
And after he had fixed things so thorny and well,
He said, "I'll be d—d if this don't beat hell!"
Then he flopped his wings and away he flew,
And vanished from earth in a blaze of blue.

And now, no doubt, in some corner of hell
He gloats o'er the work he has done so well,
And vows that Arizona cannot be beat
For scorpions, tarantulas, snakes and heat;
For with his own realm it compares so well
He feels assured it surpasses hell.

CHARLES O. BROWN

The Old Santa Fe Trail

It wound through strange scarred hills, down
    cañons lone
Where wild things screamed, with winds for
    company;
Its mile-stones were the bones of pioneers.
Bronzed, haggard men, often with thirst
    a-moan,

Lashed on their beasts of burden toward the
    sea:
An epic quest it was of elder years,
For fabled gardens or for good, red gold,
The trail men strove in iron days of old.

To-day the steam-god thunders through the
    vast,
While dominant Saxons from the hurtling trains
Smile at the aliens, Mexic, Indian,
Who offer wares, keen-colored, like their past;
Dread dramas of immitigable plains
Rebuke the softness of the modern man;
No menace, now, the desert's mood of sand;
Still westward lies a green and golden land.

For, at the magic touch of water, blooms
The wilderness, and where of yore the yoke
Tortured the toilers into dateless tombs,
Lo! brightsome fruits to feed a mighty folk.

RICHARD BURTON

Drifting

Out beyond the grasses growing,
Out beyond each marching hill,
Out where desert winds are blowing . . .
    Let me wander at my will.

There where yucca bells are ringing,
There where chollas guard the dead,
There where desert things are singing . . .
    All around my sandy bed.

Drifting down the ranges, dreaming;
Drifting and not caring why . . .

Drifting to the desert gleaming
Underneath a jewelled sky.

D. MAITLAND BUSHBY

An Adobe House

In a house born of the brown earth
And dying back to earth again,
Without any desire to be more than earth
And without any particular pain,
Beside an acequia bringing water
To the corn not yet tall,
Three men were sitting with poems on their knees
And they heard the wind rise and fall.
And one of them heard his own voice rising,
And one of them heard his own voice falling,
And the other heard only the summons of the
    wind
And wondered where it was calling.

WITTER BYNNER

New Mexican Desert

A vivid hardened ocean,
A rough arrested sea,
On its imagined motion
Had so conjured me
That I was the only one not dead. . . .
Till, slowly up a wave ahead,
With a moon of a hat to know him by
And a wizard's blanket marked with red,

And his toes outswung from a burro,
Arose a man more thorough
In the uses of magic than I;
And he sang a song, and he sang it still
When, shaking like heat to the top of the hill,
He vanished through the open light
Out of the desert, out of sight,
Into the solid sky.

WITTER BYNNER

Spanish Johnny

The old West, the old time,
   The old wind singing through
The red, red grass a thousand miles,
   And, Spanish Johnny, you!
He'd sit beside the water-ditch
   When all his herd was in,
And never mind a child, but sing
   To his mandolin.

The big stars, the blue night,
   The moon-enchanted plain:
The olive man who never spoke,
   But sang the songs of Spain.
His speech with men was wicked talk—
   To hear it was a sin;
But those were golden things he said
   To his mandolin.

The gold songs, the gold stars,
   The world so golden then:
And the hand so tender to a child
   Had killed so many men.

He died a hard death long ago
   Before the Road came in;
The night before he swung, he sang
   To his mandolin.

            WILLA CATHER

The Santa Fe Trail

It winds o'er prairie and o'er crest,
   And tracks of steel now glance
Where once it lured men to the West,
   The highway of Romance.

Its furrows now are overgrown
   With snowdrift or with flower;
Lost are the graves so thickly sown
   By Death in that dim hour.

But when the night has drawn its veil
   The teams plod, span on span,
And one sees o'er the long dead trail
   A ghostly caravan.

           ARTHUR CHAPMAN

The Old Casa

The moon and I a-tiptoe peer within;
  Slim shadows cross, recross the earthen floor;
  What if *la señorita* as of yore
Dances tonight to muted violin?

Red rose, I climb with you to *balcón* high!
  My gran'-dam wore red roses in her braids
  And leaned, just here, to twilight serenades—
Was that the ghost of some fond lover's sigh?

White is the moonlight on *adobe* wall
  That soon is dust—gone with the company
  That danced and loved and passed but yesterday.
And I am here to see the last rose fall!

TORREY CONNOR

Dead on the Desert

"Have mercy, God!" and on the dune sun-curs'd
He fell, his gourd crushed in his shrunken hand;
Yet in the anguish of consuming thirst
His purple lips touched but the burning sand.
The spiteful sun, mocking his feeble cry,
Drank his red sap as from its solstice-throne
It slow dropped down behind the western sky,
Leaving him there on the wide waste—alone!
Alone? Nay, for the slimy lizard crept
Across his blistered flesh; and soon the long
Thin serpent came, and, coiling where he slept,
Hissed in his ear and sang its deadly song;
While harsh the wind made sport against his cheek
And starved coyotes answered shriek on shriek.

HARRISON CONRARD

In Old Tucson

In old Tucson, in old Tucson,
What cared I how the days ran on?
A brown hand trailing the viol-string,
Hair as black as the raven's wing,
Lips that laughed and a voice that clung
To the sweet old airs of the Spanish tongue
Had drenched my soul with a mellow rime
Till all life shone, in that golden clime,
With the tender glow of the morning-time.
In old Tucson, in old Tucson,
How swift the merry days ran on!

In old Tucson, in old Tucson,
How soon the parting day came on!
But I oft turn back in my hallowed dreams,
And the low adobe a palace seems,
Where her sad heart sighs and her sweet voice sings
To the notes that throb from her viol-strings.
Oh, those tear-dimmed eyes and that soft brown
    hand!
And a soul that glows like the desert sand—
The golden fruit of a golden land!
In old Tucson, in old Tucson,
The long, lone days, O Time, speed on!

                                HARRISON CONRARD

Juan Quintana

The goat-herd follows his flock
    Over the sandy plain,
And the goats nibble the rabbit-bush
    Acrid with desert rain.

Old Juan Quintana's coat
  Is a faded purple blue,
And his hat is a warm plum-brown,
  And his trousers a tawny hue.

He is sunburnt like the hills,
  And his eyes have a strange goat-look;
And when I came on him alone,
  He suddenly quivered and shook.

Out in the hills all day
  The trees do funny things—
And a horse shaped like a man
  Rose up from the ground on wings.

And a burro came and stood
  With a cross, and preached to the flock,
While old Quintana sat
  As cold as ice on a rock.

And sometimes the mountains move,
  And the mesa turns about;
And Juan Quintana thinks he's lost,
  Till a neighbor hears him shout.

And they say with a little laugh
  That he isn't quite right, up here;
And they'll have to get a *muchacho*
  To help with the flock next year.

                              ALICE CORBIN

The Painted Hills of Arizona

The rainbows all lie crumpled on these hills,
The red dawns scattered on their colored sills.
These hills have caught the lightning in its flight,

Caught colors from the skies of day and night
And shine with shattered stars and suns; they hold
Dyed yellow, red and purple, blue and gold.

Red roses seem within their marble blown,
A painted garden chiseled in the stone;
The rose and violet trickling through their veins,
Where they drop brilliant curtains to the plains—
A ramp of rock and granite, jeweled and brightening,
Like some great colored wall of lightning!

EDWIN CURRAN

Desert Song

There's no hiding here in the glare of the desert.
   If your coat is sham the sun shines through;
Here with the lonely things and the silence
   There is no crowd for saving you.

Here love lasts a little longer
   And hate leaves here a heavy scar—
But we, with the desert's beauty of distance,
   Are always dreaming of places far.

If you have come to start a kingdom—
   Our eyes have looked on Rome and Tyre!
But if you come with dreams for baggage
   Sit with us by the cedar fire!

GLENN WARD DRESBACH

Mexican Quarter

By an alley lined with tumble-down shacks,
And street-lamps askew, half-sputtering,
Feebly glimmering on gutters choked with filth, and dogs
Scratching their mangy backs:
Half-naked children are running about,
Women puff cigarettes in black doorways,
Crickets are crying.
Men slouch sullenly
Into the shadows.
Behind a hedge of cactus,
The smell of a dead horse
Mingles with the smell of tamales frying.

And a girl in a black lace shawl
Sits in a rickety chair by the square of unglazed window,
And sees the explosion of the stars
Fiercely poised on the velvet sky.
And she seems humming to herself:
"Stars, if I could reach you
(You are so very near that it seems as if I could reach you),
I would give you all to the Madonna's image
On the gray plastered altar behind the paper flowers,
So that Juan would come back to me,
And we could live again those lazy burning hours,
Forgetting the tap of my fan and my sharp words,
And I would only keep four of you—
Those two blue-white ones overhead,
To put in my ears,
And those two orange ones yonder
To fasten on my shoe-buckles."

A little further along the street
A man squats stringing a brown guitar.
The smoke of his cigarette curls round his hair,
And he too is humming, but other words:
"Think not that at your window I wait.

New love is better, the old is turned to hate.
Fate! Fate! All things pass away;
Life is forever, youth is but for a day.
Love again if you may
Before the golden moons are blown out of the sky
And the crickets die.
Babylon and Samarkand
Are mud walls in a waste of sand."

                            JOHN GOULD FLETCHER

Rain in the Desert

The huge red-buttressed mesa over yonder
Is merely a far-off temple where the sleepy sun is burning
Its altar fires of pinyon and toyon for the day.

The old priests sleep, white-shrouded;
Their pottery whistles lie beside them, the prayer-sticks closely
    feathered.
On every mummied face there glows a smile.

The sun is rolling slowly
Beneath the sluggish folds of the sky-serpents,
Coiling, uncoiling, blue black, sparked with fires.

The old dead priests
Feel in the thin dried earth that is heaped about them,
Above the smell of scorching, oozing pinyon,
The acrid smell of rain.

And now the showers
Surround the mesa like a troop of silver dancers:
Shaking their rattles, stamping, chanting, roaring,
Whirling, extinguishing the last red wisp of light.

JOHN GOULD FLETCHER

Desert Song

When I came on from Santa Fe,
The desert road by night and day,
The desert wilds ran far and free
Beneath the wind of desert sea.

But—ah! my heart!—to know again
The scent of rain, the scent of rain!

And I'd in fancy scale the air
Beyond those yellow mountains bare,
And so with dizzy bird survey
A thousand miles of shining day.

But—oh! my heart!—to feel again
The wet of rain, the wet of rain!

And wakeful all the night I'd lie
And watch the dark infinity,
And count the stars that wheel and spin,
And drink the frosty ether in;
And I would hear the desert song
That silence sings the whole night long,
And day by day the whisper pass
Of parching heat through desert grass.

But—oh! my heart!—to hear again
The drip of rain, the drip of rain!

When I rode on from Santa Fe,
That desert road by night and day,
There came at last a little sigh,
A puff of white across the sky.

And—ah! my heart!—I knew again
The scent of rain, the scent of rain!

JOHN GALSWORTHY

Quivira

Francisco Coronado rode forth with all his
  train,
Eight hundred savage bowmen, three hundred
  spears of Spain,

To seek the desert's glory whereof the tale is told—
The City of Quivira, whose walls are rich with gold.

Oh, gay they rode with plume on crest and gilded
    spur at heel,
With gonfalon of Aragon and banner of Castile;
While High Emprise and Joyous Youth, twin
    marshals of the throng,
Awoke Sonora's mountain peaks with trumpet
    note and song.

Beside that brilliant army, beloved by serf and
    lord,
There walked a gallant soldier, no braver smote
    with sword,
Though naught of knightly harness his russet
    gown revealed;
The cross he bore as weapon, the missal was his
    shield.

But rugged oaths were changed to prayers and
    angry hearts grew tame,
And fainting spirits waxed in faith where Fray
    Padilla came;
And brawny spearmen bowed their heads to kiss
    the helpful hand
Of him who spake the simple truth that brave men
    understand.

What pen may paint their daring, those doughty
    cavaliers!
The cities of the Zuñi were humbled by their
    spears;
And Arizona's barrens grew pallid in the glow
Of blades that won Granada and conquered
    Mexico.

They fared by lofty Acoma; their rally call was blown
Where Colorado rushes down through God-hewn
    walls of stone.

Then, north and east, where deserts spread and
    treeless prairies rolled,
That fairy city lured them on with pinnacles of gold.

  On all their weary marches to gain the flitting goal
  They turned to Fray Padilla for aid of heart
    and soul.
  He salved the wounds that lance thrust and flinty
    arrow made,
  He cheered the sick and failing, above the dead
    he prayed.

Two thousand miles of war and woe behind their
    banners lay,
And sadly fever, drought, and toil had lessened their
    array,
When came a message fraught with hope for all the
    steadfast band:
"Good tidings from the northward, friends!
    Quivira lies at hand!"

  How joyously they spurred them! how sadly
    drew the rein.
  There gleamed no golden palace, there blazed
    no jeweled fane;
  Rude tents of hide of bison, dog-guarded, met
    their view—
  A squalid Indian village, the lodges of the Sioux!

Then Don Francisco bowed his head. He spake
    unto his men:
"Our search is vain, true hearts of Spain, now turn
    we home again.
And would to God that I could give that phantom
    city's pride
In ransom for the gallant souls that here have
    drooped and died!"

  Back, back to Compostela the wayworn
    handful bore;

But sturdy Fray Padilla took up the quest once
    more.
His soul still longed for conquest, though not by
    lance or sword;
He burned to show the heathen the pathway to
    the Lord.

For this he trudged the flinty hills and parching
    desert sands,
While few were they that walked with him and
    weaponless their hands—
But cheerily the man-at-arms, Docampo, rode
    him near,
Like Great Heart warding Christian's way through
    wastes of Doubt and Fear.

Where still in silken harvests the prairie-lilies
    toss,
Among the red Quiviras, Padilla reared his cross.
Beneath its sacred shadow the tribesmen of the
    Kaw
In wonder heard the gospel of love and peace
    and law.

They gloried in their brown-robed priests; and
    often, dark in thought,
The warriors grouped, a silent ring, to hear the
    word he brought,
While round the kindly man-at-arms their
    lithe-limbed children played
And shot their arrows at his shield and rode his
    guarded blade.

When thrice the silver crescent had filled its
    curving shell
The friar rose at dawning and bade his flock
    farewell:
"—And if your brothers northward be cruel,
    even so,

My Master bids me teach them; and dare I
    answer, 'No'?"

But where he trod in quenchless zeal the path of
    thorns once more,
A savage cohort swept the plain in paint and plume
    of war.
Then Fray Padilla spake to them whose hearts were
    most his own:
"My children, bear the tidings home; let me die
    here alone."

He knelt upon the prairie, begirt by yelling
    Sioux.—
"Forgive them, O my Father, they know not
    what they do!"
The twanging bowstrings answered. Before his
    eyes, unrolled
The City of Quivira whose streets are paved
    with gold.

ARTHUR GUITERMAN

In Old Tucson

In old Tucson, in old Tucson,
How swift the happy days ran on!
How warm the yellow sunshine beat
Along the white caliche street!
The flat roofs caught a brighter sheen
From fringing house leeks thick and green,
And chiles drying in the sun;
Splashes of crimson 'gainst the dun
Of clay-spread roof and earthen floor;
The squash vine climbing past the door
Held in its yellow blossoms deep
The drowsy desert bees asleep.

By one low wall, at one shut gate,
The dusty roadway turned to wait;
The pack mules loitered, passing where
The muleteers had sudden care
Of cinch and pack and harness bell.
The oleander blossoms fell,
Wind-drifted flecks of flame and snow;
The fruited pomegranate swung low,
And in the patio dim and cool
The gray doves flitted round the pool
That caught her image lightly as
The face that fades across a glass.

In old Tucson, in old Tucson,
The pool is dry, the face is gone.
No dark eyes through the lattice shine,
No slim brown hand steals through to mine;
There where her oleander stood
The twilight shadows bend and brood,
And through the glossed pomegranate leaves
The wind remembering waits and grieves;
Waits with me, knowing as I know,
She may not choose as come or go—
She who with life no more has part
Save in the dim pool of my heart.

And yet I wait—and yet I see
The dream that was come back to me;
The green leek springs above the roof,
The dove that mourned alone, aloof,
Flutes softly to her mate among
The fig leaves where the fruit has hung
Slow-purpling through the sunny days;
And down the golden desert haze
The mule bells tinkle faint and far;—
But where her candle shone, a star;
And where I watched her shadow fall—
The gray street and a crumbling wall.

SHARLOT M. HALL

Two Bits

Where the shimmering sands of the desert beat
  In waves to the foot-hills' rugged line,
And cat-claw and cactus and brown mesquite
  Elbow the cedar and mountain pine;
Under the dip of a wind-swept hill,
  Like a little gray hawk Fort Whipple clung;
The fort was a pen of peeled pine logs
  And forty troopers the army strong.

At the very gates when the darkness fell,
  Prowling Mohave and Yavapai
Signalled with shrill coyote yell,
  Or mocked the night owl's piercing cry;
Till once when the guard turned shuddering
  For a trace in the east of the welcome dawn,
Spent, wounded, a courier reeled to his feet:—
  "Apaches—rising—Wingate—warn!"

"And half the troop at the Date Creek Camp!"
  The captain muttered: "Those devils heard!"
White-lipped he called for a volunteer
  To ride Two Bits and carry the word.
"Alone, it's a game of hide and seek;
  One man may win where ten would fail."
Himself the saddle and cinches set
  And headed Two Bits for the Verde Trail.

Two Bits! How his still eyes woke to the chase!
  The bravest soul of them all was he!
Hero of many a hard-won race,
  With a hundred scars for his pedigree.
Wary of ambush and keen of trail,
  Old in wisdom of march and fray;
And the grizzled veteran seemed to know
  The lives that hung on his hoofs that day.

"A week. God speed you and make it less!
  Ride by night from the river on."

Caps were swung in a silent cheer,
  A quick salute, and the word was gone.
Sunrise, threading the Point of Rocks;
  Dusk, in the cañons dark and grim,
Where coiled like a rope flung down the cliffs
  The trail crawls up to the frowning Rim.

A pebble turned, a spark out-struck
  From steel-shod hoofs on the treacherous
    flint—
Ears strain, eyes wait, in the rocks above
  For the faintest whisper, the farthest glint;
But shod with silence and robed with night
  They pass untracked, and mile by mile
The hills divide for the flying feet,
  And the stars lean low to guide the while.

Never a plumed quail hid her nest
  With the stealthiest care that a mother may,
As crouched at dawn in the chaparral
  These two, whom a heart-beat might betray.
So, hiding and riding, night by night;
  Four days, and the end of the journey near;
The fort just hid in the distant hills—
  But hist! A whisper—a breath of fear!

They wheel and turn—too late. Ping! Ping!
  From their very feet a fiery jet.
A lurch, a plunge, and the brave old horse
  Leaped out with his broad breast torn and yet.
Ping! Thud! On his neck the rider swayed;—
  Ten thousand deaths if he reeled and fell!
Behind, exultant, the painted horde
  Poured down like a skirmish line from Hell.

Not Yet! Not Yet! Those ringing hoofs
  Have scarred their triumph on many a course;
And the desperate, blood-trailed chase swept on—
  Apache sinews 'gainst wounded horse.

Hour crowding hour till the yells died back,
   Till the pat of the moccasined feet was gone;
And dumb to heeding of foe or fear
   The rider dropped—but the horse kept on.

Stiff and stumbling and spent and sore,
   Plodding the long miles doggedly;
Till the daybreak bugles of Wingate rang
   And a faint neigh answered the reveille.
Wide swung the gates—a wounded horse—
   Red-dabbled pouches and riding gear;
A shout, a hurry, a quick-flung word—
   And "Boots and Saddles" rang sharp and
     clear.

Like a stern commander the old horse turned
   As the troop filed out, and straight to the head
He guided them back on that weary trail
   Till he fell by his fallen rider—dead—
But the man and the message saved—and he
   Whose brave heart carried the double load;
With his last trust kept and his last race won,
   They buried him there on the Wingate Road.

SHARLOT M. HALL

The Desert

'Twas the lean coyote told me, baring his
     slavish soul,
  As I counted the ribs of my dead cayuse and
     cursed at the desert sky,
The tale of the Upland Rider's fate while I dug in
     the water hole
  For a drop, a taste of the bitter seep; but the
     water hole was dry!

"He came," said the lean coyote, "and he cursed
    as his pony fell;
  And he counted his pony's ribs aloud; yea, even
    as you have done.
He raved as he ripped at the clay-red sand like an
    imp from the pit of hell,
  Shriveled with thirst for a thousand years and
    craving a drop—just one."

"His name?" I asked, and he told me, yawning to
    hide a grin:
  "His name is writ on the prison roll and many
    a place beside;
Last, he scribbled it on the sand with a finger seared
    and thin,
  And I watched his face as he spelled it out—
    laughed as I laughed, and died.

"And thus," said the lean coyote, "his need is the
    hungry's feast,
  And mine." I fumbled and pulled my gun—
    emptied it wild and fast,
But one of the crazy shots went home and silenced
    the waiting beast;
  There lay the shape of the Liar, dead! 'Twas I
    that should laugh the last.

Laugh? Nay, now I would write my name as the
    Upland Rider wrote;
  Write? What need, for before my eyes in a
    wide and wavering line
I saw the trace of a written word and letter by letter
    float
  Into a mist as the world grew dark; and I knew
    that the name was mine.

Dreams and visions within the dream; turmoil and
    fire and pain;
  Hands that proffered a brimming cup—empty,
    ere I could take;

Then the burst of a thunder-head—rain! It was
  rude, fierce rain!
  Blindly down to the hole I crept, shivering,
  drenched, awake!

Dawn—and the edge of the red-rimmed sun
  scattering golden flame,
  As stumbling down to the water hole came the
  horse that I thought was dead;
But never a sign of the other beast nor a trace of a
  rider's name;
  Just a rain-washed track and an empty gun—
  and the old home trail ahead.

HENRY HERBERT KNIBBS

The Oro Stage

Around the bend we streaked it with the leaders
  swingin' wide;
  Round the bend and down the mountain from the
  old El Oro mines:

Jim Waring he was ridin', gun—a sawed-off at his side,
   And the sun was settin' level through the pines.
      We was late—and come a-reelin',
      With the gritty brakes a-squealin',
   And the slack a-dancin' lively down the lines.

Jim Waring he said nothin', for he weren't the talkin'
      kind;
   He left that to his lawyer—and his lawyer was a gun;
But I seen as plain as daylight he had somethin' on
      his mind,
   'Cause he kept a-glancin' sideways at the sun:
      And we hit the grade a-glidin',
      With the smokin' tires a-slidin',
   Then I give the broncs a chanct, and let 'em run.

And them broncs was doin' noble—layin' clost and
      reachin' far,
   With the Concord chains a-snappin' and the brakes
      a-swingin' free,
And the Notch below a-loomin' plumb ag'inst the
      evenin' star,
   And nothin' in the road that I could see:
      Stage a-rollin'—hosses reekin',
      With the heavin' springs a-squeakin'—
When Jim Waring touched me gentle with his knee.

Oh, I knowed just what was comin'. We was packin'
      Oro dust—
   And that hombre there beside me didn't know what
      quittin' meant:
We was bustin' on a holdup. It was Salvador, or bust:
   With our chanct of winnin' worth about a cent:
      Now I weren't no outlaw stopper,
      But I sure could shoot the popper,
So I shot it to the broncs—and in we went.

I seen a bridle shinin' and a shadder in the brush,
   Then a streak of red come flittin' and a-spittin'
      through the black:

I seen a empty saddle in the ruckus and the rush,
  And the leaders pawin' air, and traces slack.
    Hell it sure was loose and hoppin'
    With Jim Waring's gun a-poppin',
  And a-spreadin' his ideas in his track.

If the game was worth the glory, then we ought to had
    a crown,
  For we sure was nominated, biddin' high for all we
    got:
I was watchin' of the hosses when I seen Jim's gun
    come down,
  And I smelt the powder-smoke a-blowin' hot,
    As we took the grade a-flyin'
    With the pinto wheeler dyin'
  And Jim doin' business every time he shot.

We made it! And the wind was fannin' cool ag'inst
    my face:
  But the scare was still a-boilin' where I aim to keep
    my brains:
The wheeler he was weavin' and a-saggin' on the trace,
  When San Salvador loomed up acrost the plains.
    And we hit the town a-reelin',
    With the gritty brakes a-squealin',
  And the pinto wheeler draggin' in the chains.

                                   HENRY HERBERT KNIBBS

Death Valley

    'Twas silent below on the desert
    Where the night comes swift and strange,
    And a deadly pall hung over all
    From the top of the Funeral Range.
    Startling and clear, the sibilant hiss

Of a rattlesnake's slithering tone;
Not a creature stirred, nor the sound of a bird;
Death Valley was holding its own.

High o'er the crest of the Panamint peaks
The ghost of a whispering breeze;
And its wavering breath, in the valley of death,
Seems weird and ill at ease.
Brilliantly shining the stars disappear,
And the mountains stand sombre and grand;
Till the blazing sun, on its endless run,
Bursts forth o'er the shimmering sand.

Like spirits they come—a beast and man,
With painful gait, and slow.
For the canteens clink in the burning sink,
And the animal's ears hang low.
The man staggers forward calling to God,
Then drops with a whimpering moan;
The burro faint calls, stumbles and falls,
But Death Valley answers alone.

A lizard circles an arc below,
And a vulture overhead;
The poison air drifts here and there
From the pits of the borax bed.
The Palo Verdes and Yucca Palms
Stand guard with the Joshua trees
But the sun glares bright on the skeletons white
With a vigil that never may cease.

And this is the price of the quest for gold
By saddle and frying pan,
The rustling tones of the bleaching bones
And the crumbling skull of a man.
Slowly the sun tips the Panamint peaks
For the space of a fleeting breath,
Then follows its rays in a crimson haze.
'Tis night in the Valley of Death.

JACK H. LEE

Spring in the Desert

Like the rusty bronze of a copper kettle
The rattler coils in the sun;
The lizard lies, an emerald green,
On the armored blade of a cactus,
Or, blushing red, on its bloom;
The coyote sprawls at the mouth of his cave
Maw-sick of his carrion-trove,
And sheds his coat of the winter gone.
Bees buzz in the thralls of the yucca cups,
And midges dance o'er the fetid pool.
The gorgeous dyes of the desert floor
Are like the robes of a medicine-man,
Or the loom of a Zuñi maid.
Old Chief Lone Man squats in the sun,
Back propped against an orange cliff,
He mutters anon, or smokes or sleeps in the sun;
And miles up there in the desert sky
A vulture specks the blue.

ARTHUR TRUMAN MERRILL

The Toll of the Desert

This is the toll of the desert,
    These bleaching bones in the sun;
Ever the price of its grueling,
    If all its treasures are won.

Stern is the sway of the desert,
    Ever and always the same;
The strong and the sturdy survive it,
    But woe to the weak and lame.

These bleaching bones on the hillside
　　Bear witness for others to see,
Where someone has paid the ransom,
　　The desert's toll and its fee.

Take heed from this gruesome warning,
　　Take care lest you might stay too,
To bleach on the sands of the desert,
　　And the coyotes howl over you.

ARTHUR W. MONROE

In the Yucca Land

The rim of the desert is the Yucca land,
Behind it the snow-peaked ranges stand.
Beyond it, and out, the desert lies,—
And far as the line of the tenting skies.
"The ship of the desert" sails there at dawn
In the swift mirage; and there, up-drawn
From violet seas, in the sunrise glow
Are the coral reefs the mermen know;
And the perfumed plains where the iris grow.
Out there where the web of the gossamer flies
The shoals of the purple islands rise,
Out there are the pink gray mists unrolled,
And the sun goes down on a world of gold,
　　　　In the Yucca land.

The grimness of time, is the Yucca land,
When twilight reaches her specter hand,
When the moon bends down, a living thing,
And the midnight stars are whispering!
The Yucca glades are peopled, then,
With naiads and gnomes and the ghosts of men;
From the inner earth, from the Everywhere,

They come, and they walk in the moonlight there.
The dryads step from the Yucca trees
And lean white arms on the wavering breeze.
There, a pallid priestess counts her beads,
Yon arch to a Druid temple leads.
Aye; and yonder Yucca, whose grim shape warns,
Is the cross of Him, and His crown of thorns.
There are stealthy shadows, a phantom whir—
The night vibrates with a soundless stir;
And oh, the silence! so tense, so terse,
You can hear the heart of the Universe.
The desert its mystery unbars
To you and the moon and the whispering stars,
            In the Yucca land.

The newness of earth, is the Yucca land,
The tang of the first-made gleam of sand,
Not ever a plow profaned its sod,—
The world is so new you could talk with God,
            In the Yucca land.

                                    MADGE MORRIS

¿ Quién Sabe?

"Where do the waters go that go
        To the sands of bleached Mojave?"
        I asked of an ancient Indian man
(Lingering trace of his vanished race):
        "Do they sink in the sand
        To the underland?"
With never a bend of his stately head,
Nor look, or the lurk of a smile, he said:

        "¿Quién sabe?"

"Surely thou knowest, thou primal man!
Brood of the desert's birth, and ban,—

Wise as the rattlesnake, old as the sun,
Where do the rivers run that run
To the sands of thy grim Mojave?
          Do they sink in the sand
          To the underland?—
Down where the red volcano's glow
Lieth await for the underflow?
Down where the salt-sea left its scum
When the earth was void and the deep was
          dumb?"

          "¿*Quién sabe?*"

                              MADGE MORRIS

To the Colorado Desert

Thou brown, bare-breasted, voiceless mystery,
Hot sphinx of nature, cactus-crowned, what hast
          thou done?
Unclothed and mute as when the groans of chaos
          turned
Thy naked burning bosom to the sun.
The mountain silences have speech, the rivers
          sing.
Thou answerest never unto anything.
Pink-throated lizards pant in thy slim shade;
The horned toad runs rustling in the heat;
The shadowy gray coyote, born afraid,
Steals to some brackish spring and laps, and
          prowls
Away; and howls, and howls and howls and
          howls,
Until the solitude is shaken with an added
          loneliness.
Thy sharp mescal shoots up a giant stalk,
Its century of yearning, to the sunburnt skies,

And drips rare honey from the lips
Of yellow waxen flowers, and dies.
Some lengthwise sun-dried shapes with feet and
    hands
And thirsty mouths pressed on the sweltering
    sands,
Mark here and there a gruesome graveless spot
Where someone drank thy scorching hotness,
    and is not.
God must have made thee in His anger, and
    forgot.

MADGE MORRIS

Mi Corazón

Spanish is the tongue of lovers,
Music light as fountain-spray;
And a *señorita* taught me
Every promise it can play.
Still her seal of love is on me
Though the raveling years unwind,
Though my rose-lipped *señorita*
Blossoms only in my mind.

Pepper trees recite their rosary
When the psalm of night appears,
Telling over their crimson berries
Strung on drooping cordeliers.
And I stand there by the Mission
With my love, my one-alone,
When she whispered on the moonlight:
"Mi amor, mi corazón!"

Down the long bright road of summer
Mission roses bloom again;
But their scent is only perfume—

It was breath of heaven then!
Night winds never moan the silence
But the vanished years restore,
Mourning doves will never sorrow
But she echoes, *"Mi amor!"*

The white stars came to move in heaven
Like a flock of grazing sheep,
While a shepherd moon among them
Watched—the world was dreams asleep.
Then I kissed my love in the moonlight,
By her door I held her close,
And her lips were trembling summer
When she whispered, *"Adios!"*

Spanish is the tongue of lovers;
And the plea of Spanish eyes
Cried their promise in the moonlight—
But I wasn't very wise.
Heyday rode my prancing saddle
When I left my love alone . . .
Now the years forever echo,
"Mi amor, mi corazón!"

But a horse is meant to gallop,
Trails are made and meant to know,
Every young *vaquero*'s saddle
Meant for him to mount and go.
Only youth, too quick for silence,
Finds love was not meant for this—
Trails are armless brides to fancy,
Giving only dust to kiss.

But I never came to claim her.
It is all so far away,
Yet the knife-edge pain of heartache
Comes as if it were yesterday.
I spurred back to old San Gabriel
Like a wind on darkness blown,

When I heard her call on the mountain:
"Mi amor, mi corazón!"

Where the pepper trees were shaking
Silver moon-drops through their hair,
Padre led my beat of torment
To the *campo santo*. There
Was the raw earth, brute against her,
In its arms it held her close,
And I felt her lips caress me
With her final *"Adios!"*

Spanish is the tongue of lovers,
Music light as fountain-spray;
But the one who taught me vanished
With the promise it can play.
Now the night wind, in its sorrow,
Sings a low heart-breaking tone:
Still my *señorita,* calling,
"Mi amor, mi corazón!"

GORDON W. NORRIS

Song of the Border

South of the Border and north of the sea,
The moon hangs ripe in the mango tree,
Night is an orchard of apricot glow:
South of the Border, in Mexico.
Guitarras were stringing hearts on a tune—
And the heart of a *gringo* was never immune!
Her eyes spoke of April, but June were her lips,
South of the Border and dreams from the ships.
Our idyl was broken one rattlesnake night
In gambling and cards, then shooting and flight . . .
I saddled—I kissed her, my bright *corazón,*

And space in my breast, flew northward alone.
Spur-driven hoofs, a pattern of pain,—
Galloping hoofs kept pounding my brain
And spurs in my soul kept raking: Obey!—
Till, north of the Border, I cursed on the day!
I've never returned: there's a price on my head.
But the cantering years find love thoroughbred.
My breast is a desert, no reason nor chart—
For, south of the Border, I left her my heart!

GORDON W. NORRIS

Spring Morning—Santa Fe

The first hour was a word the color of dawn;
The second came, and gorgeous poppies stood
Backs to the wall. The yellow sun rode on:
A mockingbird sang from a nest of wood.

The water in the acequia came down
At the stroke of nine, and watery clouds were lifting
Their velvet shadows from the little town:
Gold fired the pavement where the leaves were shifting.

At ten, black shawls of women bowed along
The Alameda. Sleepy burros lay
In the heat, and lifted up their ears. A song
Wavered upon the wind and died away,

And the great bells rang out a golden tune:
Words grew in the heart and clanged, the color of noon.

LYNN RIGGS

Bones in the Desert

We found him there on the Desert,
At the end of the trail where he died,
With his old gray head on a boulder,
With an empty canteen by his side.

Tenderly we laid him
In a shallow grave to rest,
His tattered coat for a pillow,
With hands across his breast.

Who he was, or where he came from,
Never will be known;
For the desert keeps her secrets,
When she has claimed her own.

NED WHITE

I Wanted to Die in the Desert

I wanted to die in the desert,
I planned it for twenty year;
Alone with my God and my conscience,
And not a sky-pilot near.

I meant what I said when I doped it,
For it threw a spell over me.
Its mesas, its sand, and its deadness—
It was the place I wanted to be.

I've hoofed with my jack all over it;
I've stood on the brink of hell;
I wooed it, I coaxed it, I fought it,
And was caught in its deadly spell.

I said when I croaked that I'd go
To the desert to find my hole,
With snakes and toads to watch over me,
And my headstone a yucca pole.

But the death I've cheated so often
Has pulled its freight into town,
And I can't get back to the desert;
I'm broke—not a penny—I'm down.

Life is a burden and not worth the while;
So I'll play the ace up my sleeve.
It's poison—quick stuff—and Saint Peter;
Adios to the world I leave.

Just throw my old hide in the cactus,
Out where the desert wind moans;
For I wanted to die in the desert,
Where the buzzards would peck at my bones.

                                        UNKNOWN

The Railroad Cars Are Coming

The great Pacific railway,
    For California hail!
Bring on the locomotive,
    Lay down the iron rail;
Across the rolling prairies
    By steam we're bound to go,
The railroad cars are coming, humming
    Through New Mexico,
The railroad cars are coming, humming
    Through New Mexico.

The little dogs in dog-town
    Will wag each little tail;

They'll think that something's coming
   A-riding on a rail.
The rattle-snake will show its fangs,
   The owl tu-whit, tu-who,
The railroad cars are coming, humming
   Through New Mexico,
The railroad cars are coming, humming
   Through New Mexico.

UNKNOWN

VIII

From the Mountains
to the Prairies

The Sheep-Herder's Lament

The cowboy has his bunkie
    To share his tarpaulin—
To joke with him and smoke with him
    And listen to his chin.
But a sheep-herder, doggone it!
    When lonesome breezes moan,
Must grit his teeth and stand it—
    He's got to fight alone.

The nester he is married—
    Contentment is his lot—
There's laughin' and there's chaffin'
    At his ranch (which here there's not).
For the sheep-herder, doggone it!
    Don't hear a human voice;
It's enough fer him to listen
    While the kyo-tes rejoice.

The city man is bothered
    With too many men around;
There's rushin' and there's crushin'
    Like when ants swarm o'er the ground.
But the sheep-herder, doggone it!
    Has miles of space to fill
And nary soul to help him
    Watch the sheep feed on the hill.

                ARTHUR CHAPMAN

Ode to the Norther

Thrice welcome to the Norther,
    The Norther roaring free,
Across the rolling prairies
    Straight from the Arctic sea!

Avaunt, ye western breezes,
   And southern zephyrs warm!
Here's to the cold, blue Norther,
   The stern, relentless storm!

I'm tired of love and laughter,
   Tonight I long for war;
For the bugle blasts are sounding
   From the heights of Labrador.
"Whoo-hoo!" the winds are wailing
   Their muffled réveilles,
And 'round my chimney fortress
   Roar angry, shoreless seas.

Wild storms and wants and dangers
   Will thrill a poet's heart,
And free a Viking's spirit
   Far more than feeble art.
So welcome to the storm-wind!
   The Northers I invoke.
Here's to the strong, gray weather
   That makes the heart of oak!

   WILLIAM LAWRENCE CHITTENDEN

The Sheep-herder

All day across the sagebrush flat,
   Beneath the sun of June,
My sheep they loaf and feed and bleat
   Their never-changin' tune.
And then, at night time, when they lay
   As quiet as a stone,
I hear the gray wolf far away,
   "Alo-one!" he says, "alo-one!"

A-a! ma-a! ba-a! eh-eh-eh!
 The tune the woollies sing;
It's rasped my ears, it seems, for years,
 Though really just since Spring;
And nothin', far as I can see
 Around the circle's sweep,
But sky and plain, my dreams and me
 And them infernal sheep.

I've got one book—it's poetry—
 A bunch of pretty wrongs
An Eastern lunger gave to me;
 He said 'twas "shepherd songs."
But, though that poet sure is deep
 And has sweet things to say,
He never seen a herd of sheep
 Or smelt them, anyway.

A-a! ma-a! ba-a! eh-eh-eh!
 My woollies greasy gray,
An awful change has hit the range
 Since that old poet's day.
For you're just silly, on'ry brutes
 And I look like distress,
And my pipe ain't the kind that toots
 And there's no "shepherdess."

Yet 'way down home in Kansas State,
 Bliss Township, Section Five,
There's one that's promised me to wait,
 The sweetest girl alive;
That's why I salt my wages down
 And mend my clothes with strings,
While others blow their pay in town
 For booze and other things.

A-a! ma-a! ba-a! eh-eh-eh!
 My Minnie, don't be sad;
Next year we'll lease that splendid piece
 That corners on your dad.

We'll drive to "literary," dear,
   The way we used to do
And turn my lonely workin' here
   To happiness for you.

Suppose, down near that rattlers' den,
   While I sit here and dream,
I'd spy a bunch of ugly men
   And hear a woman scream.
Suppose I'd let my rifle shout
   And drop the men in rows,
And then the woman should turn out—
   My Minnie!—just suppose.

A-a! ma-a! ba-a! eh-eh-eh!
   The tune would then be gay;
There is, I mind, a parson kind
   Just forty miles away.
Why, Eden would come back again,
   With sage and sheep corrals,
And I could swing a singin' pen
   To write her "pastorals."

I pack a rifle on my arm
   And jump at flies that buzz;
There's nothin' here to do me harm;
   I sometimes wish there was.
If through that brush above the pool
   A red should creep—and creep—
Wah! cut down on 'im!—Stop, you fool!
   That's nothin' but a sheep.

A-a! ma-a! ba-a!—Hell!
   Oh, sky and plain and bluff!
Unless my mail comes up the trail
   I'm locoed, sure enough.
What's that?—a dust-whiff near the butte
   Right where my last trail ran,
A movin' speck, a—wagon! Hoot!
   Thank God! here comes a man.

        CHARLES BADGER CLARK, JR.

The Snowstorm

Across the plain the wind whines through the sage,
  And boots the tumbleweeds with veering whim;
The day is dimming through the merging mists
  And huddled herds head south against the rim.

On flurried wing the snowbirds, wheeling low,
  In shrill, staccato chorus whir away;
In vagrant gust the snowflakes eddy by,
  And closer swirls the circling wall of gray.

Unleashed, the north wind swings his whistling whip.
  The air is blinded by a whirling veil;
And riding through the maelstrom, madly free
  Exultant shriek the demons of the gale!

PEARL RIGGS CROUCH

The Plains

Give me the plains,—the barren and sun-beaten plains!
Free in the vague indeterminate murmur of winds,
High on the arched and tremendous back of the world,
Alone and close up under the skies,
Let me lie dark in the grass like an Indian,
Hearing loud footfalls afar in the rumbling sod,
And know that it knows me!—Up from the grass to the sky,
From the skies again back to the grass—I go to the plains!

Give me the plains—the lonely and rain-beaten plains!
There no escape, nor to hide from the all-seeing heavens,—
There no evasion,—open and wide and above;
No thought-guiding trails,—high up and flat under Heaven;
Free with fierce winds to follow the flicker of lightnings,—
Free with the soft-rustling rains that govern the grasses,—
Free with the long sandy rivers—I go to the plains!

Give me the plains—the solemn and sun-hallowed plains!
There the outcroppings of curious rock where the coulee
Breaks to the far-fading slant of the shallow-cut valley;
Away by the distant diminutive cottonwood groves
Run the wild-roaming bands of mustangs, their changeable colors
Passing in white-whirling dust—I go to the plains!

Give me the plains—the ancient mysterious plains!
Low to the grass-tufted world wheels the black-pinioned buzzard,
Skimming his shadow over endless undulations of prairie;
(So passes my soul's own shadow over the plains that it longs for!)
Dim in the grass leads the shadowy track of the Blackfeet;
Far are their camps,—they are lost along the blue wave
    of the mountains;
Dim are their smokes, receding, fading, a phantom, a ghost-song;
Memory-smokes, receding, dissolving over the prairies,—
Trail of my own lost footprints—I go to the plains!

MAYNARD DIXON

At Cheyenne

Young Lochinvar came in from the West,
With fringe on his trousers and fur on his vest;
The width of his hat-brim could nowhere be beat,
His No. 10 brogans were chuck full of feet,
His girdle was horrent with pistols and things,
And he flourished a handful of aces on kings.

The fair Mariana sat watching a star,
When who should turn up but the young Lochinvar!
Her pulchritude gave him a pectoral glow,
And he reined up his hoss with stentorian "Whoa!"
Then turned on the maiden a rapturous grin,
And modestly asked if he mightn't step in.

With presence of mind that was marvellous quite,
The fair Mariana replied that he might;
So in through the portal rode young Lochinvar,
Pre-empted the claim, and cleaned out the bar.
Though the justice allowed he wa'n't wholly to blame,
He taxed him ten dollars and costs, just the same.

EUGENE FIELD

The Wanderer

Upon a mountain's height, far from the sea,
    I found this shell,
And to my curious ear this lonely thing
Ever a song of ocean seemed to sing—
    Ever a tale of ocean seemed to tell.

How came this shell upon the mountain height?
    Ah, who can say
Whether there dropped by some too careless hand—

Whether there cast when oceans swept the land
    Ere the Eternal had ordained the Day.

Strange was it not? Far from its native sea,
    One song it sang—
Sang of the mighty mysteries of the tide—
Sang of the awful, vast profound and wide—
    Softly with echoes of the ocean rang.

And as the shell upon the mountain's height
    Sings of the sea,
So do I ever, leagues and leagues away—
So do I ever, wandering where I may,
    Sing, O my home—sing, O my home, of thee.

EUGENE FIELD

On Recrossing the Rocky Mountains
After Many Years

Long years ago I wandered here,
In the midsummer of the year,—
    Life's summer too;
A score of horsemen here we rode,
The mountain world its glories showed,
    All fair to view.

These scenes, in glowing colors drest,
Mirrored the life within my breast,
    Its world of hopes;
The whispering woods and fragrant breeze
That stirred the grass in verdant seas
    On billowy slopes,

And glistening crag in sunlit sky,
'Mid snowy clouds piled mountains high,
    Were joys to me;
My path was o'er the prairie wide,
Or here on grander mountain side,
    To choose, all free.

The rose that waved in morning air,
And spread its dewy fragrance there,
    In careless bloom,
Gave to my heart its ruddiest hue,
O'er my glad life its color threw
    And sweet perfume.

Now changed the scene and changed the eyes,
That here once looked on glowing skies,
    Where summer smiled;
These riven trees, this wind-swept plain,
Now show the winter's dread domain,
    Its fury wild.

The rocks rise black from storm-packed snow,
All checked the river's pleasant flow,
    Vanished the bloom;
These dreary wastes of frozen plain
Reflect my bosom's life again,
    Now lonesome gloom.

The buoyant hopes and busy life
Have ended all in hateful strife,
    And thwarted aim.
The world's rude contact killed the rose;
No more its radiant color shows
    False roads to fame.

Backward, amidst the twilight glow,
Some lingering spots yet brightly show
    On hard roads won,
Where still some grand peaks mark the way

Touched by the light of parting day
    And memory's sun.

But here thick clouds the mountains hide,
The dim horizon, bleak and wide,
    No pathway shows,
And rising gusts, and darkening sky,
Tell of the night that cometh nigh,
    The brief day's close.

JOHN CHARLES FRÉMONT

Color in the Wheat

Like liquid gold the wheat-field lies,
   A marvel of yellow and green,
That ripples and runs, that floats and flies,
   With the subtle shadows, the change, the sheen
That plays in the golden hair of a girl.
     A cloud flies there—
     A ripple of amber—a flare
Of light follows after. A swirl
In the hollows like the twinkling feet
   Of a fairy waltzer; the colors run
   To the westward sun,
Through the deeps of the ripening wheat.

I hear the reapers' far-off hum,
   So faint and far it seems the drone
Of bee or beetle, seems to come
   From far-off, fragrant, fruity zone,
    A land of plenty, where
    Toward the sun, as hasting there,
    The colors run
    Before the wind's feet
    In the wheat.

The wild hawk swoops
   To his prey in the deeps;
The sunflower droops
   To the lazy wave; the wind sleeps;
Then, moving in dazzling links and loops,
   A marvel of shadow and shine,
A glory of olive and amber and wine,
   Runs the color in the wheat.

HAMLIN GARLAND

The Old Settler's Song

I'd wandered all over the country
Prospecting and digging for gold—
I'd tunnelled, hydraulicked, and cradled,
And I had been frequently sold.
For one who gets riches by mining,
Perceiving that hundreds grow poor,
I made up my mind to try farming—
The only pursuit that is sure.
So rolling my grub in my blankets,
I left all my tools on the ground,
And started one morning to shank it
For a country they call Puget Sound.
Arriving flat broke in mid-winter,
I found it enveloped in fog,
And covered all over with timber
Thick as hair on the back of the dog.
As I looked on the prospect so gloomy
The tears trickled over my face,
For I felt that my travels had brought me
To the edge of the jumping-off place.
I took up a claim in the forest,
And sat myself down to hard toil;
For two years I chopped and I niggered,

But I never got down to the soil.
I tried to get out of the country,
But poverty forced me to stay
Until I became an Old Settler—
Then nothing could drive me away.
And now that I'm used to the climate,
I think if a man ever found
A spot to live easy and happy,
That Eden is on Puget Sound.
No longer the slave of ambition,
I laugh at the world and its shams,
As I think of my pleasant condition,
Surrounded by acres of clams.

FRANCIS HENRY

Cheyenne Mountain

By easy slope to west as if it had
No thought, when first its soaring was begun,
Except to look devoutly to the sun,
It rises and has risen, until glad,
With light as with a garment, it is clad,
Each dawn, before the tardy plains have won
One ray; and after day has long been done
For us, the light doth cling reluctant, sad to leave its brow.
    Beloved mountain, I
Thy worshipper as thou the sun's each morn
My dawn, before the dawn, receive from thee;
And think, as thy rose-tinted peaks I see
That thou were great when Homer was not born,
And ere thou change all human song shall die!

HELEN HUNT JACKSON

Ranchers

They went off on the buckboard in the rain,
The children in the straw. I didn't know
Which one of the long roads they'd have to go,
But I saw them just as plain.

For anywhere they chose to turn the horses
There'd be the same gray miles of tableland,
The same rank smell of sage, the same wet sand
In the windy watercourses.

And anywhere in time there'd be red hills
Rising, raw rock against the rain. I saw
The plunge and splash across a lonely draw,
The long slow climb with red mud on the
    hills.

And somewhere, in good time, I knew they'd
    pass
As if in secret from the road they travelled,
To follow out like a thread of rope unravelled
Some faint mark in the grass,

And come to a gate, perhaps where a stray
    steer
Breathed in the dusk, or slipped on the wet
    stone there;
And come to a house . . . I knew they'd be alone
    there
Most of the year.

The earth would slowly change where they had
    stepped,
The air would fill up softly with the sound
Of teams, voices . . . I thought the red hills
    must have slept
Until they woke the ground.

I thought no words could make, on anybody's
    mouth,
As true an image as their hills would keep of
    them,
Where on our world spread westward like a cloth
They worked a homely hem.

MAURICE LESEMAN

An Indian Summer Day on the Prairie

(IN THE BEGINNING)

The sun is a huntress young,
The sun is a red, red joy,
The sun is an Indian girl,
Of the tribe of the Illinois.

(MID-MORNING)

The sun is a smouldering fire,
That creeps through the high gray plain,
And leaves not a bush of cloud
To blossom with flowers of rain.

(NOON)

The sun is a wounded deer,
That treads pale grass in the skies,
Shaking his golden horns,
Flashing his baleful eyes.

(SUNSET)

The sun is an eagle old,
There in the windless west.
Atop of the spirit-cliffs
He builds him a crimson nest.

VACHEL LINDSAY

Dead in the Sierras

His footprints have failed us,
Where berries are red,
And madroños are rankest,
The hunter is dead!

The grizzly may pass
By his half-open door;
May pass and repass
On his path, as of yore;

The panther may crouch
In the leaves on his limb;
May scream and may scream,—
It is nothing to him.

Prone, bearded, and breasted
Like columns of stone;
And tall as a pine—
As a pine overthrown!

His camp-fires gone,
What else can be done
Than let him sleep on
Till the light of the sun?

Ay, tombless! what of it?
Marble is dust,
Cold and repellent;
And iron is rust.

JOAQUIN MILLER

The Forest Fire

Rolling clouds of greasy smoke,
    Crashing giant trees;
Roaring, flashing, fiendish flames,
    Upon an angry breeze.
Frightened, fleeing, bird and beast,
    Shrieking in despair—
The ugly demon, forest fire,
    Is on another tear.

ARTHUR W. MONROE

Sheep Country

In spring the sheep are driven over the mountain
While there is still snow knee-deep in every shadow
And the wind's edge is sharp in the Valle country.
The sheep come up from the canyons
Like a gray cloud. They move slowly. They leave unnibbled
Not a low-growing leaf, not a sliver of grass,
Not a flower.

In Capulín canyon the river crossings are muddied
Before the wild chokecherries are in flower;
There are a hundred twisted trails on Rabbit Mountain
Made by the sheep that come up from Peña Blanca,
From Cienaga and Cochití, from Santo Domingo,
From the dirty corrals, from the flat, dusty mesas
Where they have fed all winter.

I have seen them going up Santa Clara canyon in April
When Tsacoma mountain is still a white cloud of brightness
Lifted against the sky; when the wind is bitter
And there is only a haze of green around the aspens

You can see by looking slantwise, never directly,
Never in a second glance, never by coming closer.
I have seen the sheep move up Santa Clara canyon
And over the ridge
And down the Rio de los Indios and onward into
The long, curved Valle San Antonio.

And I have seen the names of the sheepherders written
On the aspen trees halfway up Tsacoma
And on Redondo Mountain where the aspens fight for their rootholds
In the black rocks, in the frozen lava.
Casimiro Chaves, I have seen written; Juan Pino, Reyes Contreras,
From Chamita and Abiquiu and Española,
Nambé and Pojuaque.

These are the names of boys, carved here and written,
Whose wits, they say, aren't fit for any other work,
Or men whose minds are still the minds of children,
Who do not desire anything more of living
Than to lie in the glittering shadow of an aspen
On the rim of the Valles where the sheep feed
And move downward slowly.

There are men who desire much more and find much less.
Must we all be madmen, I wonder, or innocents
To follow the sheep along the ridge of the Valles,
Looking down, west, to the sea of grasses,
The far-off, tangled, grass-hidden threads of water,
And the nets of rain through which the farther mountains
Shine like a shadow?

                                        MARGARET POND

The Yellow Witch of Caribou

The hills are high in Caribou—
The air is clear, the skies are blue;
But where a black ledge seams the ground
The yellow witch's tracks are found,
And men grow drunk with ravishment
Once they have caught the witch's scent.

The aspens on the mountain side
Were green when Carlo brought his bride,
The cherry-cheeked Selina, to
The haunted hills of Caribou.

"You better take your man and go,"
The old wives warned, "before the snow.
The yellow witch hides in these hills,
And gets our men against their wills."

Selina shook her bold, black head.
"My Carlo will not leave my bed
And hammer on a speckled door
A-huntin' for a yellow whore.
He's signed up with the sawmill crew,
He's safe enough in Caribou.

"Who minds the talk of wrinkled crones,
Their skin a-stickin' to their bones,
Their men folks might go trailin' round
A-chasin' witch tracks in the ground;
But my man's *mine!* I'm not afraid
I'll lose him to a stealin' jade."

"Child, we were all the same as you,
When we were brought to Caribou.
We know, as only old wives can,
The curse of havin' half a man.
We know the end of these old tracks—
The blinded eyes—and broken backs."

But when the mountain side grew red
And pulsing as a wanton's bed
Young Carlo's eyes flamed with the fire
Of an unhallowed, mad desire.
Selina knew his passion meant
"Her man" had caught the witch's scent.

Before the first snow veiled the crest,
Like lace upon a woman's breast,
She saw him leave the sheltering mills
To roam among the siren hills.

But no man yet has come to know
Which way the yellow witch may go.
She burrows deep in porphyry rocks
And bars her trail with granite blocks.
So Carlo did, as all men do
That chase the witch of Caribou.

At last upon a sloping crest,
As rounded as a woman's breast,
Beneath a snow of winding lace,
He tracked her to her hiding place.
Here, in an evil blackened niche,
He mated with the yellow witch.

At dawn, Selina found him there
Strangled by a golden hair.

CLYDE ROBERTSON

Summer on the Great American Desert

Ye dreary plains, that round me lie,
     So parch'd with summer's heat,
No more ye please my wand'ring eye,
     Or woo my weary feet.

Why hath the spring your beauty borne
    Into his hiding place,
And left the widow'd winds to mourn
    The charms they would embrace?

Why should those flowers, whose honey'd breath
    With incense filled the breeze,
Drooping and wither'd, lie in death,
    And now no longer please?

That grassy carpet, green and wide,
    Why turn'd to stubble now?
Save 'chance along some streamlet's side,
    Where less'ning waters flow!

And why those gently murm'ring rills,
    Whose soft melodious strains
Were wont to echo 'mong the hills
    No longer reach the plains?

The lark no longer meets the morn,—
    Nor linnet pours his throat,—
Nor feather'd warbler hails the dawn
    With his sweet, mellow note;—

Nor even insect cheers the scene,
    Where Solitude alone,
In wither'd garb, as Desert Queen,
    Rears her eternal throne!

These thirsty plains, with open mouth,
    Implore the gentle shower;
But vainly plead, while summer's drouth
    In scorching heat doth pour!

Nor grateful shade, of spreading tree,
    Invites my feet to rest;
Nor cooling stream, in melody,
    Attempts my quicken'd zest.

So dismal all! why should I stay
    And sicken by their view?
Thrice gladly will I turn away,
    And bid these scenes adieu!

RUFUS B. SAGE

Wind Song

Wind of the Prairie, sweeping adown from the hills
Bending the upstarting grass of the early spring,
    Tell me what you are singing.
Summers and winters uncounted; unknown,
Over the wilderness roaming,
So you have learned if you will but tell,
All that in the long years befell;
    Sing to me, then, of the Coming.

"Tread of the moccasin'd Indian, trailing the deer in the
    timber,
Stalking the bison and antelope grazing the open plains;
Flying with stolen ponies snatcht from the Utes of the West,
Plumes of the war-parties riding—past, like the wind in the
    grass.

"Tramp of the cavalry horses, and gleam of the council
    fires burning;
Sound of the axe and of hammer where forts arise at their
    bidding;
Dim trails over the prairie where longhorns journey
    northward—
I lift the mists from the river, and these are gone as the
    vapors.

"Creaking of laden wagons in lonely and desolate places,
Ring of the wires drawn taut as the staples are driven home;

Grazing herds in the pastures; long lines winding down to
  the river;
They drink, and I ripple the water, and these are gone like
  the ripples.

"Alone in the smile of the springtide the land lies waiting
  before me.
The jackrabbit leisurely lopes on quest of his own, and the
  coyote
Howls in the night at the camp fires that gleam in the
  darkness before him;
Men and women and children about them gather'd and
  waiting,
Faces and hearts alight with a wonderful hope and desiring;
Soldiers riding before them, as the sun climbs high in the
  heavens;
I scatter the smoke of their guns, and the throngs are melted
  as quickly.

"Over the land they are pour'd, in a flood resistless,
  unyielding;
Toiling with stubborn patience, a winter light in their faces;
Steadfast thru days that are dark, till the first great struggle
  is over;
Winter winds have they borne, but now the joy of the
  springtime
Wells in their hearts once more, as they who remain are
  foregathered;
Past on the breath of the wind, pioneers who blazed the way
  for them.
But these are they who have conquer'd and kept, the People
  of Eighty-Nine."

ZOE A. TILGHMAN

Creede

Here's a land where all are equal—
　　Of high or lowly birth—
A land where men make millions,
　　Dug from the dreary earth.
Here the meek and mild-eyed burro
　　On mineral mountains feed—
It's day all day, in the day-time,
　　And there is no night in Creede.

The cliffs are solid silver,
　　With wond'rous wealth untold;
And the beds of running rivers
　　Are lined with glittering gold.
While the world is filled with sorrow,
　　And hearts must break and bleed—
It's day all day in the day-time,
　　And there is no night in Creede.

CY WARMAN

The Rise and Fall of Creede

A thousand burdened burrows filled
　　The narrow, winding, wriggling trail.
A hundred settlers came to build,
　　Each day, new houses in the vale.
A hundred gamblers came to feed
　　On these same settlers—this was Creede.

Slanting Annie, Gambler Joe
　　And bad Bob Ford, Sapolio,
Or Soapy Smith, as he was known,—
　　Ran games peculiarly their own,

And everything was open wide,
    And men drank absinthe on the side.

*   *   *   *   *   *

And now the Faro Bank is closed,
    And Mr. Faro's gone away
To seek new fields, it is supposed,—
    More verdant fields. The gamblers say
The man who worked the shell and ball
    Has gone back to the Capital

The winter winds blow bleak and chill,
    The quaking, quivering aspen waves
About the summit of the hill—
    Above the unrecorded graves
Where halt, abandoned burros feed
    And coyotes call—and this is Creede.

Lone graves whose head-boards bear no name,
    Whose silent owners lived like brutes
And died as doggedly,—but game,
    And most of them died in their boots.
We mind among the unwrit names
    The man who murdered Jesse James.

We saw him murdered, saw him fall,
    And saw his mad assassin gloat
Above him. Heard his moans and all,
    And saw the shot holes in his throat,
And men moved on and gave no heed
    To life or death—and this is Creede.

CY WARMAN

Sheep Ranching

It's none too sociable herdin' sheep
    Ten thousand feet up in the air,
With yelping coyotes spoilin' your sleep,
    Or Injuns on a tear—
An' nothin' for company or for fun
But a collie, a pony and a gun.

                OWEN WISTER

The Water-hole

I'd rather lie on a rye-grass bed
Where the sun fights with the willow,
My saddle underneath my head,
My blanket for a pillow,

Than on the silk of palaces.
On the rye-grass let me lie
Between the desert quietness
The bigness of the sky.
I'd rather lie on the dry rye-grass
Than the softest bed of all:
By the water-hole, where the cattle pass
And the piebald magpies call,
To chew my soul as a cow her cud.
No human voice or sound:
The sky above and the desert flood
Of silence all around.

CHARLES ERSKIN SCOTT WOOD

The Buffalo Skinners

Come all you jolly skinners and listen to my song,
There are not many verses, it will not detain you long;
It's concerning some young fellows who did agree to go
And spend one summer pleasantly on the range of the buffalo.

'Twas in the town of Jacksboro in the spring of Sev'nty-three,
A man by the name of Crego came stepping up to me,
Saying, "How do you do, young fellow, and how would you like
    to go
And spend one summer pleasantly on the range of the buffalo?"

"It's me being out of employment," this to Crego I did say,
"This going out on the buffalo range depends upon the pay.
But if you will pay good wages and transportation, too,
I think, sir, I will go with you to the range of the buffalo."

"Yes, I will pay good wages, give transportation too,
Provided you will go with me and stay the summer through;
But if you should grow homesick, come back to Jacksboro,
I won't pay transportation from the range of the buffalo."

It's now our outfit was complete—seven able-bodied men,
With navy six and needle gun—our troubles did begin;
Our way it was a pleasant one, the route we had to go,
Until we crossed Pease River on the range of the buffalo.

It's now we've crossed Pease River, our troubles have begun.
The first damned tail I went to rip, Christ! how I cut my thumb!
While skinning the damned old stinkers our lives they had no
    show,
For the Indians watched to pick us off while skinning the buffalo.

He fed us on such sorry chuck I wished myself most dead,
It was old jerked beef, croton coffee, and sour bread.
Pease River's as salty as hell fire, the water I could never go—
O God! I wished I had never come to the range of the buffalo.

Our meat it was buffalo hump and iron wedge bread,
And all we had to sleep on was a buffalo robe for a bed;
The fleas and graybacks worked on us, O boys, it was not slow,
I'll tell you there's no worse hell on earth than the range of the
    buffalo.

Our hearts were cased with buffalo hocks, our souls were cased with
    steel,
And the hardships of that summer would nearly make us reel.
While skinning the damned old stinkers our lives they had no
    show,
For the Indians waited to pick us off on the hills of Mexico.

The season being near over, old Crego he did say
The crowd had been extravagant, was in debt to him that day.
We coaxed him and we begged him and still it was no go—
We left old Crego's bones to bleach on the range of the buffalo.

Oh, it's now we've crossed Pease River and homeward we are
    bound,
No more in that hell-fired country shall ever we be found.
Go home to our wives and sweethearts, tell others not to go,
For God's forsaken the buffalo range and the damned old buffalo.

                                                        UNKNOWN

Bury Me Not on the Lone Prairie

"O bury me not on the lone prairie!"
These words came low and mournfully
From the pallid lips of a youth who lay
On his dying bed at the close of day.

"O bury me not on the lone prairie,
Where the wild coyotes will howl o'er me,
Where the buzzards beat and the wind goes free;
O bury me not on the lone prairie!

"O bury me not on the lone prairie,
In a narrow grave six foot by three,
Where the buffalo paws o'er a prairie sea;
O bury me not on the lone prairie!

"O bury me not on the lone prairie,
Where the wild coyotes will howl o'er me,
Where the rattlesnakes hiss and the crow flies free;
O bury me not on the lone prairie!

"O bury me not," and his voice faltered there,
But we took no heed of his dying prayer;
In a narrow grave just six by three
We buried him there on the lone prairie.

UNKNOWN

Bury Me Out on the Prairie

Now, I've got no use for the women,
A true one may seldom be found.
They use a man for his money;
When it's gone they turn him down.

They're all alike at the bottom;
Selfish and grasping for all,
They'll stay with a man while he's winning,
And laugh in his face at his fall.

My pal was an honest puncher,
Honest and upright and true,
But he turned to a hard-shooting gunman,
On account of a girl named Lou.
He fell in with evil companions,
The kind that are better off dead;
When a gambler insulted her picture,
He filled him full of lead.

All through the long night they trailed him,
Through mesquite and thick chaparral,
And I couldn't help think of that woman,
As I saw him pitch and fall.
If she'd been the pal that she should have,
He might have been raising a son,
Instead of out there on the prairie,
To die by a ranger's gun.

Death's sharp sting did not trouble,
His chances for life were too slim;
But where they are putting his body
Was all that worried him.
He lifted his head on his elbow;
The blood from his wounds flowed red;
He gazed at his pals grouped about him,
As he whispered to them and said:

"Oh, bury me out on the prairie,
Where the coyotes may howl o'er my grave.
Bury me out on the prairie,
But from them my bones please save.
Wrap me up in my blankets
And bury me deep in the ground,
Cover me over with boulders,
Of granite gray and round."

So we buried him out on the prairie,
Where the coyotes can howl o'er his grave,
And his soul is now a-resting,
From the unkind cut she gave;
And many another young puncher,
As he rides past that pile of stone,
Recalls some similar woman,
And thinks of his mouldering bones.

UNKNOWN

Dakota Land

We've reached the land of desert sweet,
Where nothing grows for man to eat.
The wind it blows with feverish heat
Across the plains so hard to beat.

O Dakota land, sweet Dakota land,
As on thy fiery soil I stand
I look across the plains
And wonder why it never rains,
Till Gabriel blows his trumpet sound
And says the rain's just gone around.

We have no wheat, we have no oats,
We have no corn to feed our shoats;
Our chickens are so very poor
They beg for crumbs outside the door.

Our horses are of broncho race;
Starvation stares them in the face.
We do not live, we only stay;
We are too poor to get away.

UNKNOWN

The Dreary Black Hills

Now friends if you'll listen to a horrible tale,
It's getting quite dreary and it's getting quite stale,
I gave up my trade selling Ayers' Patent Pills
To go and hunt gold in the dreary Black Hills.

Stay away, I say, stay away if you can
Far from that city they call Cheyenne,
Where the blue waters roll and Comanche Bill
Will take off your scalp, boys, in those dreary Black
    Hills.

Now, friends, if you'll listen to a story untold
Don't go to the Black Hills a-digging for gold;
For the railroad speculators their pockets will fill,
While taking you a round trip to the dreary Black Hills.

I went to the Black Hills, no gold could I find.
I thought of the free land I'd left far behind;
Through rain, snow, and hail, boys, froze up to the gills,
They called me the orphan of the dreary Black Hills.

The roundhouse at Cheyenne is filled every night
With loafers and beggars of every kind of sight;
On their backs there's no clothes, boys, in their pockets
    no bills.
And they'll take off your scalp in those dreary Black
    Hills.

UNKNOWN

For Sale

One hay-wire sawmill, nice new location,
Ten-mile haul to the shipping station.
Half-mile of plank road, rest of it mud,
Six bridges all condemned, but otherwise good.
Timber—yellow pine, very few knots,
Awfully sound between rotten spots.
Fire box, boiler, flues leak some,
Injector patched with chewin' gum.
Darn good whistle and carriage track,
Nine feet left of old smoke stack,
Belt's a little ragged, rats ate the laces,
Head-saw is cracked in a couple of places.
The engine knocks and is loose on its base,
And the fly wheel's broke in just one place.
There's a pile of side lumber and a few cull ties,
And they've been attached by some creditor guys.
There's a mortgage on the land
That's now past due,
And I still owe for the machinery, too.
But if you want to get rich,
Here's the place to begin,
For it's a darn good layout
For the shape it's in.

UNKNOWN

Home on the Range

Oh, give me a home where the buffalo roam,
Where the deer and the antelope play,
Where seldom is heard a discouraging word
And the skies are not cloudy all day.

CHORUS:
Home, home on the range,
Where the deer and the antelope play;
Where seldom is heard a discouraging word
And the skies are not cloudy all day.

Where the air is so pure, the zephyrs so free,
The breezes so balmy and light,
That I would not exchange my home on the range
For all of the cities so bright.
CHORUS

The red man was pressed from his part of the West,
He's likely no more to return
To the banks of Red River where seldom if ever
Their flickering camp-fires burn.
CHORUS

How often at night when the heavens are bright
With the light from the glittering stars,

Have I stood here amazed and asked as I gazed
If their glory exceeds that of ours.
    CHORUS

Oh, I love these wild flowers in this dear land of ours,
The curlew I love to hear scream,
And I love the white rocks and the antelope flocks
That graze on the mountain-tops green.
    CHORUS

Oh, give me a land where the bright diamond sand
Flows leisurely down the stream;
Where the graceful white swan goes gliding along
Like a maid in a heavenly dream.
    CHORUS

Then I would not exchange my home on the range,
Where the deer and the antelope play;
Where seldom is heard a discouraging word
And the skies are not cloudy all day.
    CHORUS

UNKNOWN; JOHN A. LOMAX COLLECTION

An Idaho Cowboy Dance

Git yo' little sage hens ready, trot 'em out upon the floor;
Line up there, you cusses; steady, lively now, one couple more.
Shorty, shed that old sombrero; Bronco, douse that cigarette;
Stop that cussin', Casimero, 'fore the ladies. Now all set!

S'lute your ladies all together, ladies opposite the same;
Hit the lumber with your leathers, balance all an' swing your dame.
Bunch the heifers to the middle, circle stags and do-se-do;
Pay attention to the fiddle, swing her round and off you go!

First four forward, back to your places; second follow, shuffle back;
Now you've got it down to cases, swing 'em till your trotters crack.

Gents all right, a-heel-and-toeing. Swing 'em, kiss 'em if you kin;
On to next and keep a-goin' till you hit your pards again!

Gents to center, ladies round 'em; form a circle, balance all.
Whirl your gals to where you found 'em, promenade around the hall.
Balance to your pards and trot 'em round the circle double quick,
Grab and kiss 'em while you've got 'em, hold 'em to it if they kick!

Ladies, left hand to your sonnies, alamain, grand right and left;
Balance all and swing your honeys, pick 'em up and feel their heft.
Promenade like skeery cattle, balance all and swing your sweets;
Shake yer spurs and make 'em rattle. Kino! Promenade to seats!

UNKNOWN

The Little Old Sod Shanty on the Claim

I am looking rather seedy now,
While holding down my claim,
And my victuals are not always served the best;
And the mice play slyly round me,
As I nestle down to sleep
In my little old sod shanty in the West.

The hinges are of leather, and the windows have
no glass
While the board roof lets the howling blizzard in,
And I hear the hungry coyote
As he sneaks up through the grass
Around the little old sod shanty on my claim.

Yet I rather like the novelty of living in this way,
Though my bill of fare is always rather tame,
But I'm as happy as a clam
On this land of Uncle Sam's,
In my little old sod shanty on my claim.

But when I left my Eastern home, a bachelor so gay,
To try to win my way to wealth and fame,
I little thought that I'd come down to burning twisted
    hay
In my little old sod shanty on my claim.

UNKNOWN

My Little Buckaroo

Close your sleepy eyes,
  My little buckaroo,
While the light of western skies
  Is shining down on you.
Don't you know it's time for bed?
  Another day is through.
So go to sleep,
  My little buckaroo.

Don't you realize,
  My little buckaroo,
It was from a little acorn
  That the oak tree grew?
And remember that your dad
  Was once a kid like you,
So go to sleep,
  My little buckaroo, hmm, humm.

Soon you're gonna ride the range
  Like grown-up cowboys do,
Now it's time that you
  Were roundin' up a dream or two.
So go to sleep,
  My little buckaroo.

UNKNOWN

Pete Orman

I'll tell all you skinners
    From John Day to Bend
That the road south o' Shaniko
    Ain't got no end;
It's rut-holes and boulders,
    It's alkali dust,
But the jerkliners gotta make
    Maupin or bust.

They rolled out Pete Orman
    A quarter past three
He never had time
    To get over the spree
That he'd started at noon
    Only two days before;
When the call-boy come 'round,
    Old Pete was right sore.

"Now what in the hell
    Are they fixin' for me?"
He wanted to know,
    "Get out, let me be;
Last night my poor side-kick
    Was throwed in the can,
Today we ride jerk-line
    For no God-damn man!"

They rolled out Pete Orman
    And bailed out McBee,
They set a stiff price
    With oats and grub free;
The boys had to take it,
    The contract was made,
They watered, fed, harnessed,
    And then hit the grade.

The sun was just risin',
   The weather was fine,
They figured clear sailin'
   To the Cow Canyon line;
But while they was startin'
   Up Shaniko Hill,
Orm tickled Old Tommy
   With a porcupine quill.

"Put in the oats
   And shovel in the hay,
We're goin' to make it through
   If we can find a way;
We ain't quite as fast
   As the Oregon Trunk,
But we'll pull 'em into Bend
   If we are both drunk."

UNKNOWN

Pike's Peak

I'm looking at your lofty head
   Away up in the air.
Eight thousand feet above the plain
   Where grows the prickly-pear.
A great big thing with ice on,
   You seem to be up there.

Away above the timber-line
   You lift your frosty head,
Where lightnings are engendered;
   And thunderstorms are bred;
But you'd be a bigger tract of land
   If you were thin out-spread.

UNKNOWN

Prairie Lullaby

Shadows slowly creeping
   Down the prairie trail,
Everything is sleeping,
   All but the nightingale.
Moon will soon be climbing
   In the purple sky,
Night winds are a-humming
   This tender lullabye.

Cares of the day have fled,
   My little sleepy head,
The stars are in the sky,
   Time that your prayers were said.
My little sleepy head,
   To a prairie lullabye.

Saddle up your pony,
   The sandman's here
To guide you down
   The trail of dreams.
Tumble in bed, my baby,
   My little sleepy head,
To a prairie lullabye.

UNKNOWN

Ranch at Twilight

The soothing sigh of the night wind, the whine of a coyote's call,
The lonesome bawl of a maverick, a hush as the shadows fall.

A gleam of light from the ranch house, the smell of food from
   the door,

The laughter of men well contented, the clink of their spurs on
    the floor.

The cool, sweet smell of the prairie, the twang of a cowboy's guitar,
The deep, gleaming blue of the heavens with its brand of a
    silver star.

Saddles hung over the gate-posts, dusty boots lining the wall,
Rest for the hard-riding waddies, peace and contentment for all!

UNKNOWN

Red River Valley

From this valley they say you are going,
I shall miss your sweet face and your smile;
Because you are weary and tired,
 You are changing your range for a while.
I've been thinking a long time, my darling,
Of the sweet words you never would say;
Now, alas, must my fond hopes all vanish?
For they say you are going away.

REFRAIN:
Then come sit here awhile e'er you leave us,
Do not hasten to bid us adieu,
Just remember the Red River Valley
And the cowboy who loves you so true.

I have promised you, darling, that never
Will words from my lips cause you pain;
And my life it will be yours forever,
If you only will love me again.
Must the past with its joys all be blighted
By the future of sorrow and pain?

Must the vows that were spoken be slighted?
Don't you think you could love me again?
REFRAIN

There never could be such a longing
In the heart of a poor cowboy's breast,
As dwells in the heart you are breaking,
As I wait in my home in the West.
Do you think of the valley you're leaving?
Oh, how lonely and dreary it'll be!
Do you think of the kind hearts you're hurting,
And the pain you are causing to me?
REFRAIN

UNKNOWN

Starving to Death on a Government Claim

Frank Baker's my name, and a bachelor I am.
I'm keeping old batch on an elegant plan,
You'll find me out west in the county of Lane,
A-starving to death on a government claim.

My house is constructed of natural soil,
The walls are erected according to Hoyle,
The roof has no pitch, but is level and plain,
And I never get wet till it happens to rain.

Hurrah for Lane county, the land of the free,
The home of the grasshopper, bed-bug, and flea,
I'll holler its praises, and sing of its fame,
While starving to death on a government claim.

How happy I am as I crawl into bed,
The rattlesnakes rattling a tune at my head,
While the gay little centipede, so void of all fear,
Crawls over my neck, and into my ear;

And the gay little bed-bug so cheerful and bright,
He keeps me a-going two-thirds of the night.

My clothes are all ragged, my language is rough,
My bread is case-hardened, both solid and tough,
The dough it is scattered all over the room,
And the floor would get scared at the sight of a broom.

The dishes are scattered all over the bed,
All covered with sorghum, and government bread,
Still I have a good time, and I live at my ease,
On common sop sorghum, an' bacon an' cheese.

How happy I am on my government claim,
I've nothing to lose, I've nothing to gain,
I've nothing to eat and I've nothing to wear,
And nothing from nothing is honest and fair.

Oh, here I am safe, so here I will stay,
My money's all gone, and I can't get away,
There's nothing to make a man hard and profane,
Like starving to death on a government claim.

Now come on to Lane county, there's room for you all,
Where the wind never ceases, and the rains never fall,
Come join in our chorus to sing for its fame,
You sinners that're stuck on your government claim.

Now hurrah for Lane county, where the blizzards arise,
The wind never ceases, and the moon never rise,
Where the sun never sets, but it always remains,
Till it burns us all out on our government claims.

Now don't get discouraged, you poor hungry men.
You're all just as free as the pig in the pen,
Just stick to your homestead, and battle the fleas,
And look to your Maker to send you a breeze.

Hurrah for Lane county, the land of the West,
Where the farmers and laborers are ever at rest;

There's nothing to do but to stick and remain,
And starve like a dog on a government claim.

Now, all you poor sinners, I hope you will stay,
And chew the hard rag till you're toothless and gray,
But as for myself, I'll no longer remain,
To starve like a dog on a government claim.

Farewell to Lane county, farewell to the West,
I'll travel back east to the girl I love best,
I'll stop at Missouri and get me a wife,
Then live on corn dodgers, the rest of my life.

UNKNOWN

Way Out in Idaho

Come all you jolly railroad men, and I'll sing you if I can
Of the trials and tribulations of a godless railroad man,
Who started out from Denver his fortunes to make grow
And struck the Oregon Short Line way out in Idaho.

CHORUS:
Way out in Idaho, way out in Idaho,
A-working on the narrow-gauge, way out in Idaho.

I was roaming around in Denver one luckless rainy day
When Kilpatrick's man-catcher stepped up to me and did say,
"I'll lay you down five dollars as quickly as I can
And you'll hurry up and catch the train, she's starting for Cheyenne."
CHORUS

He laid me down five dollars, like many another man,
And I started for the depot—was happy as a clam.
When I got to Pocatello, my troubles began to grow,
A-wading through the sagebrush in frost and rain and snow.
CHORUS

When I got to American Falls, it was there I met Fat Jack.
They said he kept a hotel in a dirty canvas shack,
Said he, "You are a stranger and perhaps your funds are low,
Well, yonder stands my hotel tent, the best in Idaho."
    CHORUS

I followed my conductor into his hotel tent,
And for one square and hearty meal I paid him my last cent.
Jack's a jolly fellow, and you'll always find him so,
A-working on the narrow-gauge way out in Idaho.
    CHORUS

They put me to work next morning with a cranky cuss called Bill,
And they give me a ten-pound hammer to strike upon a drill.
They said if I didn't like it I could take my shirt and go,
And they'd keep my blankets for my board way out in Idaho.
    CHORUS

Oh it filled my heart with pity as I walked along the track
To see so many old bummers with their turkeys on their backs.
They said the work was heavy and the grub they couldn't go,
Around Kilpatrick's dirty tables way out in Idaho.
    CHORUS

But now I'm well and happy, down in the harvest camp,
And I'll—there I will continue till I make a few more stamps.
I'll go down to New Mexico and I'll marry the girl I know,
And I'll buy me a horse and buggy and go back to Idaho.
    CHORUS

UNKNOWN

IX

Poems of the People

Caller of the Buffalo

Whenever the summer-singed plains,
Past my car window
Heave and fall like the flanks of trail-weary cattle,
When the round-backed hills go shouldering down
To drink of western rivers,
And dust, like ceremonial smoke,
Goes up from the long-dried wallows,
Then I remember the Caller of Buffalo.

Then I think I see him,
Head feathers slant in the wind,
Shaking his medicine robe.
From the buttes of Republican River,
At Pawnee bluffs
Offering sacred smoke to the Great White Buffalo.
Then at dawn, between jiggling curtains, I wake
To the star-keen note of his deer-shin whistle.

O Caller of Buffalo!
Hunt no more on the ancient traces
Pale and emptied of grong as a cast snake-skin;
Come into my mind and hunt the herding thoughts
The White Buffalo
Of the much desired places.
Come with your medicine making,
O Caller of Buffalo!

MARY AUSTIN

The Heart's Friend

(Shoshone Love Song)

Fair is the white star of twilight,
And the sky clearer
At the day's end;
But she is fairer, and she is dearer,
She, my heart's friend!

Fair is the white star of twilight,
And the moon roving
To the sky's end;
But she is fairer, better worth loving,
She, my heart's friend.

MARY AUSTIN

Lament of a Man for His Son

Son, my son!
I will go up to the mountain
And there I will light a fire
To the feet of my son's spirit,
And there will I lament him;
Saying,
O my son,
What is my life to me, now you are departed!

Son, my son,
In the deep earth
We softly laid thee in a chief's robe,
In a warrior's gear.
Surely there,
In the spirit land
Thy deeds attend thee!

Surely,
The corn comes to the ear again!

But I here,
I am the stalk that the seed-gatherers
Descrying empty, afar, left standing.
Son, my son!
What is my life to me, now you are departed!

MARY AUSTIN

Neither Spirit nor Bird

(*Shoshone Love Song*)

Neither spirit nor bird;
That was my flute you heard
Last night by the River.
When you came with your wicker jar
Where the river drags the willows,
That was my flute you heard,
Wacoba, Wacoba,
Calling, Come to the willows!

Neither the wind nor a bird
Rustled the lupin blooms,
That was my blood you heard
Answer your garment's hem
Whispering through the grasses;
That was my blood you heard
By the wild rose under the willows.

That was no beast that stirred,
That was my heart you heard
Pacing to and fro
In the ambush of my desire,

To the music my flute let fall.
Wacoba, Wacoba,
That was my heart you heard
Leaping under the willows.

MARY AUSTIN

Prayer to the Mountain Spirit

(From the Navajo)

Lord of the Mountain,
Reared within the Mountain,
Young Man, Chieftain,
Hear a young man's prayer!
Hear a prayer for cleanness.
Keeper of the strong rain,
Drumming on the mountain;
Lord of the small rain
That restores the earth in newness;
Keeper of the clean rain,
Hear a prayer for wholeness.

Young Man, Chieftain,
Hear a prayer for fleetness.
Keeper of the deer's way,
Reared among the eagles,
Clear my feet of slothness.
Keeper of the paths of men,
Hear a prayer for straightness.

Hear a prayer for courage.
Lord of the thin peaks,
Reared amid the thunders;
Keeper of the headlands
Holding up the harvest,
Keeper of the strong rocks
Hear a prayer for staunchness.

Young Man, Chieftain,
Spirit of the Mountain!

MARY AUSTIN

Song of a Passionate Lover

(From the Yokut)

Come not near my songs,
You who are not my lover,
Lest from out that ambush
Leaps my heart upon you!

When my songs are glowing
As an almond thicket
With the bloom upon it,
Lies my heart in ambush
All amid my singing;
Come not near my songs,
You who are not my lover!

Do not hear my songs,
You who are not my lover,
Over-sweet the heart is
Where my love has bruised it,
Breathe you not that fragrance,
You who are not my lover!
Do not stoop above my heart
With its languor on you,
Lest I should not know you
From my own belovèd,
Lest from out my singing
Leaps my heart upon you!

MARY AUSTIN

Song of a Woman Abandoned by the Tribe Because She Is Too Old to Keep Up With Their Migration

(Southern Shoshone)

Alas, that I should die,
That I should die now,
I who know so much!

It will miss me,
The twirling fire stick;
The fire coal between the hearth stones,
It will miss me.

The Medicine songs,
The songs of magic healing;
The medicine herbs by the water borders,
They will miss me;
The basket willow,
It will miss me;
All the wisdom of women,
It will miss me.

Alas, that I should die,
Who know so much.

MARY AUSTIN

Warrior's Song

Weep not for me, Loved Woman,
Should I die;
But for yourself be weeping!

Weep not for warriors who go
Gladly to battle.
Theirs to revenge
Fallen and slain of our people;
Theirs to lay low
All our foes like them,
Death to make, singing.

Weep not for warriors,
But weep for women!
Oh, weep for all women!

Theirs to be pitied
Most of all creatures,
Whose men return not!
How shall their hearts be stayed
When we are fallen?

Weep not for me, Loved Woman,
For yourself alone be weeping!

MARY AUSTIN

Hopi Lament

Aa Mihoya (*Little Buried One*)

Why does it tear so
At my heart?
Why did he fare so
Far apart
From his mother?
Little buried one!

On the side of a hill
Where the soft rains in April

Patter the stones that fill
The crypt that we made.
The God-of-warm-sunshine
Helped us lay him there—
And then go away.
Dull are my wings now
And quiet each day
When I hear by my door
Some children at play
And I go to look for him—
But he is not with them,
Little buried one!
Aa mihoya!

CHARLES BEGHTOL

Hopi Prayer

Rain, lean down
And touch my lands,
For I have many mouths to feed.
Sunshine, give me both
Your hands
To lift the flowers I need.

Wind, blow gently
From the west,
My harvest time is near.
Spirit, Thou hast
Done thy best
To allay my fear.

CHARLES BEGHTOL

A Dance for Rain

You may never see rain, unless you see
A dance for rain at Cochiti,
Never hear thunder in the air
Unless you hear the thunder there,
Nor know the lightning in the sky
If there's no pole to know it by. . . .
They dipped the pole just as I came,
And I can never be the same
Since those feathers gave my brow
The touch of wind that's on it now,
Bringing over the arid lands
Butterfly gestures from Hopi hands
And holding me, till earth shall fail,
As close to earth as a fox's tail.
   I saw them, naked, dance in line
Before the candles of a leafy shrine;
Before a saint in a Christian dress
I saw them dance their holiness,
I saw them reminding him all day long
That death is weak and life is strong
And urging the fertile earth to yield
Seed from the loin and seed from the field.
A feather in the hair and a shell at the throat
Were lifting and falling with every note
Of the chorus-voices and the drum,
Calling for the rain to come.
A fox on the back, and shaken on the thigh
Rain-cloth woven from the sky,
And under the knee a turtle-rattle
Clacking with the toes of sheep and cattle—
These were the men, their bodies painted
Earthen, with a white rain slanted;
These were the men, a windy line,
Their elbows green with a growth of pine.
And in among them, close and slow,
Women moved the way things grow,
With a mesa-tablet on the head

And a little grassy creeping tread
And with sprays of pine moved back and forth,
While the dance of the men blew from the north,
Blew from the south and east and west
Over the field and over the breast.
And the heart was beating in the drum,
Beating for the rain to come.

   Dead men out of earlier lives,
Leaving their graves, leaving their wives,
Were partly flesh and partly clay,
And their heads were corn that was dry and gray.
They were ghosts of men and once again
They were dancing like a ghost of rain;
For the spirits of men, the more they eat,
Have happier hands and lighter feet,
And the better the dance the better they know
How to make corn and children grow.

   And so in Cochiti that day
They slowly put the sun away
And they made a cloud and they made it break
And they made it rain for the children's sake.
And they never stopped the song or the drum
Pounding for the rain to come.

   The rain made many suns to shine,
Golden bodies in a line
With leaping feather and swaying pine.
And the brighter the bodies, the brighter the rain
As thunder heaped it on the plain.
Arroyos had been empty, dry,
But now were running with the sky;
And the dancers' feet were in a lake,
Dancing for the people's sake.
And the hands of a ghost had made a cup
For scooping handfuls of water up;
And he poured it into a ghostly throat,
And he leaped and waved with every note
Of the dancers' feet and the songs of the drum
That had called the rain and made it come.

   For this was not a god of wood,
This was a god whose touch was good,

You could lie down in him and roll
And wet your body and wet your soul;
For this was not a god in a book,
This was a god that you tasted and took
Into a cup that you made with your hands,
Into your children and into your lands—
This was a god that you could see,
Rain, rain in Cochiti!

WITTER BYNNER

The Blanket Injun

Jest a worthless blanket Injun,
    With the turquoise in his ears—
Jest a-loafin' round the trader's,
    'Stead of herdin' sheep or steers;
Not a thing to cause him worry,
    Not a care to give him pain—
Just a worthless blanket Injun
    With no thought for earthly gain.

Jest a worthless blanket Injun,
    Blinkin' lazy in the sun;
Smokin' cigarettes past number,
    While the precious hours run;
Never seen a railroad engine,
    Never wants to, it would seem—
Rather roll up in his blanket
    And jest watch the blaze and dream.

Jest a worthless blanket Injun—
    Scorns a bid for honest work;
Rather jog off on his pony—
    He's the reservation shirk;

Jest a worthless blanket Injun;
 Never does a tap—and won't—
But I envy him, in secret,
 Dash me, partner, if I don't!

ARTHUR CHAPMAN

Little Papoose

Your eyes are as black as twin pools at night,
 Little papoose;
And down in their depths I can see Love's light,
 Little papoose;
Let the winter wind round the teepee whine:
My song shall you hear—not the creak of the pine,
 Little papoose of mine!

I love you—how much I cannot tell,
 Little papoose;
I hope you shall love me but half as well,
 Little papoose;
Few are our people and weak have they grown:
We must live, we must love, we must fight alone,
 Little papoose, my own!

In the days when the buffalo roamed the plain,
 Little papoose,
This heart of mine would have known no pain,
 Little papoose;
But—woe to the red when the white comes nigh!—
An alien dwells 'neath our Western sky—
 Little papoose, we die!

ARTHUR CHAPMAN

A Hopi Prayer

Rain! rain!
For the growing grain,
For the high white mesa, the pale wide plain!
To the gods that fly
The clouds in the sky
Child of the Snake Woman, run with our cry!
Rain! rain!
For the thirsting plain,
For the sad, pale melon, the squash, and the grain!
Our prayer in your breast,
Go forth to the west,
The east, south, north, with your soft skin pressed
Down hard on the sand
Of our dry, harsh land,
That the gods may see that you bear the brand
Of the woeful need
Of the plant and the seed:
For your tongue will droop and your breast will
    bleed.
Then the gods will know
That the wind should blow
The black clouds up from the far below,
And our prayer and cry,
In your breast that lie,
The gods that whirl the clouds through the sky
Will know are true,
And the rain and the dew
With a hand of fire o'er the plain will strew.
Rain! rain!
For the dying plain:
For the sad, pale melon, the squash, and the grain!

HARRISON CONRARD

Buffalo Dance

(*Chippewa*)

Strike ye our land
With curved horns!
Now with cries
Bending our bodies,
Breathe fire upon us;
Now with feet
Trampling the earth,
Let your hoofs
Thunder over us!
Strike ye our land
With curved horns!

ALICE CORBIN

Courtship

(*Chippewa*)

When I go I will give you surely
What you will wear if you go with me;
A blanket of red and a bright girdle,
Two new moccasins and a silver necklace.
When I go I will give you surely
What you will wear if you go with me!

ALICE CORBIN

The Green Corn Dance

San Ilderonso

Far in the east
The gods beat
On thunder drums. . . .

With rhythmic thud
The dancers' feet
Answer the beat
Of the thunder drums.

Eagle feather
On raven hair,
With bright tablita's
Turquoise glare.

Tasselled corn
Stands tall and fair
From rain-washed roots
Through lambent air.

Corn springs up
From the seed in the ground,
The cradled corn
By the sun is found.

Eagle feather
And turkey plume
From the wind-swept cloud
Bring rain and gloom.

Hid in the cloud
The wind brings rain,
And the water-song
To the dust-parched plain.

Far in the east
The gods retreat

As the thunder drums
Grow small and sweet.

The dancers' feet
Echo the sound
As the drums grow faint
And the rain comes down.

ALICE CORBIN

Indian Death

Out of blue nowhere came guns,
Came, horses—dogs—men
Clothed in blue steel.

Slow disintegrating fingers
Touched the trees,
Touched mountains—plains—buffaloes—
Touched men. . . .

The Indians did not know
They were dead men, walking;

Columbus did not know
He brought that time to an end.

Think deep of that world,
And remember
That world's end—
Ticked off by an accidental stop-watch,
Not now—but then. . . .

ALICE CORBIN

Listening

(*Chippewa*)

The noise of passing feet
On the prairie—
Is it men or gods
Who come out of the silence?

ALICE CORBIN

Parting

Now I go, do not weep, woman—
Woman, do not weep;
Though I go from you to die,
We shall both lie down
At the foot of the hill, and sleep.

Now I go, do not weep, woman—
Woman, do not weep;
Earth is our mother and our tent the sky.
Though I go from you to die,
We shall both lie down
At the foot of the hill, and sleep.

ALICE CORBIN

Sand Paintings

The dawn breeze
Loosens the leaves
Of the trees,
The wide sky quivers
With awakened birds.

Two blue runners
Come from the east,
One has a scarf of silver,

One flings pine-boughs
Across the sky.

Noon-day stretched
In gigantic slumber—
Red copper cliffs
Rigid in sunlight.

An old man stoops
For a forgotten faggot,
Forehead of bronze
Between white locks
Bound with a rag of scarlet.

Where one door stands open,
The female moon
Beckons to darkness
And disappears.

ALICE CORBIN

Where the Fight Was

(*Chippewa*)

In the place where the fight was
Across the river,
In the place where the fight was
Across the river:
A heavy load for a woman
To lift in her blanket,
A heavy load for a woman
To carry on her shoulder.
In the place where the fight was
Across the river,
In the place where the fight was
Across the river:

The women go wailing
To gather the wounded,
The women go wailing
To pick up the dead.

ALICE CORBIN

The Wind

(*Chippewa*)

The wind is carrying me round the sky;
The wind is carrying me round the sky.
My body is here in the valley—
The wind is carrying me round the sky.

ALICE CORBIN

Navajo Song

A-zláy, A-zláy, you who have clambered the mountains, A-zláy,
  Where is the little juniper growing up green?
  Over the line of blue mesas,
  Out of the yellow edges of dawn
Come on the curled-up toe of your moccasins, A-zláy.

A-zláy, you who have wandered the hill-trails, A-zláy,
  Where does the little fawn come down from the rim?
  Over the band of red mesas,
  The turquoise hollow of noon
Touch with the softness of white corn-tassels, A-zláy.

A-zláy, you who have followed the canyons, A-zláy,
  Where does the he-bear come at evening to drink?

Over the wall of black mesas,
  Into the velvet of night
Go, stepping soft in your star-buttoned moccasins, A-zláy.

MAYNARD DIXON

The Lost Lagoon

It is dusk on the Lost Lagoon,
And we two dreaming the dusk away,
Beneath the drift of a twilight gray—
Beneath the drowse of an ending day
And the curve of a golden moon.

It is dark on the Lost Lagoon,
And gone are the depths of haunting blue,
The grouping gulls, and the old canoe,
The singing firs, and the dusk and—you,
And gone is the golden moon.

O lure of the Lost Lagoon—
I dream tonight that my paddle blurs
The purple shade where the seaweed stirs—
I hear the call of the singing firs
In the hush of the golden moon.

PAULINE JOHNSON

The Song My Paddle Sings

West wind, blow from your prairie nest,
Blow from the mountains, blow from the
    west.
The sail is idle, the sailor too;

O! wind of the west, we wait for you.
Blow, blow!
I have wooed you so,
But never a favor you bestow.
You rock your cradle the hills between,
But scorn to notice my white lateen.

I stow the sail, unship the mast:
I wooed you long but my wooing's past;
My paddle will lull you into rest.
O! drowsy wind of the drowsy west,
Sleep, sleep,
By your mountain steep,
Or down where the prairie grasses sweep!
Now fold in slumber your laggard wings,
For soft is the song my paddle sings.

August is laughing across the sky,
Laughing while paddle, canoe and I,
Drift, drift,
Where the hills uplift
On either side of the current swift.
The river rolls in its rocky bed;
My paddle is plying its way ahead;
Dip, dip,
While the waters flip
In foam as over their breast we slip.

And oh, the river runs swifter now;
The eddies circle about my bow.
Swirl, swirl!
How the ripples curl
In many a dangerous pool awhirl!

And forward far the rapids roar,
Fretting their margin for evermore.
Dash, dash,
With a mighty crash,
They seethe, and boil, and bound, and
    splash.

Be strong, O paddle! be brave, canoe!
The reckless waves you must plunge into.
Reel, reel.
On your trembling keel,
But never a fear my craft will feel.

We've raced the rapid, we're far ahead!
The river slips through its silent bed.
Sway, sway,
As bubbles spray
And fall in tinkling tunes away.
And up on the hills against the sky,
A fir tree rocking its lullaby,
Swings, swings,
Its emerald wings,
Swelling the song that my paddle sings.

PAULINE JOHNSON

Indian Song

The fire on the hearth is the woman's fire,
Yellow and warm and pale with desire;
But the fire on the hill beneath the trees
Is red and green against men's knees.

The indoor fire is dim with tears,
Nursing women and their fears;
The campfire, flaring to a star,
Fans the wind where hunters are.

WILLARD JOHNSON

Indian Sky

The old squaw
Is one
With the old stone behind her.
Both have squatted there—
Ask mesa
Or mountain how long?
The bowl she holds—
Clay shawl of her art,
Clay ritual of her faith—
Is one
With the thought of the past,
And one with the now;
Though dim, a little old, strange.
The earth holds her
As she holds the bowl—
Ask kiva
Or shrine how much longer?
No titan,
No destroyer,
No future thought,
Can part
Earth and this woman,
Woman and bowl:
The same shawl
Wraps them around.

ALFRED KREYMBORG

Blackfoot Sin-ka-ha

Hoo-Kee hear me
Take pity on me
I am very poor
I am going whither I go.

Give me this day a spotted horse to ride on my return.
Take care of my going and take heed of my coming.
Let no mishaps delay me.
Preserve my fellow friends, that with me go.
Do not deliver us to death.

Our safety hither and thither make thou sure.
Thus, O Sun, I speak to thee,
Art thou not very powerful and good?
As thou art powerful and good, pity me.
Thou powerful one, help me to bring also a scalp of my foe, that
     my people may rejoice at my coming.

WILLIAM S. LEWIS

Flathead and Nez Perce Sin-ka-ha

Where art thou?
I see thee not,
Not before me, not behind me;
I look at all, but thou art not.
When my song is done
I go, I go to find our enemy.
Is it to find the dead?
When thou hearest that I am dead, thine eyes will flow;
They will pour down their tears.
Then thou within thy heart will say,
Thou will say it with thy mouth:
"Ah, I was not with him in death."
Thou moreover will say:
"Why did I descend by the rivers;
Why did I not sign with him?
Why did I not stand by his side?
Why was I not there to die with him?"
I hearken, what is there to sing; behind me,
"Do not go, Oh, do not go."
Hear not the voice that would stop me,

I go to the sands of the plains.
My song is my own, which I'll sing for you.
Women of my people;
When you are cutting skins,
When you take the awl and the sinew,
Intent on sewing the shoes,
Be your thought afar on those that are away.
When ye enter the forests for wood and the solitudes sing with you,
Think voices of the trees and the rocks are echoes of my song.
Let thoughts of thee make me steadfast;
Let thoughts of the women of my people
Find speech and strength in my limbs
That I may not fatigue:
Nor be weary
Nor be left behind,
In days of war.

WILLIAM S. LEWIS

The Revenge of Rain-in-the-Face

In that desolate land and lone,
Where the Big Horn and Yellowstone
   Roar down their mountain path,
By their fires the Sioux Chiefs
Muttered their woes and griefs
   And the menace of their wrath.

"Revenge!" cried Rain-in-the-Face,
"Revenge upon all the race
   Of the White Chief with yellow hair!"
And the mountains dark and high
From their crags reëchoed the cry
   Of his anger and despair.

In the meadow, spreading wide
By woodland and river-side
   The Indian village stood;
All was silent as a dream,
Save the rushing of the stream
   And the blue-jay in the wood.

In his war paint and his beads,
Like a bison among the reeds,
   In ambush the Sitting Bull
Lay with three thousand braves
Crouched in the clefts and caves,
   Savage, unmerciful!

Into the fatal snare
The White Chief with yellow hair
   And his three hundred men
Dashed headlong, sword in hand;
But of that gallant band
   Not one returned again.

The sudden darkness of death
Overwhelmed them like the breath
   And smoke of a furnace fire:
By the river's bank, and between
The rocks of the ravine,
   They lay in their bloody attire.

But the foemen fled in the night,
And Rain-in-the-Face, in his flight,
   Uplifted high in air
As a ghastly trophy, bore
The brave heart, that beat no more,
   Of the White Chief with yellow hair.

Whose was the right and the wrong?
Sing it, O funeral song,
   With a voice that is full of tears,

And say that our broken faith
Wrought all this ruin and scathe,
  In the Year of a Hundred Years.

HENRY WADSWORTH LONGFELLOW

Geronimo

Beside that tent and under guard in majesty alone he stands
As some chained eagle, broken-winged, with eyes that gleam like
    smouldering brands.
A savage face, streaked o'er with paint, and coal-black hair in
    unkempt mane,
Thin, cruel lips, set rigidly—a red Apache Tamerlane.

As restless as the desert winds, yet here he stands like carven stone,
His raven locks by breezes moved, and backward o'er his
    shoulders blown:
Silent, yet watchful as he waits, robed in his strange, barbaric guise,
While here and there go searchingly the cat-like wanderings
    of his eyes.

The eagle feather on his head is dull with many a bloody stain,
While darkly on his lowering brow forever rests the mark of Cain.
Have you but seen a tiger caged and sullen through his
    barriers glare?
Mark well his human prototype, the fierce Apache fettered there.

ERNEST MCGAFFEY

Rain Chant

Come the little clouds out of the Ice-Caves,
Bringing rain and snow.
They come because we call them;
They come because we ask them;
They come because the Spider-Woman loves
    us;
Come the little clouds out of the Northland!

Our yellow meal we throw to the sky.
It is our offering to the gods.

We have placed the images of clay,
Shaped like desert toads, by the
    water-courses,
To guide the water along the canals,
That it may flow over our fields.
Come the little clouds out of the Ice-Caves,
To bring us rain for our harvests!

LOUIS MERTINS

The Death of Crazy Horse

And now 'twas done.
Spring found the waiting fort at Robinson
A half-moon ere the Little Powder knew;
And, doubting still what Crazy Horse might do
When tempted by the herald geese a-wing
To join the green rebellion of the spring,
The whole frontier was troubled. April came,
And once again his undefeated name
Rode every wind. Ingeniously the West
Wrought verities from what the East had guessed
Of what the North knew. Eagerly deceived,

The waiting South progressively believed
The wilder story. April wore away;
Fleet couriers, arriving day by day
With but the farthing mintage of the fact,
Bought credit slowly in that no one lacked
The easy gold of marvelous surmise.
For, gazing northward where the secret skies
Were moody with a coming long deferred,
Whoever spoke of Crazy Horse, still heard
Ten thousand hoofs.

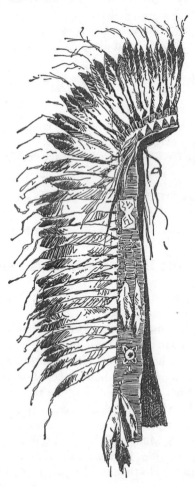

But yonder, with the crow
And kiote to applaud his pomp of woe,
The last great Sioux rode down to his defeat.
And now his people huddled in the sleet
Where Dog Creek and the Little Powder met.
With faces ever sharper for the whet
Of hunger, silent in the driving rains,
They straggled out across the blackened plains
Where Inyan Kara, mystically old,
Drew back a cloudy curtain to behold,
Serene with Time's indifference to men.
And now they tarried on the North Cheyenne
To graze their feeble ponies, for the news
Of April there had wakened in the sloughs
A glimmering of pity long denied.
Nor would their trail across the bare divide
Grow dimmer with the summer, for the bleach
Of dwindled herds—so hard it was to reach
The South Cheyenne. O sad it was to hear
How all the pent-up music of the year
Surged northward there the way it used to do!
In vain the catbird scolded at the Sioux;
The timid pewee queried them in vain;
Nor might they harken to the whooping crane
Nor heed the high geese calling them to come.
Unwelcome waifs of winter, drab and dumb,
Where ecstacy of sap and thrill of wing
Made shift to flaunt some color or to sing
The birth of joy, they toiled a weary way.
And giddy April sobered into May
Before they topped the summit looking down
Upon the valley of the soldier's town
At Robinson.

Then eerily began
Among the lean-jowled warriors in the van
The chant of peace, a supplicating wail
That spread along the clutter of the trail
Until the last bent straggler sang alone;

And camp dogs, hunger-bitten to the bone,
Accused the heavens with a doleful sound;
But, silent still, with noses to the ground,
The laden ponies toiled to cheat the crows,
And famine, like a wag, had made of those
A grisly jest.
                    So Crazy Horse came in
With twice a thousand beggars.
                                      And the din
Died out, though here and there a dog still howled,
For now the mighty one, whom Fate had fouled,
Dismounted, faced the silent double row
Of soldiers haughty with the glint and glow
Of steel and brass. A little while he stood
As though bewildered in a haunted wood
Of men and rifles all astare with eyes.
They saw a giant shrunken to the size
Of any sergeant. Now he met the glare
Of Dull Knife and his warriors waiting there
With fingers itching at the trigger-guard.
How many comrade faces, strangely hard,
Were turned upon him! Ruefully he smiled,
The doubtful supplication of a child
Caught guilty; loosed the bonnet from his head
And cast it down. "I come for peace," he said;
"Now let my people eat." And that was all.

The summer ripened. Presages of fall
Now wanted nothing but the goose's flight.
The goldenrods had made their torches bright
Against the ghostly imminence of frost.
And one, long brooding on a birthright lost,
Remembered and remembered. O the time
When all the prairie world was white with rime
Of mornings, and the lodge smoke towered
    straight
To meet the sunlight, coming over late
For happy hunting! O the days, the days
When winds kept silence in the far blue haze
To hear the deep-grassed valleys running full

With fatling cows, and thunders of the bull
Across the hills! Nights given to the feast
When big round moons came smiling up the east
To listen to the drums, the dancing feet,
The voices of the women, high and sweet
Above the men's!

               And Crazy Horse was sad.
There wasn't any food the white man had
Could find his gnawing hunger and assuage.
Some saw a blood-mad panther in a cage,
And some the sulking of a foolish pride,
For there were those who watched him
    narrow-eyed
The whole day long and listened for a word,
To shuttle in the warp of what they heard
A woof of darker meaning.

              Then one day
A flying tale of battles far away
And deeds to make men wonder stirred the land:
How Nez Perce Joseph led his little band,
With Howard's eager squadrons in pursuit,
Across the mountains of the Bitter Root
To Big Hole Basin and the day-long fight;
And how his women, fleeing in the night,
Brought off the ponies and the children too.
O many a heart beat fast among the Sioux
To hear the way he fled and fought and fled
Past Bannack, down across the Beaverhead
To Henry's Lake, relentlessly pursued;
Now swallowed by the dreadful solitude
Where still the Mighty Spirit shapes the
    dream
With primal fires and prodigies of steam,
As when the fallow night was newly sown;
Now reappearing down the Yellowstone,
Undaunted yet and ever making less
That thousand miles of alien wilderness
Between a people's freedom and their need!

O there was virtue in the tale to feed
The withered heart and make it big again!
Not yet, not yet the ancient breed of men
Had vanished from the aging earth! They say
There came a change on Crazy Horse the day
The Ogalala village buzzed the news.
So much to win and only life to lose;
The bison making southward with the fall,
And Joseph fighting up the way to Gall
And Sitting Bull!

                        Who knows the dream he had?
Much talk there was of how his heart was bad
And any day some meditated deed
Might start an irresistible stampede
Among the Sioux—a human prairie-fire!
So back and forth along the talking wire
Fear chattered. Yonder, far away as morn,
The mighty heard—and heard the Little Horn
Still roaring with the wind of Custer's doom.
And there were troopers moving in the gloom
Of midnight to the chaining of the beast;
But when the white light broke along the east,
There wasn't any Ogalala town
And Crazy Horse had vanished!

                            Up and down
The dusty autumn panic horsemen spurred
Till all the border shuddered at the word
Of how that terror threatened every trail.
They found him in the camp of Spotted Tail,
A lonely figure with a face of care.
"I am afraid of what might happen there"
He said. "So many listen what I say
And look and look. I will not run away.
I want my people here. You have my guns."

But half a world away the mighty ones
Had spoken words like bullets in the dark
That wreak the rage of blindness on a mark
They can not know.

            Then spoke the one who led
The soldiers: "Not a hair upon your head
Shall suffer any harm if you will go
To Robinson for just a day or so
And have a parley with the soldier chief."
He spoke believing and he won belief,
So Crazy Horse went riding down the west;
And neither he nor any trooper guessed
What doom now made a rutted wagon road
The highway to a happier abode
Where all the dead are splendidly alive
And summer lingers and the bison thrive
Forever.

        If the better hope be true,
There was a gate of glory yawning through
The sunset when the little cavalcade
Approached the fort.

              The populous parade,
The straining hush that somehow wasn't peace,
The bristling troops, the Indian police
Drawn up as for a battle! What was wrong?
What made them hustle Crazy Horse along
Among the gleaming bayonets and eyes?
There swept a look of quizzical surprise
Across his face. He struggled with the guard.
Their grips were steel; their eyes were cold and
    hard—
Like bayonets.

           There was a door flung wide.
The soldier chief would talk with him inside
And all be well at last!

             The stifling, dim
Interior poured terror over him.
He blinked about—and saw the iron bars.

O nevermore to neighbor with the stars
Or know the simple goodness of the sun!

Did some swift vision of a doom begun
Reveal the monstrous purpose of a lie—
The desert island and the alien sky,
The long and lonely ebbing of a life?
The glimmer of a whipped-out butcher knife
Dismayed the shrinking squad, and once again
Men saw a face that many better men
Had died to see! Brown arms that once were
    kind,
A comrade's arms, whipped round him from
    behind,
Went crimson with a gash and dropped aside.
"Don't touch me! I am Crazy Horse!" he
    cried,
And, leaping doorward, charged upon the world
To meet the end. A frightened soldier hurled
His weight behind a jabbing belly-thrust,
And Crazy Horse plunged headlong in the dust,
A writhing heap. The momentary din
Of struggle ceased. The people, closing in,
Went ominously silent for a space,
And one could hear men breathing round the
    place
Where lay the mighty. Now he strove to rise,
The wide blind stare of anguish in his eyes,
And someone shouted, *Kill that devil quick!*

A throaty murmur and a running click
Of gun-locks woke among the crowding Sioux,
And many a soldier whitened. Well they knew
What pent-up hate the moment might release
To drop upon the bungled farce of peace
A bloody curtain.

          One began to talk;
His tongue was drunken and his face was chalk;
But when a halfbreed shouted what he spoke
The crowd believed, so few had seen the stroke,
Nor was there any bleeding of the wound.

It seemed the chief had fallen sick and swooned;
Perhaps a little rest would make him strong!
And silently they watched him borne along,
A sagging bundle, dear and mighty yet,
Though from the sharp face, beaded with the
    sweat
Of agony, already peered the ghost.

They laid him in an office of the post,
And soldiers, forming in a hollow square,
Held back the people. Silence deepened there.
A little while it seemed the man was dead,
He lay so still. The west no longer bled;
Among the crowd the dusk began to creep.
Then suddenly, as startled out of sleep
By some old dream-remembered night alarm,
He strove to shout, half rose upon an arm
And glared about him in the lamp-lit place.

The flare across the ashes of his face
Went out. He spoke; and, leaning where he lay,
Men strained to gather what he strove to say,
So hard the panting labor of his words.
"I had my village and my pony herds
On Powder where the land was all my own.
I only wanted to be let alone.
I did not want to fight. The Gray Fox sent
His soldiers. We were poorer when they went;
Our babies died, for many lodges burned
And it was cold. We hoped again and turned
Our faces westward. It was just the same
Out yonder on the Rosebud. Gray Fox came.
The dust his soldiers made was high and long.
I fought him and I whipped him. Was it wrong
To drive him back? That country was my own.
I only wanted to be let alone.
I did not want to see my people die.
They say I murdered Long Hair and they lie.
His soldiers came to kill us and they died."

He choked and shivered, staring hungry-eyed
As though to make the most of little light.
Then like a child that feels the clutching
    night
And cries the wilder, deeming it in vain,
He raised a voice made lyrical with pain
And terror of a thing about to be.
"I want to see you, Father! Come to me!
I want to see you, Mother!" O'er and o'er
His cry assailed the darkness at the door;
And from the gloom beyond the hollow square
Of soldiers, quavered voices of despair:
"We can not come! They will not let us come!"

But when at length the lyric voice was dumb
And Crazy Horse was nothing but a name,
There was a little withered woman came
Behind a bent old man. Their eyes were dim.
They sat beside the boy and fondled him,
Remembering the little names he knew
Before the great dream took him and he grew
To be so mighty. And the woman pressed
A hand that men had feared against her breast
And swayed and sang a little sleepy song.
Out yonder in the village all night long
There was a sound of mourning in the dark.
And when the morning heard the meadowlark,
The last great Sioux rode silently away.
Before the pony-drag on which he lay
An old man tottered. Bowed above the bier,
A little wrinkled woman kept the rear
With not a sound and nothing in her eyes.

Who knows the crumbling summit where he lies
Alone among the badlands? Kiotes prowl
About it, and the voices of the owl
Assume the day-long sorrow of the crows,
These many grasses and these many snows.

JOHN G. NEIHARDT

Red Cloud

Sullenly a gale
That blustered rainless up the Bozeman Trail
Was bringing June again; but not the dear
Deep-bosomed mother of a hemisphere
That other regions cherish. Flat of breast,
More passionate than loving, up the West
A stern June strode, lean suckler of the lean,
Her rag-and-tatter robe of faded green
Blown dustily about her.

                    Afternoon
Now held the dazzled prairie in a swoon;
And where the Platte and Laramie unite,
The naked heavens slanted blinding light
Across the bare Fort Laramie parade.
The groping shadow-arm the flag-pole swayed
To nightward, served to emphasize the glare;
And 'mid Saharan hollows of the air
One haughty flower budded from the mast
And bloomed and withered as the gale soughed past
To languish in the swelter.

Growing loud,
When some objection wakened in the crowd,
Or dwindling to a murmur of assent,
Still on and on the stubborn parley went
Of many treaty makers gathered here.
Big talk there was at Laramie that year
Of 'sixty-six; for lo, a mighty word
The Great White Father spoke, and it was heard
From peep of morning to the sunset fires.
The southwind took it from the talking wires
And gave it to the gusty west that blew
Its meaning down the country of the Sioux
Past Inyan Kara to Missouri's tide.
The eager eastwind took and flung it wide
To where lush valleys gaze at lofty snow
All summer long. And now Arapahoe
The word was; now Dakota; now Cheyenne;
But still one word: "Let grass be green again
Upon the trails of war and hatred cease,
For many presents and the pipe of peace
Are waiting yonder at the Soldier's Town!"
And there were some who heard it with a frown
And said, remembering the White Man's guile:
"Make yet more arrows when the foemen smile."
And others, wise with many winters, said:
"Life narrows, and the better days are dead.
Make war upon the sunset! Will it stay?"
And some who counselled with a dream would say:
"Great Spirit made all peoples, White and Red,
And pitched one big blue teepee overhead
That men might live as brothers side by side.
Behold! Is not our country very wide,
With room enough for all?" And there were some
Who answered scornfully: "Not so they come;
Their medicine is strong, their hearts are bad;
A little part of what our fathers had
They give us now, tomorrow come and take.
Great Spirit also made the rattlesnake
And over him the big blue teepee set!"

So wrought the Great White Father's word;
  and yet,
Despite remembered and suspected wrong,
Because the Long Knife's medicine was strong,
There lacked not mighty chieftains who obeyed.
A thousand Ogalalas Man Afraid
And Red Cloud marshalled on the council trail;
A thousand Brulés followed Spotted Tail.
Cheyennes, Arapahoes came riding down
By hundreds; till the little Soldier Town
Was big with teepees.

                    Where the white June drowse
Beat slanting through a bower of withered
  boughs
That cast a fretwork travesty of shade,
Now sat the peace-commissioners and made
Soft words to woo the chieftains of the bands.
"They wanted but a roadway through the lands
Wherein the Rosebud, Tongue and Powder
  head,
That white men, seeking for the yellow lead
Along the Madison, might pass that way.
There ran the shortest trail by many a day
Of weary travel. This could do no harm;
Nor would there be occasion for alarm
If they should wish to set a fort or two
Up yonder—not against Cheyenne and Sioux,
But rather that the Great White Father's will
Might be a curb upon his people still
And Red Men's rights be guarded by the laws."

Adroitly phrased, with many a studied pause,
In which the half-breed spokesmen, bit by bit,
Reshaped the alien speech and scattered it,
The purpose of the council swept at last
Across the lounging crowd. And where it passed
The feathered headgear swayed and bent
  together
With muttering, as when in droughty weather

A little whirlwind sweeps the tasseled corn.
Some bull-lunged Ogalala's howl of scorn
Was hurled against the few assenting "hows"
Among the Brulés. Then the summer drowse
Came back, the vibrant silence of the heat;
For Man Afraid had gotten to his feet,
His face set hard, one straight arm rising slow
Against the Whites, as though he bent a bow
And yonder should the fleshing arrow fly.
So stood he, and the moments creeping by
Were big with expectation. Still and tense,
The council felt the wordless eloquence
Of Man Afraid; and then:

　　　　　　　　　　"I tell you no!
When Harney talked to us ten snows ago
He gave us all that country. Now you say
The White Chief lied. My heart is bad today,
Because I know too well the forkéd tongue
That makes a promise when the moon is young,
And kills it when the moon is in the dark!"

The Ogalalas roared; and like a spark
That crawls belated when the fuse is damp,
The words woke sequent thunders through
　　the camp
Where Cheyennes heard it and Arapahoes.
Then once again the chieftain's voice arose:
"Your talk is sweet today. So ever speak
The white men when they know their hands
　　are weak
That itch to steal. But once your soldiers pitch
Their teepees yonder, will the same hands itch
The less for being stronger? Go around.
I do not want you in my hunting ground!
You scare my bison, and my folk must eat.
Far sweeter than your words are, home is sweet
To us, as you; and yonder land is home.
In sheltered valleys elk and bison roam
All winter there, and in the spring are fat.

We gave the road you wanted up the Platte.
Make dust upon it then! But you have said
The shortest way to find the yellow lead
Runs yonder. Any trail is short enough
That leads your greedy people to the stuff
That makes them crazy! It is bad for you.
I, Man Afraid, have spoken. *Hetchetu!*"

How, how, how, how! A howl of fighting men
Swept out across the crowd and back again
To break about the shadow-mottled stand
Where Colonel Maynadier, with lifted hand,
Awaited silence. "As a soldier should,
He spoke straight words and few. His heart
    was good.
The Great White Father would be very sad
To know the heart of Man Afraid was bad
And how his word was called a crooked word.
It could not be that Man Afraid had heard.
The council had not said that Harney lied.
It wanted but a little road, as wide
As that a wagon makes from wheel to wheel.
The Long Knife chieftains had not come to steal
The Red Men's hunting ground."

                        The half-breeds cried
The speech abroad; but where it fell, it died.
One heard the flag a-ripple at the mast,
The bicker of the river flowing past,
The melancholy crooning of the gale.

Now 'mid the bodeful silence, Spotted Tail
Arose, and all the people leaned to hear;
For was he not a warrior and a seer
Whose deeds were mighty as his words were wise?
Some droll, shrewd spirit in his narrowed eyes
Seemed peering past the moment and afar
To where predestined things already are;
And humor lurked beneath the sober mien,
But half concealed, as though the doom foreseen

Revealed the old futility of tears.
Remembering the story of his years,
His Brulé warriors loved him standing so.
And some recalled that battle long ago
Far off beside the upper Arkansaw,
When, like the freshet of a sudden thaw,
The Utes came down; and how the Brulés,
    caught
In ambush, sang the death-song as they fought,
For many were the foes and few were they;
Yet Spotted Tail, a stripling fresh from play,
Had saved them with his daring and his wit.
How often when the dark of dawn was lit
With flaming wagon-tops, his battle-cry
Had made it somehow beautiful to die,
A whirlwind joy! And how the leaping glare
Had shown by fits the snow-fall of despair
Upon the white men's faces! Well they knew
That every brave who followed him was two,
So mighty was the magic of his name.
And none forgot the first time Harney came—
His whetted deaths that chattered in the sheath,
The long blue snake that set the ground beneath
A-smoulder with a many-footed rage.
What bleeding of the Brulés might assuage
That famished fury? Vain were cunning words
To pay the big arrears for harried herds
And desolated homes and settlers slain
And many a looted coach and wagon-train
And all that sweat of terror in the land!
Who now went forth to perish, that his band
Might still go free? Lo, yonder now he stood!
And none forgot his loving hardihood
The day he put the ghost paint on his face
And, dressed for death, went singing to the place
Where Harney's soldiers waited.

                    "Brothers, friends!"
Slow words he spoke. "The longest summer ends,
And nothing stays forever. We are old.

Can anger check the coming of the cold?
When frosts begin men think of meat and wood
And how to make the days of winter good
With what the summer leaves them of its cheer.
Two times I saw the first snow deepen here,
The last snow melt; and twice the grass was brown
When I was living at the Soldier's Town
To save my Brulés. All the while I thought
About this alien people I had fought,
Until a cloud was lifted from my eyes.
I saw how some great spirit makes them wise.
I saw a white Missouri flowing men,
And knew old times could never be again
This side of where the spirit sheds its load.
Then let us give the Powder River road,
For they will take it if we do not give.
Not all can die in battle. Some must live.
I think of those and what is best for those.
Dakotas, I have spoken."

                    Cries arose
From where his band of Brulé warriors sat—
The cries that once sent Panic up the Platte,
An eyeless runner panting through the gloom.
For though their chief had seen the creeping doom
Like some black cloud that gnaws the prairie rim,
Yet echoes of their charges under him
Had soared and sung above the words he said.
Now silence, like some music of the dead
That holds a throng of new-born spirits awed,
Possessed the brooding crowd. A lone crow cawed.
A wind fled moaning like a wildered ghost.

So clung that vatic hush upon the host
Until the Bad Face Ogalala band
Saw Red Cloud coming forward on the stand,
Serene with conscious might, a king of men.
Then all the hills were ululant again
As though a horde of foes came charging there;
For here was one who never gave despair

A moral mien, nor schooled a righteous hate
To live at peace with evil. Tall and straight
He stood and scanned the now quiescent crowd;
Then faced the white commissioners and bowed
A gracious bow—the gesture of a knight
Whose courage pays due deference to might
Before the trumpets breathe the battle's breath.
Not now he seemed that fearful lord of death,
Whose swarm of charging warriors, clad in red,
Were like a desolating thunder-head
Against an angry sunset. Many a Sioux
Recalled the time he fought alone and slew
His father's slayers, Bull Bear and his son,
While yet a fameless youth; and many a one
About the fort, remembering Grattán
And all his troopers slaughtered by a man
So bland of look and manner, wondered much.
Soft to the ear as velvet to the touch,
His speech, that lacked but little to be song,
Caressed the fringing hushes of the throng
Where many another's cry would scarce be clear.

"My brothers, when you see this prairie here,
You see my mother. Forty snows and four
Have blown and melted since the son she bore
First cried at Platte Forks yonder, weak and blind;
And whether winter-stern or summer-kind,
Her ways with me were wise. Her thousand laps
Have shielded me. Her ever-giving paps
Have suckled me and made me tall for war.
What presents shall I trade my mother for?
A string of beads? A scarlet rag or two?"

Already he was going ere they knew
That he had ceased. Among the people fled
A sound as when the frosted oaks are red
And naked thickets shiver in the flaws.
Far out among the lodges keened the squaws,
Shrill with a sorrow women understand,

As though the mother-passion of the land
Had found a human voice to claim the child.

With lifted brows the bland commission smiled,
As clever men who share a secret joke.

At length the Brulé, Swift Bear, rose and spoke,
'Twixt fear and favor poised. He seemed a man
Who, doubting both his ponies, rode the span
And used the quirt with caution. Black Horse then
Harangued the crowd a space, the words, Cheyenne,
Their sense, an echo of the White Man's plea,
Rebounding from a tense expectancy
Of many pleasing gifts.

               But all the while
These wrestled with the question, mile on mile
The White Man's answer crept along the road—
Two hundred mule-teams, leaning to the load,
And seven hundred soldiers! Middle May
Had seen their dust cloud slowly trail away
From Kearney. Rising ever with the sun
And falling when the evening had begun,
It drifted westward. When the low-swung
   moon
Was like a cradle for the baby June,
They camped at Julesburg. Yet another week
Across the South Platte's flood to Pumpkin Creek
They fought the stubborn road. Beneath the towers
Of Court House Rock, awash in starry showers,
Their fagged herd grazed. Past Chimney Rock
   they crawled;
Past where the roadway narrows, dizzy walled;
Past Mitchell Post. And now, intent to win
Ere dusk to where the Laramie comes in,
The surly teamsters swore and plied the goad.
The lurching wagons grumbled at the road,
The trace-chains clattered and the spent mules brayed,
Protesting as the cracking lashes played
On lathered withers bitten to the red;

And, glinting in the slant glare overhead,
A big dust beckoned to the Soldier's Town.

It happened now that Red Cloud, peering down
The dazzling valley road with narrowed eyes,
Beheld that picture-writing on the skies
And knitted puzzled brows to make it out.
So, weighing this and that, a lonely scout
Might read a trail by moonlight. Loudly still
The glib logicians wrangled, as they will,
The freer for the prime essential lacked—
A due allowance for the Brutal Fact,
That, by the vulgar trick of being so,
Confounds logicians.

             Lapsing in a flow
Of speech and counter-speech, a half hour passed
While Red Cloud stared and pondered. Then at last
Men saw him rise and leave his brooding place,
The flinty look of battle on his face,
A gripping claw of wrath between his brows.
Electric in the sullen summer drowse,
The silence deepened, waiting for his word;
But still he gazed, nor spoke. The people heard
The river lipping at a stony brink,
The rippling flag, then suddenly the clink
Of bridle-bits, the tinkling sound of spurs.
The chieftains and the white commissioners
Pressed forward with a buzzing of surprise.
The people turned.

             Atop a gentle rise
That cut the way from fort to ford in half,
Came Carrington a-canter with his staff,
And yonder, miles behind, the reeking air
Revealed how many others followed there
To do his will.

             Now rising to a shout,
The voice of Red Cloud towered, crushing out

The wonder-hum that ran from band to band:
"These white men here have begged our
   hunting land.
Their words are crookéd and their tongues are split;
For even while they feign to beg for it,
Their soldiers come to steal it! Let them try,
And prove how good a warrior is a lie,
And learn how Ogalalas meet a thief!
You, Spotted Tail, may be the beggar's chief—
I go to keep my mother-land from harm!"
He tapped his rifle nestled in his arm.
"From now I put my trust in this!" he said
With lowered voice; then pointing overhead,
"Great Spirit, too, will help me!"

                With a bound
He cleared the bower-railing for the ground,
And shouting "Bring the horses in," he made
His way across the turbulent parade
To where the Ogalala lodges stood.
So, driving down some hollow in a wood,
A great wind shoulders through the tangled ruck
And after it, swirled inward to the suck,
The crested timber roars.

              Then, like a bird
That fills a sudden lull, again was heard
The clink of steel as Carrington rode through
The man-walled lane that cleft the crowd in two;
And, hobbling after, mindless of the awe
That favors might, a toothless, ancient squaw
Lifted a feeble fist at him and screamed.

                    JOHN G. NEIHARDT

On the Capture and Imprisonment
of Crazy Snake, January, 1900

Down with him! chain him! bind him fast!
  Slam to the iron door and turn the key!
The one true Creek, perhaps the last
  To dare declare, "You have wronged me!"
Defiant, stoical, silent,
  Suffers imprisonment!

Such coarse black hair! such eagle eye!
  Such stately mien!—how arrow-straight!
Such will! such courage to defy
  The powerful makers of his fate!
A traitor, outlaw,—what you will,
  He is the noble red man still.

Condemn him and his kind to shame!
  I bow to him, exalt his name!

ALEXANDER L. POSEY

Buffalo Dusk

The buffaloes are gone.
And those who saw the buffaloes are gone.
Those who saw the buffaloes by thousands and how they pawed the
  prairie sod into dust with their hoofs, their great heads down
  pawing on in a great pageant of dusk,
Those who saw the buffaloes are gone.
And the buffaloes are gone.

CARL SANDBURG

Early Moon

The baby moon, a canoe, a silver papoose
canoe, sails and sails in the Indian
West.
A ring of silver foxes, a mist of silver
foxes, sit and sit around the Indian
moon.
One yellow star for a runner, and rows of
blue stars for more runners, keep a
line of watchers.
O foxes, baby moon, runners, you are the
panel of memory, fire-white writing
tonight of the Red Man's dreams.

Who squats, legs crossed, and arms folded,
   matching its look against the moon-face,
   the star-faces, of the West?
Who are the Mississippi Valley ghosts, of
   copper foreheads, riding wiry ponies
   in the night?—no bridles, love arms on
   the pony necks, riding in the night, a
   long old trail?
Why do they always come back when the
   silver foxes sit around the early moon,
   a silver papoose, in the Indian West?

CARL SANDBURG

Homesick Song

Said the very old man at the drum:
It is a homesick song—

Of lonely deserts,
Of grinding the corn,
Of a roof overhead,
The love of woman;
Of the Path to the Sunset,
Where we go to-morrow.

Ah! then I knew;
Knew why it sang in my heart.

WILLIAM HASKEL SIMPSON

Navajo

Your desert land is—
An old squaw,
Crooning old words
Beside dead embers of old thoughts.

What she has told you
Is not told to me,
Though I ask.

Your desert land is—
Coyote,
Running alongside white horses
As the wolves howl.

What it has found out, running,
Is not told to me,
Though I ask.

WILLIAM HASKEL SIMPSON

Saddle

Hastin Dot Klish, just Navajo,
Of lonesome place, Chilchinbito—

'Tis you in truth that I would be;
Good-bye to towns, their jest with me.

A horse, a blanket, a smoke or two;
Foot into stirrup and off with you. . . .

Chuska hills, and the Chinle trails;
Shiprock, waiting to spread its sails;

That lonely place, Chilchinbito—
With shooting stars, slip loose, let go!

WILLIAM HASKEL SIMPSON

Taos Drums

I have crouched in your kivas by night;
Kept step with your dancers by day;
Wrapped myself in your garments of white,
And laughed with your maidens at play.

Your songs have I sung, and your drums
Have I beaten in rhythmic tattoo;
Have eaten your feast and your crumbs—
Yet never in truth have known you.

There's a door no one may unlatch,
A silence that speaks not at all,
A music the ear fails to catch,
And a mist that shuts down like a pall.

With your flocks safe in fold, from the steeps
You watch the stars glow in the blue.
There's a hush in the deeps beyond deeps
That is kin to the hush within you!

WILLIAM HASKEL SIMPSON

Three Songs from the Haida:
Queen Charlotte's Island, B.C.

THE BEAR'S SONG

*(Whoever can sing this song is admitted
forever to the friendship of the bears)*

I have taken the woman of beauty
For my wife;
I have taken her from her friends.
I hope her kinsmen will not come
And take her away from me.
I will be kind to her.
Berries, berries I will give her from the
    hill
And roots from the ground.
I will do everything to please her.
For her I made this song and for her I
    sing it.

LOVE SONG

Beautiful is she, this woman,
As the mountain flower;
But cold, cold, is she,
Like the snowbank
Behind which it blooms.

SONG FOR FINE WEATHER

O good Sun,
Look thou down upon us:
Shine, shine on us, O Sun,
Gather up the clouds, wet, black, under thy
    arms—
That the rains may cease to fall.
Because thy friends are all here on the
    beach
Ready to go fishing—

Ready for the hunt.
Therefore look kindly on us, O Good Sun!
Give us peace within our tribe
And with all our enemies.
Again, again, we call—
Hear us, hear us, O Good Sun!

CONSTANCE LINDSAY SKINNER

Song of Basket-Weaving

O Cedar-tree, Cedar, my Mother,
I sit at thy knee
Weaving my basket of grasses,
Weaving for my harvest of berries when the Ripe Days come.
Thy fingers gently touch my hair with fragrance,
Thy mouth drips a song, for the wind has kissed it.
   (Love sings in thy mouth!)
The soil listens and answers;
I feel a stirring beneath me and hear buds opening,
The river chants thy song, and the clouds dance to it.
Tonight the stars will float upon thy singing breath,
Gleaming like slanting flocks above the sea.
All the Earth sings: and its voices are one song!

I alone am silent: I alone, a maid waiting him, the Fate,
The Stirring One, the Planter of the Harvest,
The Basket-Filler.
Cedar, Cedar-tree, Mother!
See how beautiful, how liberal, is my basket,
How tightly woven for the waters of love,
How soft for the treading of children's feet,
How strong to bear them up!
Cedar, Cedar-tree, Mother, remember me—
Ere the Sunset and the Drooping Leaf!

CONSTANCE LINDSAY SKINNER

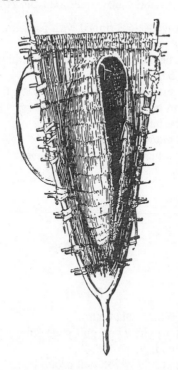

Hopi Woman

The children play with doll Katchinas
But not my child.
He lies in a secret place
Who came nine moons from the night
My squash-blossom hairdress uncoiled
Into lengths of the bearing vine.
He lived one sleep in this upper world.
The guide-string is in his still hand:
It points toward the pueblo
And my breast.
O Tiponi, Corn-Mother, I dress your bright ear grandly
That you may nurse him for me!

O pahos, prayer-sticks tipped with feathers,
Hidden, like my babe among the rocks,
Send to our fields and my eyes the holy rain!
We are not barren but abandoned.
Our sacred snakes have not brought back the clouds
And my man has gone with the runners.
Little son, he has forgotten us:
Come, lead me where you are!
They say, mothers of the dead are never alone.

LILLIAN WHITE SPENCER

Bear Song

(Haida)

Chief, chief, that I am,
Be careful how you pull your grandfather
   around.
Be careful how you pull around your
   grandfather
As you sit beside him.
I am too much of a boy for you.
Chief, chief that I am.

Chief, chief that I am,
I am already far away.
At the cliff, coming from my passage
   through the mountains,
I hold up my head grandly.
Chief, chief that I am,

I am already far away from it.
From my blue mountain I am now far
   away.
On the Island I travel, led about proudly.
From it I am far away.
Chief, chief that I am.

Chief, chief that I am,
They say that I have green mountains.
They say that I went into the creek I own
    which stretches its length afar.
Chief, chief that I am.

Chief, chief that I am,
When the sun rises I start traveling about.
Now I am lying under a deadfall.
Chief, chief that I am.

Chief, chief that I am,
My power is all taken away,
My power is all taken away.
Chief, chief that I am,
My power is all taken away,
Chief, chief that I am.

Chief, chief, whither did my great brother
    wander proudly?
My mind shakes as I go about.
Chief, chief.

Chief, chief,
Tell me where he fell.
I do not know the place.
Chief, chief, chief.

JOHN R. SWANTON

The Golden Stallion

Out of all the wild horse bands
That crossed the great salt plain,
He alone escaped the death
That the others were glad to gain.

When the cowboys started the drive,
The horses' heads were high.
With streaming manes and waving tails
The stallions seemed to fly.

With a rumble of hoofs on the hard earth,
With arched necks and brightened eyes,
Wild horses were hitting the last trail
Into pastures beyond the skies.

One of the stallions was beautiful,
With silver mane and body of gold.
His head was held as a king's should be,
And his eyes were fierce and bold.

But as the march went on and on
Beneath the blazing sky,
The stallions' heads began to droop
And the mares began to die.

But the Golden Stallion would not quit—
His fight for life was on.
With a screaming neigh he wheeled,
And the golden horse was gone.

The half-breed Injun, Tomahawk Bill,
Raised a rifle to eagle eye;
But the drive boss shouted, "Let 'im go,
Fer in th' desert he will die."

Out across the sun-baked desert,
With heaving flanks and chest,
The stallion ran in the blazing sun
Without a stop for rest.

When next they saw the Golden Stallion,
He was king of another herd,
Still the king of the sunburnt desert—
As swift as a startled bird.

PAUL THOMPSON

Alibi

Six foot two in his moccasins,
  Stately, unbowed with age,
Eagle Bull came down the sun-parched street,
  And I questioned the old Osage.

For the drouth was sore in the country.
  "When will it rain? Can you say?"
He nodded. "Rain pretty soon," he said,
  "Hoot owl holler in day."

But the days went on and it still was dry,
  And I said to the chief, "Oho!
What about rain?" "I mistake," he said.
  "That was young owl. He don't know!"

ZOE A. TILGHMAN

How Our Forefather Got
His Wife

Our forefather once wished a wife,
A woman from another tribe.
He knew that she would not marry him
Neither for love nor bribe,
So he changed into a yellow dog
And followed her up the trail.
She patted his head, and fed him deer
And stepped upon his tail.
He followed her out into the woods
Very far away,
There he changed into a man again
And carried her off like a sack of hay.

EDA LOU WALTON

Indian Death

Land of the Horizontal Yellow,
Walking I come to you.
In my old age I come to you,
Searching for night.
Once I ran with Dawn-Boy
Down the land of Horizontal White;
He climbed the sky-road toward the West
And found his rest;
As he has done, so I do,
Land of the Horizontal Yellow,
Walking I come to you.

EDA LOU WALTON

Love Medicine

(*Blackfoot Indian Song*)

A yellow dot on her forehead,
While she lies asleep in the sun,
A black dot over her beating heart,
And my charm is done, is done.
Tonight she will slip to my tipi
With wondering, half-breathed sigh.
She will part the painted curtains,
I shall watch her with half-shut eye.
The sacred charm will bind her,
Yet she will never know why.
And then if she pleases me not
I can wash my charm away
And laugh when I see her hiding
From my mocking eyes all day.

EDA LOU WALTON

The Marriage Dance

(Blackfoot Indian Song)

I weave my blanket red,
I weave my blanket blue,
I weave my blanket all my life
Until I come to you.

I bring my blanket red,
I bring my blanket blue,
They are the story of the wife
The gray chief sold to you.

I spread my blanket red,
I spread my blanket blue,
I spread my blankets for your bed;
We belong now to you.

EDA LOU WALTON

Apache Kid

Ye traced me on the desert wide,
Ye traced me on the mountain side,
Through the forest, o'er the flood
For my trail was marked with blood—
And ye dare not venture near,
Now that I'm surrounded here—

Like a beast far from his ken
A wild thing, hunted down by men.
Some foul crime you say was done;
You are many—I but one.
A hated Indian—that is all—
So on me all blame must fall.

Here beneath the sunny sky
Now, I am prepared to die.
Beware, man-hunters, come not near;
For my life my price is dear.
Come and take me if you can—
Come and fight me, Man to Man!

NED WHITE

X

Wild Critters and Prairie Flowers

Elf Owl

Elf owl, elf owl, what do you see,
All day winking and blinking?

I see the smut-nosed badger run
And the rattlesnake coiled asleep in the sun
And the gray coyote slinking.

Elf owl, elf owl, what do you hear?

I hear the nighthawk chirring,
The horned toads scuttering past in fear,
And the rabbit squeal where the red fox is stirring.

Elf owl, elf owl, what do you do
When all of us are sleeping?

I go down to the water hole to wait
Where the frisk-tailed things come creeping,
And the little gray mice by the grass stalks climb
To the moon of the mesa, and bide my time
To mark the blind mole's furrow.
And I strike my kill,
And eat my fill,
And get me back to my burrow.

MARY AUSTIN

Grizzly Bear

If you ever, ever, ever meet a grizzly bear,
You must never, never, never ask him *where*
He is going,
Or *what* he is doing;

For if you ever, ever dare
To stop a grizzly bear,
You will never meet *another* grizzly bear.

MARY AUSTIN

Prairie-Dog Town

Old Peter Prairie-Dog
Builds him a house
In Prairie-Dog Town,
With a door that goes down
And down and down,
And hall that goes under
And under and under,
Where you can't see the lightning,
You can't hear the thunder
In Prairie-Dog Town.

Old Peter Prairie-Dog
Digs him a cellar

In Prairie-Dog Town,
With a ceiling that is arched
And a wall that is round,
And the earth he takes out he makes
   into a mound.
And the hall and the cellar
Are dark as dark,
And you can't see a spark,
Not a single spark;
And the way to them cannot be found.

Old Peter Prairie-Dog
Knows a very clever trick
Of behaving like a stick
When he hears a sudden sound,
Like an old dead stick;
And when you turn your head
He'll jump quick, quick,
And be another stick
When you look around.
It is a clever trick,
And it keeps him safe and sound
In the cellar and the halls
That are under the mound
In Prairie-Dog Town.

MARY AUSTIN

The Sandhill Crane

Whenever the days are cool and clear
The sandhill crane goes walking
Across the field by the flashing weir
Slowly, solemnly stalking.
The little frogs in the tules hear
And jump for their lives when he comes near,

The minnows scuttle away in fear,
When the sandhill crane goes walking.

The field folk know if he comes that way,
Slowly, solemnly stalking,
There is danger and death in the least delay
When the sandhill crane goes walking.
The chipmunks stop in the midst of their play,
The gophers hide in their holes away
And hush, oh, hush! the field mice say,
When the sandhill crane goes walking.

MARY AUSTIN

The White Steed of the Prairies

Mount, mount for the chase! let your lassos be strong,
And forget not sharp spur and tough buffalo thong;
For the quarry ye seek hath oft baffled, I ween,
Steeds swift as your own, backed by hunters as keen.

Fleet barb of the prairie, in vain they prepare
For thy neck, arched in beauty, the treacherous snare;
Thou wilt toss thy proud head, and with nostrils stretched wide,
Defy them again, as thou still hast defied.

Trained nags of the course, urged by rowel and rein,
Have cracked their strong thews in thy pursuit in vain;
While a bow-shot in front, without straining a limb,
The wild courser careered as 'twere pastime to him.

Ye may know him at once, though a herd be in sight,
As he moves o'er the plain like a creature of light—
His mane streaming forth from his beautiful form
Like the drift from a wave that has burst in the storm.

Not the team of the Sun, as in fable portrayed,
Through the firmament rushing in glory arrayed,
Could match in wild majesty, beauty and speed,
That tireless, magnificent, snowy-white steed.

Much gold for his guerdon, promotion and fame,
Wait the hunter who captures that fleet-footed game;
Let them bid for his freedom, unbridled, unshod,
He will roam till he dies through these pastures of God.

And ye think on his head your base halters to fling!
So ye shall—when yon Eagle has lent you his wing;
But no slave of the last that your stables contain
Can e'er force to a gallop the steed of the Plain!

His fields have no fence save the mountain and sky;
His drink the snow-capped Cordilleras supply;
'Mid the grandeur of nature sole monarch is he.
And his gallant heart swells with the pride of the free.

J. BARBER

Jackrabbits

Jackrabbits are a lanky crew—
    No flaccid fat nor blubber.
Four legs they wear, the hinder two
    Composed of wire and rubber.

When food gets scarce this western hare
    Nibs vitamins from cactus.
To dine upon a prickly pear
    Must surely take some practice!

The jack's a timid creature which
    Lies low among the grasses,

Too still to even scratch his itch
  When a hungry coyote passes.

From such an ambush out he pops
  To spook the bronc you straddle,
And by the time the bucking stops
  You're short a horse and saddle.

When Mister Jack lets in to lope
  He sure gets up and drags it.
It makes him mighty hard to rope—
  The way he zigs and zags it.

Long ears like sails upon a mast,
  A short tail on his bottom—
They say what makes him flee so fast
  Is fleas—because he's got 'em!

S. OMAR BARKER

To a Jack Rabbit

Lean, lanky son of desert sage,
Gaunt galloper of mesas,
Speed king of Satan's acreage,
Gray ghost of twilight places,

Long-legged bouncer of the plains,
Long-eared cow country racer,
Pray tell me what your legs contain
That makes you such a chaser?

You're always hungry-looking, thin,
As if with bilious liver,
And yet you're droll as Harlequin,
And far outrun the flivver.

You leap across the trail and scare
My pony with your jumping,
And when you bounce up in the air
The blue sky gets a bumping.

You'd be a cousin to the mule
But for your speedy habit;
You are the frontier's clown and fool,
Though you are called "jack rabbit."

But say, gaunt racing prairie pest,
There's one good thing about you:
Although you're useless, our old West
Would not be West without you!

S. OMAR BARKER

The Horse Thief

There he moved, cropping the grass at the purple canyon's lip.
  His mane was mixed with the moonlight that silvered his
    snow-white side,
For the moon sailed out of a cloud with the wake of a spectral ship.
  I crouched and I crawled on my belly, my lariat coil looped wide.

Dimly and dark the mesas broke on the starry sky.
  A pall covered every color of their gorgeous glory at noon.
I smelt the yucca and mesquite, and stifled my heart's quick cry,
  And wormed and crawled on my belly to where he moved against
    the moon!

Some Moorish barb was that mustang's sire. His lines were beyond
    all wonder.
  From the prick of his ears to the flow of his tail he ached in my
    throat and eyes.

Steel and velvet grace! As the prophet says, God had "clothed his
     neck with thunder."
  Oh, marvelous with the drifting cloud he drifted across the skies!

And then I was near at hand—crouched, and balanced, and cast the
     coil;
  And the moon was smothered in cloud, and the rope through my
     hands with a rip!
But somehow I gripped and clung, with the blood in my brain
     a-boil,—
  With a turn round the rugged tree-stump there on the purple
     canyon's lip.

Right into the stars he reared aloft, his red eye rolling and raging.
  He whirled and sunfished and lashed, and rocked the earth to
     thunder and flame.
He squealed like a regular devil horse. I was haggard and spent and
     aging—
  Roped clean, but almost storming clear, his fury too fierce to tame.

And I cursed myself for a tenderfoot moon-dazzled to play the part,
  But I was doubly desperate then, with the posse pulled out from
     town,
Or I'd never have tried it. I only knew I must get a mount and a
     start.
  The filly had snapped her foreleg short. I had had to shoot her
     down.

So there he struggled and strangled, and I snubbed him around the
     tree.
  Nearer, a little nearer—hoofs planted, and lolling tongue—
Till a sudden slack pitched me backward. He reared right on top of
     me.
  Mother of God—that moment! He missed me . . . and up I swung.

Somehow, gone daft completely and clawing a bunch of his mane,
  As he stumbled and tripped in the lariat, there I was—up and
     astride
And cursing for seven counties! And the mustang? *Just insane!*
  Crack-bang! went the rope; we cannoned off the tree—then—gods,
     that ride!

A rocket—that's all, a rocket! I dug with my teeth and nails.
   Why, we never hit even the high spots (though I hardly remember
      things),
But I heard a monstrous booming like a thunder of flapping sails
   When he spread—well, *call* me a liar!—when he spread those
      wings, those wings!

So white that my eyes were blinded, thick-feathered and wide
      unfurled,
   They beat the air into billows. We sailed, and the earth was gone.
Canyon and desert and mesa withered below, with the world.
   And then I knew that mustang; for I—was Bellerophon!

Yes, glad as the Greek, and mounted on a horse of the elder gods,
   With never a magic bridle or a fountain-mirror nigh!
My chaps and spurs and holster must have looked it? What's the
      odds?
   I'd a leg over lightning and thunder, careering across the sky!

And forever streaming before me, fanning my forehead cool,
   Flowed a mane of molten silver; and just before my thighs
(As I gripped his velvet-muscled ribs, while I cursed myself for a
      fool),
   The steady pulse of those pinions—their wonderful fall and rise!

The bandanna I bought in Bowie blew loose and whipped from my
      neck.
   My shirt was stuck to my shoulders and ribboning out behind.
The stars were dancing, wheeling and glancing, dipping with smirk
      and beck.
   The clouds were flowing, dusking and glowing. We rode a roaring
      wind.

We soared through the silver starlight to knock at the planets' gates.
   New shimmering constellations came whirling into our ken.
Red stars and green and golden swung out of the void that waits
   For man's great last adventure. The Signs took shape—and
      then

I knew the lines of that Centaur the moment I saw him come!
   The musical box of the heavens all round us rolled to a tune

That tinkled and chimed and trilled with silver sounds that struck you
    dumb,
  As if some archangel were grinding out the music of the moon.

Melody-drunk on the Milky Way, as we swept and soared hilarious,
  Full in our pathway, sudden he stood—the Centaur of the Stars,
Flashing from head and hoofs and breast! I knew him for Sagittarius.
  He reared, and bent and drew his bow. He crouched as a boxer
    spars.

Flung back on his haunches, weird he loomed—then leapt—and
    the dim void lightened.
  Old White Wings shied and swerved aside, and fled from the
    splendor-shod.
Through a flashing welter of worlds we charged. I knew why my horse
    was frightened.
  He *had* two faces—a dog's and a man's—that Babylonian god!

Also, he followed us real as fear. Ping! went an arrow past.
  My broncho buck-jumped, humping high. We plunged . . . I
    guess that's all!
I lay on the purple canyon's lip, when I opened my eyes at last—
  Stiff and sore and my head like a drum, but I broke no bones in the
    fall.

So you know—and now you may string me up. Such was the way you
    caught me.
  Thank you for letting me tell it straight, though you never could
    greatly care.
For I took a horse that wasn't mine! . . . But there's one the heavens
    brought me,
  And I'll hang right happy, because I know he is waiting for me
    up there.

From creamy muzzle to cannon-bone, by God, he's a peerless
    wonder!
  He is steel and velvet and furnace-fire, and death's supremest
    prize,

And never again shall be roped on earth that neck that is
    "clothed with thunder. . . ."
  String me up, Dave! Go dig my grave! *I rode him across the skies!*

WILLIAM ROSE BENÉT

Vinegaroon

Bring your shears and clip him well,
His forked claws and his whipping tail,
Cut him out of his wicked shell
And leave him as clean as a flower-bell;
For he was disposed in a diagram
More intricate than the whited clam,
More scaly than the wooly lamb
And almost as evil as I am.

WITTER BYNNER

Prairie Wolves

Up where the white bluffs fringe the plain,
When heaven's lights are on the wane;
They sing their songs as demons might
Shriek wild a chorus to the night.
Gaunt, gray brutes with dripping fangs,
And eyes a-flame with hunger pangs;
With lips curled back in snarls of hate,
They wail a curse against their fate.

ROBERT V. CARR

The Mariposa Lily

Insect or blossom? Fragile, fairy thing,
Poised upon slender tip, and quivering
    To flight! a flower of the fields of air;
    A jeweled moth; a butterfly, with rare
And tender tints upon his downy wing
    A moment resting in our happy sight;
    A flower held captive by a thread so slight
Its petal-wings of broidered gossamer
Are light as the wind, with every wind astir,
    Wafting sweet odor, faint and exquisite,
O dainty nursling of the field and sky,
    What fairer thing looks up to heaven's blue
    And drinks the noontide sun, the dawning's
        dew?
Thou wingéd bloom! thou blossom—butterfly!

INA COOLBRITH

Yucca in the Moonlight

Flowers of mist and silence
    Stay when the blown mists fade,
Between the shadowed ridges,
    In this wind-haunted glade
    Of silver, blue and jade.

White flame against the silver,
    White shadow on the blue,
Above the jade a vision
    Of bloom and wind and dew,
    The yucca stands in view.

It reaches to the distance
    That ends against a cloud

Of silver in the valley,
 Lonely, aloof and proud,
 Where footsteps seem too loud . . .

Something there is within us
 Like yucca in this sand.
At times aloof and lonely
 It takes a shadowy stand
 That shames a groping hand.

GLENN WARD DRESBACH

Massasauga

A cold, coiled line of mottled lead,
He wakes where grazing cattle tread
And lifts a fanged and spiteful head.
His touch is deadly, and his eyes
Are hot with hatred and surprise.
Death waits and watches where he lies.

His hate is turned toward everything;
He is the undisputed king
Of every path and meadow spring.
His venomed head is poised to smite
All passing feet—light
Is not swifter than his bite.

His touch is deadly, and his eyes
Are hot with hatred and surprise.
Death waits and watches where he lies.

HAMLIN GARLAND

The Passing of the Buffalo

Going, the wild things of our land.
Passing, the antelope and the buffalo.
They have gone with the sunny sweep
Of the untracked plain.
They have passed away with the untrammeled
Current of our streams.

With the falling trees they fell,
With the autumn grasses they rotted,
And their bones
Lie white on the flame-charred sod,
Mixed with the antlers of the elk.

For centuries they lay down and rose
In peace and calm content.
They were fed by the rich grass
And watered by sunny streams.
The plover called to them
Out of the shimmering air,
The hawk swooped above them,
The blackbirds sat on their backs
In the still afternoons;
In the cool mud they wallowed,
Rolling in noisy sport.

They lived through centuries of struggle—
In swarming millions—till the white man came.
The snows of winter were terrible,
The dry wind was hard to bear,
But the breath of man, the smoke
Of his gun were more fatal.

They fell by the thousands.
They melted away like smoke.
Mile by mile they retreated westward;
Year by year they moved north and south
In dust-brown clouds;

Each year they descended upon the plains
In endless floods;
Each winter they retreated to the hills
Of the south.
Their going was like the ocean current,
But each spring they stopped a little short—
They were like an ebbing tide.
They came at last to meager little bands
That never left the hills—
Crawling in somber files from canyon to canyon—
Now, they are gone!

HAMLIN GARLAND

The Vulture of the Plains

He wings a slow and watchful flight,
His neck is bare, his eyes are bright,
His plumage fits the starless night.

He sits at feast where cattle lie
Withering in ashen alkali,
And gorges till he scarce can fly.

But he is kingly on the breeze!
On rigid wing in royal ease
A soundless bark on viewless seas,
Piercing the purple storm-cloud—he makes
The sun his neighbor, and shakes
His wrinkled neck in mock dismay,
Swinging his slow contemptuous way
Above the hot red lightning's play:—

Monarch of cloudland—yet a ghoul at prey.

HAMLIN GARLAND

The Ocotillo in Bloom

A flock of scarlet birds
     Against the deep blue sky:
With every wing outspread
     And yet they do not fly:
       They flutter there
     And poise in air:

A flock of scarlet birds
     Above a world of gray:

The only lively tone
        In all the desert's sway.
                They flutter there
                And poise in air.

A flock of scarlet birds
        For spring is on the wing,
In tune with silent stretches
        And yet they do not sing.
                They flutter there
                And poise in air.

MARILLA MERRIMAR GUILD

The Dance of Gray Raccoon

Curled in his black-ringed tail
    drowsed he,
Gray Raccoon of the hollow tree;
But the North Wind called and he woke
    too soon;
Out from his hole came Gray Raccoon.

Sharp-faced, keen-eared, shrewdly wise,
Mischief bright in his dark brown eyes,
Over the frost-ridged path he crept
To the bowldered cave where the Black
    Bear slept.

Warm in his fur and his donjon keep,
Moween the Black Bear slept his sleep.
Led by the light of the wintry moon,
Into the den came Gray Raccoon.

There he came and there he saw;
Quick of eye and deft of paw

He stole the Black Bear's magic flask,
His medicine lance and his medicine mask!

Warned by the cry of the Great Horned
   Owl,
Moween awoke with a wrathful growl;
Down he came like the mad typhoon
Hard on the trail of Gray Raccoon.

Gray Raccoon shook the magic flask,
He covered his face with the medicine
   mask,
He drove to the sky the wizard lance,
He danced the North Wind's medicine
   dance.

The North Wind stormed with a trumpet
   blare,
Full in the way of the raging bear
Heaping the snow like a lake-shore dune,
Saving the hide of Gray Raccoon.

Gray Raccoon is a hardened case
With the medicine mask on his elfin face,
And his dark brown eyes have an impish
   gleam
As he washes his food in the purling stream.

And you'll know that he wakes from his
   winter sleep
When the North Wind comes with a
   rollicking sweep
And the snow wraiths whirl to the eldritch
   tune
Of the medicine dance of Gray Raccoon.

                 ARTHUR GUITERMAN

Ephraim the Grizzly

This is the tale of Ephraim,
  Ephraim the Grizzly Bear,
He of the curving talons,
  He of the silvered hair.
Lord of the snow-topped ranges,
  Lord of the vales below;
This is the tale of Ephraim
  Told in the Long Ago.

Hot was the sun of August,
  Cool was the ferny glade;
Ephraim, the monster Grizzly,
  Lay in the cedar shade.
Proud of his bulk and vastness,
  Proud that his limbs were strong,
Ephraim the big and burly
  Bragged in a rumbling song:

"Great is the might of Ephraim!
  Broad are his heavy paws,
Huge are his brawny shoulders,
  Strong are his crunching jaws!
Feared by the Wolf and Panther,
  Feared by the Race of Man,
Biggest of all is Ephraim,
  Chief of the Grizzly Clan!"

There, in the glow of summer,
  Poised on his vibrant wings,
Darted the tiny Hummer,
  Swiftest of feathered things,
Trilling in elfin laughter
  Down from the crystal sky,
"Boast of your lordship, Ephraim,
  When you have learned to fly!"

Loud on the pond the Beaver
  Smote with a slapping tail:

"Big though you be, old Ephraim,
  What does your bulk avail?
When," said the craftsman Beaver,
  "When did you dream a dream?
When did you build a wigwam?
  When did you dam a stream?"

Briskly the bright-eyed Chipmunk
  Chirped from the aspen limb:
"Big are the paws of Ephraim,
  Small are the wits of him.
Dull as a barren mountain,
  How does he spend his time?
Where has he digged a storehouse?
  When did he learn to climb?"

Perched with a green pine tassel
  Back of his coat of gray,
Chattered the bold Camp-robber,
  Chided the roving Jay:
"Swift is the stroke of Ephraim,
  Sharp are his claws—and still,
What is the good of Ephraim?
  What can he do but kill?"

Full to his height, the Grizzly,
  Rearing to make his mark,
Growled as he drove his talons
  Gashing the cedar bark,
"There is the Scar of Ephraim
  High on the living tree!
Who has the reach of Ephraim?
  Who is as big as he?"

Such is the tale of Ephraim
  Told in the tents of Men.
He that will boast of Bigness,
  What can he boast of, then?

Such is the tale of Ephraim
    Told where the Klamath glides.
They that will boast of Bigness,
    Naught can they boast besides!

ARTHUR GUITERMAN

The Prairie Dog

The Gopher remarked to the Prairie Dog,
"Though widely reputed a scary dog,
You live in a room with a Rattlesnake,
A Burrowing Owl and a Cattle Snake.
Now, Burrowing Owls are lugubrious,
And Snakes I should term insalubrious;
I wonder, by all that's get-at-able,
If truly you find them compatible."
"Not wholly," responded the Prairie Dog—
First looking behind him, the wary dog!
"My quarters are scarcely commodious,
The squatters you mention are odious,
But he that is prudent negotiates
With even unpleasant associates
Who might, at a pinch, overpower him,
Evict him, or maybe devour him;
And hence, with my wonted sagacity,
I satisfy all their rapacity
And hail those too palpable realists
As brothers and fellow idealists,
While justly they laud my sublimity
Of vision and great magnanimity.
It needs just a little hypocrisy
To make the world safe for democracy."

ARTHUR GUITERMAN

The Last Longhorn

An ancient long-horned bovine
Lay dying by the river;
There was lack of vegetation
And the cold winds made him shiver;
A cowboy sat beside him
With sadness in his face,
To see his final passing—
This last of a noble race.

The ancient eunuch struggled
And raised his shaking head,
Sayin', "I care not to linger
When all my friends are dead.
These Jerseys and these Holsteins,
They are no friends of mine;
They belong to the nobility
Who live across the brine.

"Tell the Durhams and the Herefords
When they come a-grazing round,
And see me lying stark and stiff
Upon the frozen ground,
I don't want them to bellow,
When they see that I am dead,
For I was born in Texas
Near the river that is Red.

"Tell the coyotes, when they come at night
A-hunting for their prey,
They might as well go further,
For they'll find it will not pay.
If they attempt to eat me,
They very soon will see
That my bones and hide are petrified—
They'll find no beef on me.

"I remember back in the seventies,
Full many summers past,

There was grass and water plenty,
But it was too good to last.
I little dreamed what would happen
Some twenty summers hence,
When the nester came with his wife, his kids,
His dogs, and his barbed-wire fence."

His voice sank to a murmur,
His breath was short and quick;
The cowboy tried to skin him
When he saw he couldn't kick;
He rubbed his knife upon his boot
Until he made it shine,
But he never skinned old longhorn,
Caze he couldn't cut his rine.

And the cowboy riz up sadly
And mounted his cayuse,
Saying, "The time has come when longhorns
And their cowboys are no use!"
And while gazing sadly backward
Upon the dead bovine,
His bronc' stepped in a dog-hole
And fell and broke his spine.

The cowboys and the longhorns
Who partnered in Eighty-four
Have gone to their last round-up
Over on the other shore;
They answered well their purpose,
But their glory must fade and go,
Because men say there's better things
In the modern cattle show.

R. W. HALL

Road Runner

Out of the western chaparral
    Where the raw, new highways run,
He flashes swift as a rainbow flame
    And races the morning sun.
He perks and preens with lifted crest,
    He dances, heel and toe.
He will jig and flirt in the roadway dirt—
    Then—off like a shot he'll go.

SHARLOT M. HALL

Chiquita.

Beautiful! Sir, you may say so. Thar isn't her
    match in the county.
Is thar, old gal,—Chiquita, my darling, my beauty?
Feel of that neck, sir,—thar's velvet! Whoa! Steady,
    —ah, will you, you vixen!
Whoa! I say. Jack, trot her out; let the gentleman
    look at her paces.

Morgan!—She ain't nothin' else, and I've got the
    papers to prove it.
Sired by Chippewa Chief, and twelve hundred dollars
    won't buy her.
Briggs of Tuolumne owned her. Did you know Briggs
    of Tuolumne?—
Busted hisself in White Pine, and blew out his brains
    down in 'Frisco?

Hedn't no savey—hed Briggs. Thar, Jack! that'll
    do,—quit that foolin'!

Nothin' to what she kin do, when she's got her work
    cut out before her.
Hosses is hosses, you know, and likewise, too, jockeys
    is jockeys;
And 't ain't ev'ry man as can ride as knows what a hoss
    has got in him.

Know the old ford on the Fork, that nearly got
    Flanigan's leaders?
Nasty in daylight, you bet, and a mighty rough ford in
    low water!
Well, it ain't six weeks ago that me and the Jedge and
    his nevey
Struck for that ford in the night, in the rain, and the
    water all round us;

Up to our flanks in the gulch, and Rattlesnake Creek
    just a bilin',
Not a plank left in the dam, and nary a bridge on the
    river.
I had the gray, and the Jedge had his roan, and his
    nevey, Chiquita;
And after us trundled the rocks jest loosed from the top
    of the cañon.

Lickity, lickity, switch, we came to the ford, and
    Chiquita
Buckled right down to her work, and afore I could yell
    to her rider,
Took water jest at the ford, and there was the Jedge
    and me standing,
And twelve hundred dollars of hoss-flesh afloat and a
    driftin' to thunder!

Would ye b'lieve it? that night that hoss, that ar' filly,
    Chiquita,
Walked herself into her stall, and stood there, all quiet
    and dripping:
Clean as a beaver or rat, with nary a buckle of harness,

Just as she swam the Fork,—that hoss, that ar' filly,
    Chiquita.

That's what I call a hoss! and— What did you say?
    —Oh, the nevey?
Drownded, I reckon,—leastways, he never kem back
    to deny it.
Ye see the derned fool had no seat,—ye couldn't have
    made him a rider;
And then, ye know, boys will be boys, and hosses—
    well, hosses is hosses!

BRET HARTE

Coyote

Blown out of the prairie in twilight and dew,
Half bold and half timid, yet lazy all through;
Loath ever to leave, and yet fearful to stay,
He limps in the clearing,—an outcast in gray.

A shade on the stubble, a ghost by the wall,
Now leaping, now limping, now risking a fall,
Lop-eared and large-jointed, but ever alway
A thoroughly vagabond outcast in gray.

Here, Carlo, old fellow,—he's one of your kind,—
Go, seek him, and bring him in out of the wind.
What! snarling, my Carlo! So—even dogs may
Deny their own kin in the outcast in gray.

Well, take what you will,—though it be on the sly,
Marauding, or begging,—I shall not ask why;
But will call it a dole, just to help on his way
A four-footed friar in orders of gray!

BRET HARTE

Grizzly

Coward,—of heroic size,
In whose lazy muscles lies
Strength we fear and yet despise;
Savage,—whose relentless tusks
Are content with acorn husks;
Robber,—whose exploits ne'er soared
O'er the bee's or squirrel's hoard;
Whiskered chin, and feeble nose,
Claws of steel on baby toes,—
Here, in solitude and shade,
Shambling, shuffling, plantigrade,
Be thy courses undismayed!

Here, where Nature makes thy bed,
Let thy rude, half-human tread
   Point to hidden Indian springs,
Lost in ferns and fragrant grasses,
   Hovered o'er by timid wings,
Where the wood-duck lightly passes,
Where the wild bee holds her sweets,
Epicurean retreats,
Fit for thee, and better than
Fearful spoils of dangerous man.

In thy fat-jowled deviltry
Friar Tuck shall live in thee;
Thou mayest levy tithe and dole;
   Thou shalt spread the woodland cheer
From the pilgrim taking toll;
   Match thy cunning with his fear;
Eat, and drink, and have thy fill;
Yet remain an outlaw still!

                              BRET HARTE

The Broncho That Would Not Be Broken

A little colt—broncho, loaned to the farm
To be broken in time without fury or harm,
Yet black crows flew past you, shouting alarm,
Calling "Beware," with lugubrious singing . . .
The butterflies there in the bush were romancing,
The smell of the grass caught your soul in a trance,
So why be a-fearing the spurs and the traces,
O broncho that would not be broken of dancing?

You were born with the pride of the lords great and olden
Who danced, through the ages, in corridors golden.
In all the wide farm-place the person most human,
You spoke out so plainly with squealing and capering,
With whinnying, snorting, contorting and prancing,
As you dodged your pursuers, looking askance,
With Greek-footed figures, and Parthenon paces,
O broncho that would not be broken of dancing.

The grasshoppers cheered. "Keep whirling," they said.
The insolent sparrows called from the shed,
"If men will not laugh, make them wish they were dead."
But arch were your thoughts, all malice displacing,
Though the horse-killers came, with snake-whips advancing.
You bantered and cantered away your last chance.
And they scourged you, with Hell in their speech and their
    faces,
O broncho that would not be broken of dancing.

"Nobody cares for you," rattled the crows,
As you dragged the whole reaper, next day, down the rows.
The three mules held back, yet you danced on your toes.
You pulled like a racer, and kept the mules chasing.
You tangled the harness with bright eyes side-glancing,
While the drunk driver bled you—a pole for the lance—
And the giant mules bit at you—keeping their places,
O broncho that would not be broken of dancing.

In that last afternoon your boyish heart broke.
The hot wind came down like a sledge-hammer stroke.
The blood-sucking flies to a rare feast awoke,
And they searched out your wounds, your death-warrant
    tracing.
And the merciful men, their religion enhancing,
Stopped the red reaper, to give you a chance.
Then you died on the prairie, and scorned all disgraces,
O broncho that would not be broken of dancing.

                                        VACHEL LINDSAY

The Flower-Fed Buffaloes

The flower-fed buffaloes of the spring
In the days of long ago,
Ranged where the locomotives sing

And the prairie flowers lie low:—
The tossing, blooming, perfumed grass
Is swept away by the wheat,
Wheels and wheels and wheels spin by
In the spring that still is sweet.
But the flower-fed buffaloes of the spring
Left us, long ago.
They gore no more, they bellow no more,
They trundle around the hills no more:—
With the Blackfeet, lying low,
With the Pawnees, lying low,
Lying low.

VACHEL LINDSAY

The Sidewinder

A lazy loop of lozenged gray,
   I stretch amid the sand and sun;
Or writhe a sullen yard away,
   The greasewood's creeping shade to shun.

The hot earth nestles to my chin;
   My lidless orbs outstare the sky
All unabashed; and dry and thin
   My unawakened rattles sigh.

The desert glare that does to death
   Pale human shirkers of the sun—
Poor fools that court a colder breath,
   Nor know that heat and life are one—

It filters through my scaly still,
   It simmers to one drop of Fate—
The mother-tincture of To Kill,
   Quintessence of a whole world's hate.

Content I dream; content is deep
  For whom three mortal joys there be—
My lord the Sun, my ardent sleep,
  And—sleep for him that wakens me!

CHARLES F. LUMMIS

A California Idyl

A road-runner dodged through the chaparral,
  As a coin will slip through the hand of a wizard,
A black wasp droned by his sun-baked cell,
  While flat on his stone lay a sun-baked lizard.
A shy quail lowered his crested head
'Neath the rock-lined sweep of a dry creek-bed.

A sage hen scratched 'neath a cactus spike,
  While high in the sky was the noon-sun's glamor;
And, ready as ever rose anvil strike,
  Came the rat-tat-tat of a yellowhammer.
A wolf in the cleft of a sycamore,
Sat gray as a monk at his Mission door.

Out of the earth a tarantula crept
  On its hairy legs, to the road's white level,
With eyes where a demon's malice slept,
  And the general air of a devil;
And a rattlesnake by the dusty trail
Lay coiled in a mat of mottled scale.

The wolf down sprang on the sage hen there,
  The lizard snapped at the wasp and caught him.
The spider fled to his sheltering lair
  As if a shadowy foeman sought him;
The road-runner slipped through the roadside brake
And dashed his beak through the rattlesnake.

ERNEST MCGAFFEY

The Lizard

I sit among the hoary trees
With Aristotle on my knees,
And turn with serious hand the pages,
Lost in the cobweb-hush of ages;
When suddenly with no more sound
Than any sunbeam on the ground,
The little hermit of the place
Is peering down into my face—
The slim gray hermit of the rocks,
With bright inquisitive, quick eyes,
His life a round of harks and shocks,
A little ripple of surprise.

Now lifted up, intense and still,
Sprung from the silence of the hill,
He hangs upon the ledge a-glisten,
And his whole body seems to listen!
My pages give a little start,
And he is gone! to be a part
Of the old cedar's crumpled bark,
A mottled scar, a weather-mark.

How halt am I, how mean of birth,
Beside this darting pulse of earth.
I only have the wit to look
Into a big presumptuous book,
To find some sage's rigid plan
To tell me how to be a man.
Tradition lays its dead hand cold
Upon our youth—and we are old.

But this wise hermit, this gray friar,
He has no law but heart's desire.
He somehow touches higher truth,
The circle of eternal youth.

EDWIN MARKHAM

The Organ Cactus

Up from the desert desolate and bleak
   That stretches out as far as eye can reach
In wind-blown, mocking waves that never break
   On any howsoever-distant beach,
The organ cactus lifts its columns grand
   That, linked together, tower toward the sky,
A vast pipe organ in a lonely land,
   Ancient of days ere ever man came nigh.

Shall mighty touch of hurricane or storm
   Awake majestic chords to life within?
Or shall the breath of Mexic breezes warm
   Avail the sweeter melodies to win?
Perhaps in some hushed midnight's holy spell,
   When soft on desert sands the moonbeams lie,
The hand divine that shaped so wondrous well
   This organ vast shall play his symphony!

DOROTHY SCARBOROUGH

Yucca Is Yellowing

Yucca is yellowing;
Hello, yellow!
Cactus is crimsoning;
Glow, glow, red fellow!
And in the mesquite bush is seen
A splash of green—

As when sunset colors spill
Their beauty down an evening hill.

No one rides the trail to-day—
Who cares, if strange or lonely?
No one goes the desert way—
It is for beauty only.

WILLIAM HASKEL SIMPSON

The Last Longhorn's Farewell

I hear a sound, like music through the gale,
Of kindred calling down the old-time trail.

The morning winds, for many, many morns,
Have pulsed with tramping feet, and clashing horns.

And in the burning noons of summer days,
Above the dust I've seen the heat's blue blaze.

And centaur spirits flash before my eyes,
Swifter than meteors through starry skies.

And voices far and faint ring in my ears,
Now soft to soothe, now shrill to waken fears.

I see, I hear, I feel, for through me runs
Tempests of fires and floods, and stars and suns.

For there, beyond the hemming fence and hedge,
I see where earth and sky meet edge to edge.

And all the world between that bound and me,
My kindred once possessed, and roamed in, free.

There bone and sinew, and pure hardihood,
They strove with Nature in her every mood.

Hunger and thirst, these did they understand,
And flood and fire that swept the sun-scorched land.

In summer noons they sought shade-giving trees,
For winter nights they found the friendly leas.

And these were guarded by the earth and sky
Locked edge to edge, letting no foe come by.

And Nature's gifts they took, and understood,
But Man's they scorned—shelter, and care and food.

They knew the wild. There freedom was at flood,
Its spirit flowing high-tide in their blood.

But they are gone. There must be plains somewhere
Without Man's proffered shelter, food and care.

For I can hear the lowings of my kind,
Soft and content, come flowing down the wind.

And in the night a loving voice and low,
Inquiring wakes me—just like long ago.

True to the past, our common fate I face—
Death—unsubdued—the last one of my race.

JOHN P. SJOLANDER

The Pine of Whiting Wood

Not to the fury of the storm, though loud
   Above the thunders boom,
Nor to the slanting wind, or lowering cloud
   Would you succumb.

But when the storm was past, the earth sun-flashed,
   You laid you down in pride;
And loud your death-song roared, and rolled, and
    crashed
   Through field and woodland wide.

Above your fellows, watching night and day,
   A landmark fair you stood;
A guide to wanderers on the miles-wide way
   To Whiting Cove and Wood.

You seemed to beckon to the outer strife,
   Bidding the striving cease,
And come and share with you the boon of life,
   And have the strength of peace.

As you were first to frown, and feel the blast,
   And face the driving rain,
So you were first, when it had hurried past,
   To sing and smile again.

And as you stood in adoration rapt,
   Swaying your sun-bright crown,
There came a tremor, and then something snapped,
   And you went thundering down.

O grand old pine, how great your joy must be!
   And, oh, your fate how blest!
After the storm to sing of victory,
   And then lie down to rest.

JOHN P. SJOLANDER

The Black Vulture

Aloof upon the day's immeasured dome,
   He holds unshared the silence of the sky.

Far down his bleak, relentless eyes descry
The eagle's empire and the falcon's home—

Far down, the galleons of sunset roam;
    His hazards on the sea of morning lie;
    Serene, he hears the broken tempest sigh
Where cold sierras gleam like scattered foam.

And least of all he holds the human swarm—
    Unwitting now that envious men prepare
        To make their dream and its fulfillment one,
When, poised above the caldrons of the storm,
    Their hearts, contemptuous of death, shall dare
        His roads between the thunder and the sun.

GEORGE STERLING

Father Coyote

At twilight time, when the lamps are lit,
Father coyote comes to sit
At the chaparral's edge, on the mountain-side—
Comes to listen and to deride
The rancher's hound and the rancher's son,
The passer-by and everyone.
And we pause at milking-time to hear
His reckless carolling, shrill and clear,—
His terse and swift and valorous troll,
Ribald, rollicking, scornful, droll,
As one might sing in coyotedom:
"Yo ho ho and a bottle of rum!"

Yet well I wot there is little ease
Where the turkeys roost in the almond trees,
But mute forebodings, canny and grim,
As they shift and shiver along the limb.
And the dog flings back an answer brief

(Curse o' the honest man on the thief),
And the cat, till now intent to rove,
Stalks to her lair by the kitchen stove;
Not that *she* fears the rogue on the hill;
But—no mice remain, and—the night is chill.
And now, like a watchman of the skies,
Whose glance to a thousand valleys flies,
The moon glares over the granite ledge—
Pared a slice on its upper edge.
And father coyote waits no more,
Knowing that down on the valley floor,
In a sandy nook all cool and white,
The rabbits play and the rabbits fight,
Flopping, nimble, skurrying,
Careless now with the surge of Spring. . . .
Furry lover, alack! alas!
Skims your fate o'er the moonlit grass!

GEORGE STERLING

Pumas

Hushed, cruel, amber-eyed,
   Before the time of the danger of the day,
Or at dusk on the boulder-broken mountainside,
   The great cats seek their prey.

Soft-padded, heavy-limbed,
   With agate talons chiselled for love or hate,
In desolate places wooded or granite-rimmed,
   The great cats seek their mate.

Rippling, as water swerved,
   To tangled coverts overshadowed and deep,
Or secret caves where the canyon's wall is curved,
   The great cats go for sleep.

Seeking the mate or prey,
   Out of the darkness glow the insatiate eyes;
Man, who is made more terrible far than they,
   Dreams he is otherwise!

GEORGE STERLING

A Note on Lizards' Feet

Out on the desert
Where the sands are hot
The lizards don't walk—
They gallop or trot.

And you would, too;
For it ain't so sweet
To have the old sand
A-burning your feet.

Oh, a lizard's feet
Is tender things,
And it wouldn't of hurt God
To give 'em all wings!

JAMES VAN RENSSELAER

The Pinto

At Guaymas I born in this various world,
   But I spik Ingless, as ustedes see;
I was nice children's hoss, my mane was curled;
   Then for ten dollar' one day they sell me.

Then I much travel, trade from hand to hand,
And learn much languages to understand.

How ole I am? Oh, my, no more don't know!
    How much I cost? Three drinks las' time they pay.
What can I do? Why go, an' go, an' go,
    Or stand, an' stand, an' stand the whole long day.
Oh no, señor, yiou mus' not be distress'!
A hoss gets used to several things, I guess.

What that yiou say? I lie? Not tell the truth?
    I'm young an' strong, an' tryin' jus' to beg?
Gringo, get out! I bite yiou with my tooth,
    Get out, ole fool! I kick yiou with my leg.
Say, Gringo, come an' see the Injuns race
The cowboys, come an' watch me take first place.

OWEN WISTER

Sagebrush

O I am sick for the sagebrush,
The savage sagebrush plain;
And I would give the heart of me
To ride through the sage again.

To feel it scratch my stirrup,
To smell it after rain,
I would give my very heart-blood
For that bitter breath again.

To see it meet the distant hills;
Wind through a tossing mane;
Christ! for a horse between my legs
And the sagebrush once again.

CHARLES ERSKIN SCOTT WOOD

To Midnight

An Epitaph

Under this sod lies a great bucking hoss;
There never lived a cowboy he couldn't toss.
His name was Midnight, his coat was black as coal,
If there is a hoss-heaven, please, God, rest his soul.

UNKNOWN

XI

Legends and Tall Tales

The Glory Trail

'Way high up the Mogollons,
Among the mountain tops,
A lion cleaned a yearlin's bones
And licked his thankful chops,
When on the picture who should ride,
A-trippin' down the slope,
But High-Chin Bob, with sinful pride
And mav'rick-hungry rope.

"Oh, glory be to me," says he,
"And fame's unfadin' flowers!
All meddlin' hands are far away;
I ride my good top-hawse today
And I'm top-rope of the Lazy J—
Hi! kitty cat, you're ours!"

That lion licked his paw so brown
And dreamed soft dreams of veal—
And then the circlin' loop sung down
And roped him 'round his meal.
He yowled quick fury to the world
Till all the hills yelled back;
The top-hawse gave a snort and whirled
And Bob caught up the slack.

"Oh, glory be to me," laughs he,
"We hit the glory trail.
No human man as I have read
Darst loop a ragin' lion's head,
Nor ever hawse could drag one dead
Until we told the tale."

'Way high up the Mogollons
That top-hawse done his best,
Through whippin' brush and rattlin' stones,
From canyon-floor to crest.
But ever when Bob turned and hoped

A limp remains to find,
A red-eyed lion, belly roped
But healthy, loped behind.

"Oh, glory be to me," grunts he,
"This glory trail is rough,
Yet even till the Judgment Morn
I'll keep this dally 'round the horn,
For never any hero born
Could stoop to holler: 'nuff!' "

Three suns had rode their circle home
Beyond the desert's rim,
And turned their star herds loose to roam
The ranges high and dim;
Yet up and down and 'round and 'cross
Bob pounded, weak and wan,
For pride still glued him to his hawse
And glory drove him on.

"Oh, glory be to me," sighs he,
"He kaint be drug to death,
But now I know beyond a doubt
Them heroes I have read about
Was only fools that stuck it out
To end of mortal breath."

'Way high up the Mogollons
A prospect man did swear
That moon dreams melted down his bones
And hoisted up his hair:
A ribby cow-hawse thundered by,
A lion trailed along,
A rider, ga'nt, but chin on high,
Yelled out a crazy song.

"Oh, glory be to me!" cries he,
"And to my noble noose!
O stranger, tell my pards below

I took a rampin' dream in tow,
And if I never lay him low,
I'll never turn him loose!"

CHARLES BADGER CLARK, JR.

The Ballad of Pug-Nosed Lil

In Rattlesnake Gulch of the Skihootch Range
    Dwelt a miner, Cockeyed Bill,
And his little gal was his only pal,
    She was knowed as Pug-Nosed Lil.
In a cabin neat he had sought retreat
    Where he sheltered her from ills,
While he strove and toiled and delved and moiled
    For the gold in them thar hills.

She may not have been so long on looks
    And her chest was a trifle flat,
But she never played faro and she shunned mascara
    And rouge and the likes of that,
While Bill was a man with a rough hewed pan
    Who at times could be plumb tough.
You can bet this cinch that in any pinch
    They were diamonds in the rough.

On Alkali Creek just across the ridge
    Where the meadowlarks sing sweet,
Lived a young cowpoke with a heart of oak
    Who was knowed as Roundup Pete.
With a passion pure he could scarce endure
    His heart beat 'neath his vest,
For he loved Lil true as the he-men do
    In the great wide open West.

Up Spotted Calf Trail over Freeze-out Flat
   He would ride on his paint cayuse
When his work was through just to court and woo
   By the side of a placer sluice.
Well, he stood ace high and was getting by
   With Bill and the pug-nosed wren
For they both opined he'd a good pure mind,—
   One of nature's noblemen.

Now a snake in the grass lived at Hell Gate Pass,—
   His soul was as black as tar.
It had been his aim to jump Bill's claim
   On the El Dorado Bar.
He had planned, the skunk, that when Bill got drunk,
   As sometimes a miner does,
He would steal the skirt and would do her dirt
   Like the villainous fiend he wuz.

Old Bill got canned, as the slicker planned,
   Down at Shorty's Sample Bar
Where a lot of ginks let him buy them drinks
   Or a good five cent cigar.
And the villain sneered and he kind of leered
   In a most offensive style
Till he made a crack and Bill came back,
   "When you say that, stranger, smile!"

With Bill in his cups, why, the varmint ups
   And heads out to grab Bill's kid.
He was on the prowl for to do as foul
   A deed as ever was did!
Well, he found the frail waiting by the trail
   That goes to Chimney Butte.
She was lorn and sad for her cockeyed Dad
   For she loved the old galoot.

Cantankerous Nash with the dyed mustache,
   For that was the rascal's name,
Advanced on the maid who was pale and afraid
   And aware now of his game.

To this ornery guy with the shifty eye
 She uttered her favorite line.
"You low down slicker, your breath smells of likker,
 And your lips shall NOT touch mine!"

Now men were men in those old days when
 This circumstance occurred,
And Pete, of course, on his wonder horse
 Had left the thundering herd
For old Bill's shack just to get a snack
 Of the grub like Lil could cook,
When his eye so keen lit upon the scene
 Where Lil fought off the crook.

Down the mountain trail Pete rolled his tail
 To rescue the fair young wren
While the villain cursed till he almost burst
 For the skunk was foiled again.
Pete loudly cried as he reached her side,
 "Leave her be, you dastard rat!"
This Pete was a gent and what he meant
 Was a different word than that.

Nash loosed all holts and he pulled his Colts
 To plug Pete on the spot,
But like a flash Pete socked this Nash
 With a right cross that was hot.
They went to a clinch that was no soft cinch,
 It was root-hog, win, or bust.
And the canyon rang with a bang! bang!! bang!!!
 And the scoundrel bit the dust.

Then Pete took Lil and they found old Bill
 And they looked up a nice J. P.
Who made the splice for a reasonable price.
 Now they're happy as can be.
And in Rattlesnake Gulch of the Skihootch Range
 There is peace and ca'm once more
While the pale moon shineth and the woodbine twineth
 Round the old log cabin door.

ROBERT H. FLETCHER

Coyote and the Star

This is a legend from Siskiyou Bar
About "The Coyote Who Danced
　　with a Star."

Now, great were the deeds that Coyote had
　　done!
Coyote had stolen the flame of the Sun;
Coyote had opened the Frost-Wizard's
　　pen
Releasing the Salmon, desired of men.
Coyote was proud of his craft and his
　　might,
His fleetness of foot and his clearness of
　　sight,
His scent, that was choicest of all that is
　　choice,
But most was he vain of his wonderful
　　voice.
He sat like a monarch exalted on high
Where Sisson's cold summits are keen in
　　the sky
And watched on the sweep of ethereal blue
The stars and their satellites pass in review.

　　　　Aloft and alone
　　　　On Shasta's white cone
A mischievous Star-fairy twinkled and
　　shone;
　　　　So lightly she danced
　　　　That, deeply entranced,
Coyote clamated, "Empyreal Sprite,
Permit me to join in your glorious flight;
　　　　I beg,—I demand!
　　　　Oh, reach me your hand,
And over the water and over the land
We'll frolic with all of your glittering
　　band!"

How flashed the Aurora, till heaven and
  earth
Were gay with the lustre of crystalline
  mirth!
"O hairy Coyote! how stupid you are
To dream for a moment to dance with a
  Star!"

What pencil will venture, what brush will
  engage
To picture Coyote in justified rage?
He lifted his muzzle, he stiffened his tail,
Affrighting the Night with a quavering
  wail.
  With yelp and with yowl,
  With growl and with howl
He startled the Owl and the Panther
  aprowl.
He screamed like a baby bereft of his toys;
He shattered the sky with his scandalous
  noise,
  With his "Yap! yap! ki-yee!"
  In its weird minor key,
For never was singer remorseless as he.

All vainly the Fairy cajoled and denied;
He wouldn't hear reason; then, wearied,
  she cried,
  "I wish you were dumb!
  You're crazy, but—come!"
And gingerly reached him a finger and
  thumb.
He leaped!—and away, like the shaft and
  the feather,
The Star and Coyote were flying together.
And now as he fled with that Spirit of
  Light
There rushed far beneath him a glorious
  sight

Of ranges and canyons and barrens and
    plains,
Of rivers cascading with turbulent rains,
Of armies of bison, and cimarron gray,
And legions of antelopes bounding away;
The towns of the Mandans, the Nez Percé
    ranches,
The Utes and the Pi-Utes, the dashing
    Comanches
And Modocs in-reining their snorting
    cayuses
And shouting to women with wickered
    papooses,
"Look! See!"—as they waved to that vision
    afar,
"The Clever Coyote, above, with a Star!"

      To caper in style
      For many a mile
Careering the heavens, was grand!—for a
    while.
But frostily grew in Coyote apace
The awe and the horror of limitless space.
He felt on his temples the grip of a vise;
The hand of his Partner seemed colder
    than ice.
'Twas dreadful to gaze upon mountains—
    like barrows!
The tents of the Kahrocs like flint heads of
    arrows;
The silvery Klamath whose broad-bosomed
    flow
Showed meager 'mid hills like the string
    of a bow
Relaxed after battle. Grown dizzy and
    numb,
He loosened his hold on the finger and
    thumb
And dropped to the earth like a meteor,
    plumb!

> And lit with a "spat!"
> As flat as a mat!
> So here is the moral from Siskiyou Bar:
> "You Callow Coyote, don't dance with no
>   Star!

ARTHUR GUITERMAN

Silver Jack's Religion

I was on the drive in sixty, working under Silver Jack.
Which the same is now in Jackson and ain't soon expected back.
And there was a chap among us by the name of Robert Waite
Who was kinder slick and tonguey—I guess he were a graduate.

Bob could gab on any subject from the Bible down to Hoyle
And his words flowed out so easy just as smooth and slick as oil.
He was what they call a "skeptic" and he loved to sit and weave
High-falutin' words together saying what he didn't believe.

One day as we were waiting for a flood to clear the ground,
We all sat smoking niggerhead and hearing Bob expound:
Hell, he said, was a humbug, and he proved as clear as day
That the Bible was a fable: we allowed it looked that way.

As for miracles and such-like, 'twas more than he could stand.
And for Him they called the Savior. He was just a common man.
"You're a liar!" shouted someone, "and you've got to take
  that back!"
Then everybody started, 'twas the voice of Silver Jack.

Jack clicked his fists together and he shucked his coat and cried,
" 'Twas by that th'ar religion my mother lived and died.
And although I haven't always used the Lord exactly right,
When I hear a chump abuse Him he must eat his words or fight."

Now Bob he warn't no coward and he answered bold and free.
"Stack your duds and cut your capers, for you'll find no flies
   on me."
And they fit for forty minutes and the boys would hoot and cheer,
When Jack choked up a tooth or two and Bob he lost an ear.

At last Jack got Bob under and he slugged him onct or twict,
Then Bob finally admitted the divinity of Christ.
Still Jack kept reasoning with him till the cuss begun to yell,
And allowed he'd been mistaken in his views concerning Hell!

Thus that controversy ended and they riz up from the ground,
And someone found a bottle and kindly passed it round;
And we drank to Jack's Religion in a quiet sort of way,
So the spread of infidelity was checked in camp that day.

JOHN P. JONES

Étude Géographique

Out West, they say, a man's a man; the legend still persists
That he is handy with a gun and careless with his fists.
The fact is, though, you may not hear a stronger word than "Gosh!"
From Saskatoon, Saskatchewan, to Walla Walla, Wash.

In western towns 'tis many years since it was last the rage
For men to earn their daily bread by holding up the stage,
Yet story writers still ascribe such wild and woolly bosh
To Saskatoon, Saskatchewan, and Walla Walla, Wash.

The gents who roam the West today are manicured and meek,
They shave their features daily and they bathe three times
   a week.
They tote the tame umbrella and they wear the mild galosh
From Saskatoon, Saskatchewan, to Walla Walla, Wash.

But though the West has frowned upon its old nefarious games,
It still embellishes the map with sweet, melodious names,
Which grow in lush profusion like the apple and the squash
From Saskatoon, Saskatchewan, to Walla Walla, Wash.

STODDARD KING

The Lost Range

Only a few could understand his ways and his outfit queer,
His saddle-horse and his pack-horse as lean as a Winter steer,
    As he rode alone on the mesa intent on his endless quest—
    Old Tom Bright of the Pecos, a ghost of the vanished West.

His gaze was fixed on the spaces; he never had much to say
When we met him down by the river, or over in Santa Fé.
    He favored the open country with its reaches clean and wide,
    And called it his "sage-brush garden; the only place left to
        ride."

He scorned new methods and manners and stock that was under
        fence.
He had seen the last of the open range, but he kept up the old
        pretense;
    Though age made his blue eyes water, his humor was always
        dry—
    "Me? I'm huntin' The Lost Range down yonder against the
        sky."

That's what he'd say when we hailed him as we met him along
        the trail,
Hazing his old gray pack-horse, fetching some rancher's mail
    In the heat of the upland Summer, or the chill of the
        thin-spread snow;
    Any of us would have staked him, but Tom wouldn't have
        it so.

He made you think of an eagle caged up for the crowd to see,
Dreaming of crags and sunshine and glories that used to be;
Some folks called him a hobo—too lazy to work for pay;
But we old-timers knew better, for Tom wasn't built that
way.

He'd work till he got a grub stake; then drift—and he'd make
his fire
And camp on the open mesa as far as he could from wire;
Tarp and sogun and skillet, saddle and rope and gun—
And that's the way that they found him, asleep in the
noonday sun.

They were running a line that Summer surveying a right-of-way
From Buckman, down by the river, clear over to Santa Fé,
Spoiling his sage-brush garden—"the only place left to ride,"—
But Tom he had beat them to it: he had crossed to The Other
Side.

The coroner picked his jury and a livery horse apiece,
Not forgetting the shovels, and we rode to the Buckman lease,
Rolled Tom up in his slicker, and each of us said "So-long."
Tom never cared for preachers, but we knew that he liked a
song.

None of us had a hymn-book; so we didn't observe the rules,
But we sang "Git Along Little Dogies"—all cryin', we
gray-haired fools;
Kind of wishing that Tom could hear it, and know we were
standing by;
Wishing him luck on The Lost Range down yonder against
the sky.

HENRY HERBERT KNIBBS

The Ghost of the Buffaloes

Last night at black midnight I woke with a cry,
The windows were shaking, there was thunder on high,
The floor was atremble, the door was ajar,
White fires, crimson fires, shone from afar.

I rushed to the dooryard. The city was gone.
My home was a hut without orchard or lawn.
It was mud-smear and logs near a whispering stream,
Nothing else built by man could I see in my dream . . .
Then . . .
Ghost-kings came headlong, row upon row,
Gods of the Indians, torches aglow.

They mounted the bear and the elk and the deer,
And eagles gigantic, aged and sere,
They rode long-horn cattle, they cried "A-la-la."
They lifted the knife, the bow, and the spear,

They lifted ghost-torches from dead fires below,
The midnight made grand with the cry "A-la-la."
The midnight made grand with a red-god charge,
A red-god show,
A red-god show,
"A-la-la, a-la-la, a-la-la, a-la-la."

With bodies like bronze, and terrible eyes
Came the rank and the file, with catamount cries,
Gibbering, yipping, with hollow-skull clacks,
Riding white bronchos with skeleton backs,
Scalp-hunters, beaded and spangled and bad,
Naked and lustful and foaming and mad,
Flashing primeval demoniac scorn,
Blood-thirst and pomp amid darkness reborn,
Power and glory that sleep in the grass
While the winds and the snows and the great rains pass.
They crossed the gray river, thousands abreast,
They rode in infinite lines to the west.
Tide upon tide of strange fury and foam,
Spirits and wraiths, the blue was their home,
The sky was their goal where the star-flags were furled,
And on past those far golden splendors they whirled.
They burned to dim meteors, lost in the deep.
And I turned in dazed wonder, thinking of sleep.

And the wind crept by
Alone, unkempt, unsatisfied,
The wind cried and cried—
Muttered of massacres long past,
Buffaloes in shambles vast . . .
An owl said: "Hark, what is a-wing?"
I heard a cricket carolling,
I heard a cricket carolling,
I heard a cricket carolling.

Then . . .
Snuffing the lightning that crashed from on high
Rose royal old buffaloes, row upon row.
The lords of the prairie came galloping by.

And I cried in my heart "A-la-la, a-la-la,
A red-god show,
A red-god show,
A-la-la, a-la-la, a-la-la, a-la-la."

Buffaloes, buffaloes, thousands abreast,
A scourge and amazement, they swept to the west.
With black bobbing noses, with red rolling tongues,
Coughing forth steam from their leather-wrapped lungs,
Cows with their calves, bulls big and vain,
Goring the laggards, shaking the mane,
Stamping flint feet, flashing moon eyes,
Pompous and owlish, shaggy and wise.
Like sea-cliffs and caves resounded their ranks
With shoulders like waves, and undulant flanks.
Tide upon tide of strange fury and foam,
Spirits and wraiths, the blue was their home,
The sky was their goal where the star-flags are furled,
And on past those far golden splendors they whirled.
They burned to dim meteors, lost in the deep,
And I turned in dazed wonder, thinking of sleep.

I heard a cricket's cymbals play,
A scarecrow lightly flapped his rags,
And a pan that hung by his shoulder rang,
Rattled and thumped in a listless way,
And now the wind in the chimney sang,
The wind in the chimney,
The wind in the chimney,
The wind in the chimney,
   Seemed to say:—
"Dream, boy, dream,
If you anywise can.
To dream is the work
Of beast or man.
Life is the west-going dream-storms' breath,
Life is a dream, the sigh of the skies,
The breath of the stars, that nod on their pillows
With their golden hair mussed over their eyes."
The locust played on his musical wing,

Sang to his mate of love's delight.
I heard the whippoorwill's soft fret.
I heard a cricket carolling,
I heard a cricket carolling,
I heard a cricket say: "Good-night, good-night,
Good-night, good-night, . . . good-night."

VACHEL LINDSAY

A Bob-tailed Flush

There came unto me yesterday
An old man, worn and gray,
Said he, "Could you feed me, Ranger,
I've had naught to eat this day!"

As he sat at the table eating
He talked of other lands,
Of Alaska's frozen rivers,
Of the desert's parching sands.

He spoke of Paris Boulevards,
Of the streets of San Antone,
He mentioned Forty-second Street
And the Plazas of Torreón.

He spoke of Buenos Ayres
As though it were across the street;
In fact such a traveled gentleman
I had never chanced to meet.

He talked of the Versailles Treaty
As though it were a personal affair;
He juggled kings and kingdoms
And never turned a hair.

He told me he had once been wealthy
And lived in a mansion grand;

He created a feeling of opulence
With a gesture of his hand.

As I watched this palsied stranger
I wondered what misfortune in life
Had brought him to lowly condition,
This evident defeat in the strife.

Was it women, or was it only wine
Had pushed him in the mire?
In the thought that I might help him
I made bold then to inquire.

Tears in his dim eyes, he told me—
The words came with a rush—
"I've wasted my life and possessions
Trying to fill a bob-tailed flush!"

JOHN R. PAINTER

The Frozen Logger

As I sat down one ev'-nin' in a timber-town café,
A six-foot-seven waitress to me these words did say:

"I see you are a logger and not a common bum,
For no one but a logger stirs his coffee with his thumb.

"My lover was a logger. There's none like him to-day.
If you'd sprinkle whisky on it, he'd eat a bale of hay.

"He never shaved the whiskers from off his horny hide;
But he'd pound them in with a hammer, then bite 'em off inside.

"My logger came to see me, one freezing winter day.
He held me in a fond embrace that broke three vertebrae.

"He kissed me when we parted—so hard he broke my jaw,
And I could not speak to tell him he'd forgot his mackinaw.

"I watched my logger lover going through the snow,
A-sa'ntering gaily homeward at forty-eight below.

"The weather tried to freeze him. It tried its level best.
At a hundred degrees below zero, he buttoned up his vest.

"It froze clean down to China. It froze to the stars above.
At one thousand degrees below zero, it froze my logger love.

"They tried in vain to thaw him. Then, if you'll believe me, sir,
They made him into ax blades to chop the Douglas fir.

"That's how I lost my lover. And in this café I come
And here I wait till some one stirs his coffee with his thumb.

"And then I tell my story of my love they could not thaw,
Who kissed me when we parted—so hard he broke my jaw."

JAMES STEVENS

Out Where the West Begins

A Parody

Out where the talk is a little stronger,
Out where the trails are a blame sight longer,
　　That's where the West begins.
Out where the skirts are a little higher,
Where men are wilder and women shier,
Where we'll all blow away if it gets much drier—
　　That's where the West begins.

Out where the bushes are full of stickers
And the whole darn country is full of slickers,

That's where the West begins.
Where the lizards pant in the summer heat,
Where the white sands blister the kiote's feet
And we've nothing but jerky and beans to eat—
    That's where the West begins.

Where the owls at night lay hard-boiled eggs
And the jackrabbits carry canteens and kegs,
    That's where the West begins.
Where leppies are bawling the whole night through
A song more sad than the dove's sad coo;
And we never tell tourists one thing that's true,
    That's where the West begins.

Out where the rivers run upside down
And two houses together are called a town,
    That's where the West begins.
Where mules are too weary to bray or kick;
Where hens are scarce and buzzards thick;
And the devil won't stay 'cause it makes him sick—
    That's where the West begins.

Where the catclaw trees and the sagebrush grow
And their leaves get scorched when the hot winds blow,
    That's where the West begins.
Where the centipede and the rattler dwell
And where the scorpion does right well;
And the only crop we can raise is——*
    That's where the West begins.

ERNEST DOUGLAS

* Gehenna, hades, infernal regions, or something; awfully hard to get a rhyme here.

Index by Author

Index by Title